HEROES AND GODS

*Spiritual Biographies
in Antiquity*

HEROES AND GODS

Spiritual Biographies
in Antiquity

by Moses Hadas
and Morton Smith

Essay Index Reprint Series

 BOOKS FOR LIBRARIES PRESS
FREEPORT, NEW YORK

Grateful acknowledgement is made to The University of
Chicago Press for permission to quote from the following
works:

Richmond Lattimore, trans., *The Iliad of Homer*. Copyright 1951. Copyright © 1962 by The University of
Chicago.

Richmond Lattimore and David Grene (eds.), *The Complete Greek Tragedies,* William Arrowsmith's translation
of Euripides' *Heracles*. Copyright © 1956 by The University of Chicago.

INTERNATIONAL STANDARD BOOK NUMBER:

0-8369-1880-0

LIBRARY OF CONGRESS CATALOG CARD NUMBER:

77-117800

PRINTED IN THE UNITED STATES OF AMERICA

CONTENTS

RELIGIOUS PERSPECTIVES
Its Meaning and Purpose

RELIGIOUS PERSPECTIVES represents a quest for the rediscovery of man. It constitutes an effort to define man's search for the essence of being in order that he may have a knowledge of goals. It is an endeavor to show that there is no possibility of achieving an understanding of man's total nature on the basis of phenomena known by the analytical method alone. It hopes to point to the false antinomy between revelation and reason, faith and knowledge, grace and nature, courage and anxiety. Mathematics, physics, philosophy, biology, and religion, in spite of their almost complete independence, have begun to sense their interrelatedness and to become aware of that mode of cognition which teaches that "the light is not without but within me, and I myself am the light".

Modern man is threatened by a world created by himself. He is faced with the conversion of mind to naturalism, a dogmatic secularism and an opposition to a belief in the transcendent. He begins to see, however, that the universe is given not as one existing and one perceived but as the unity of subject and object; that the barrier between them cannot be said to have been dissolved as the result of recent experience in the physical sciences, since this barrier has never existed. Confronted with the question of meaning, he is summoned to rediscover and scrutinize the immutable and the permanent which constitute the dynamic, unifying aspect of life as well as the principle of differentiation; to reconcile identity and diversity, immutability and unrest. He begins to recognize that just as every person descends by his particular path, so he is able to ascend, and this ascent aims at a return to the source of creation, an inward home from which he has become estranged.

It is the hope of RELIGIOUS PERSPECTIVES that the rediscovery of man will point the way to the rediscovery of God. To this end a rediscovery of first principles should constitute part of the quest. These principles, not to be superseded by new discoveries, are not those of historical worlds that come to be and perish. They are to be sought in the heart and spirit of man, and no interpretation of a merely historical or scientific universe can guide the search. RELIGIOUS PERSPECTIVES attempts not only to ask dispassionately what the nature of God is, but also to restore to human life at least the hypothesis of God and the symbols that relate to him. It endeavors to show that man is faced with the metaphysical question of the truth of religion while he encounters the empirical question of its effects on the life of humanity and its meaning for society. Religion is here distinguished from theology and its doctrinal forms and is intended to denote the feelings, aspirations, and acts of men, as they relate to total reality.

RELIGIOUS PERSPECTIVES is nourished by the spiritual and intellectual energy of world thought, by those religious and ethical leaders who are not merely spectators but scholars deeply involved in the critical problems common to all religions. These thinkers recognize that human morality and human ideals thrive only when set in a context of a transcendent attitude toward religion and that by pointing to the ground of identity and the common nature of being in the religious experience of man, the essential nature of religion may be defined. Thus, they are committed to re-evaluate the meaning of everlastingness, an experience which has been lost and which is the content of that *visio Dei* constituting the structure of all religions. It is the many absorbed everlastingly into the ultimate unity, a unity subsuming what Whitehead calls the fluency of God and the everlastingness of passing experience.

These volumes seek to show that the unity of which we speak consists in a certitude emanating from the nature of man who seeks God and the nature of God who seeks man. Such certitude bathes in an intuitive act of cognition, participating in the divine essence and is related to the natural spirituality of intelligence. This is not by any means to say that there is an equivalence of all faiths in the traditional religions of human history. It is, however, to emphasize the distinction between the spiritual and the temporal which all religions acknowledge. For duration of thought is composed of instants superior to time, and is an intuition of the permanence of existence and is metahistorical reality. In fact, the symbol[1] itself found on cover and jacket of each volume of RELIGIOUS PERSPECTIVES is the visible sign or representation of the essence, immediacy, and timelessness of religious experience; the one immutable center, which may be analogically related to Being in pure act, moving with centrifugal and ecumenical necessity outward into the manifold modes, yet simultaneously, with dynamic centripetal power and with full intentional energy, returning to the source. Through the very diversity of its authors, the Series shows that the basic and poignant concern of every faith is to point to, and overcome the crisis in our apocalyptic epoch—the crisis of man's separation from man and of man's separation from God—the failure of love. The authors endeavor, moreover, to illustrate the truth that the human heart is able, and even yearns, to go to the very lengths of God; that the darkness and cold, the frozen spiritual misery of recent time, are breaking, cracking, and beginning to move, yielding to efforts to overcome spiritual muteness and moral paralysis. In this way, it is hoped, the immediacy of pain and sorrow, the primacy of tragedy and suffering in human life, may be transmuted into a spiritual and moral triumph.

RELIGIOUS PERSPECTIVES is therefore an effort to explore the *meaning* of God, an exploration which constitutes an aspect of man's intrinsic nature, part of his ontological substance. The Series grows out of an abiding concern that in spite of the release of man's creative energy which science has in part accomplished, this very science has overturned the essential order of nature. Shrewd as man's calculations have become concerning

[1] From the original design by Leo Katz.

his means, his choice of ends which was formerly correlated with belief in God, with absolute criteria of conduct, has become wit-less. God is not to be treated as an exception to metaphysical principles, invoked to prevent their collapse. He is rather their chief exemplification, the source of all potentiality. The personal reality of freedom and providence, of will and conscience, may demonstrate that "he who knows" commands a depth of con-sciousness inaccessible to the profane man, and is capable of that transfiguration which prevents the twisting of all good to ignominy. This religious content of experience is not within the province of science to bestow; it corrects the error of treating the scientific account as if it were itself metaphysical or religious; it challenges the tendency to make a religion of science—or a science of religion—a dogmatic act which destroys the moral dynamic of man. Indeed, many men of science are confronted with unexpected implications of their own thought and are be-ginning to accept, for instance, the trans-spatial and trans-temporal dimension in the nature of reality.

RELIGIOUS PERSPECTIVES attempts to show the fallacy of the apparent irrelevance of God in history. The Series submits that no convincing image of man can arise, in spite of the many ways in which human thought has tried to reach it, without a philo-sophy of human nature and human freedom which does not ex-clude God. This image of *Homo cum Deo* implies the highest conceivable freedom, the freedom to step into the very fabric of the universe, a new formula for man's collaboration with the creative process and the only one which is able to protect man from the terror of existence. This image implies further that the mind and conscience are capable of making genuine discrimina-tions and thereby may reconcile the serious tensions between the secular and religious, the profane and sacred. The idea of the sacred lies in what it *is,* timeless existence. By emphasizing time-less existence against reason as a reality, we are liberated, in our communion with the eternal, from the otherwise unbreakable rule of "before and after." Then we are able to admit that all forms, all symbols in religions, by their negation of error and their affirmation of the actuality of truth, make it possible to experience that *knowing* which is above knowledge, and that dynamic passage of the universe to unending unity.

The volumes in this Series seek to challenge the crisis which separates, to make reasonable a religion that binds, and to present the numinous reality within the experience of man. Insofar as the Series succeeds in this quest, it will direct mankind toward a reality that is eternal and away from a preoccupation with that which is illusory and ephemeral.

For man is now confronted with his burden and his greatness : "He calleth to me, Watchman, what of the night? Watchman, what of the night?"[1] Perhaps the anguish in the human soul may be assuaged by the answer, by the *assimilation* of the person in God : "The morning cometh, and also the night : if ye will inquire, inquire ye : return, come."[2]

RUTH NANDA ANSHEN

[1] Isaiah 21:11.
[2] Isaiah 21:12.

PREFACE

ARETALOGY IS NOT RECOGNIZED as a word in our dictionaries, nor is the type of literature it designates treated as a separate genre. The documents which may be called aretalogical and the phenomena they illustrate are familiar or accessible enough, and are acknowledged to possess high importance for religious development, but their history and internal relationships have not commonly been presented as a separate unity. The authors of the present work have thought it might be useful so to present them. We make no claim to completeness, and are well aware that reconstructions and interpretations, especially in Part I, may be open to serious question. Part I is the work of Mr. Hadas, and Part II of Mr. Smith. Each has read and given general approval to the work of his collaborator, but the ultimate responsibility for each section rests upon its own author.

Since Part II consists of a translation of Porphyry's *Life of Pythagoras* (hitherto unavailable in English) and summaries of Philo's *Life of Moses,* the Gospel according to Luke, and Philostratus's *Life of Apollonius of Tyana*, something must be said here of the ways in which the texts have been handled. The translation of Porphyry is deliberately as close to the Greek as seemed possible within the limits of a tolerable English style. Here and there explanatory phrases have been inserted in square brackets [. . .]. The summarizations of the other texts, however, are concerned only to express the essential content briefly and idiomatically. Therefore details of wording have been translated literally only when they seemed useful for this purpose or when their dramatic quality or solemnity or pomposity or

xiii

absurdity, or something of the sort, seemed worth rendition, either because of its importance as an aretalogical trait or for its own sweet sake. Consequently the use of quotation marks in the text indicates merely direct discourse, not exact translation. The texts used have been, for Porphyry, that of Nauck, for Philo, of Cohn-Wendland, for Luke, of Nestle and Kilpatrick, and for Philostratus, of Kayser, though Mr. Smith has occasionally preferred variants rejected by these editors. Though the basic rendition is, throughout, his own, he has been indebted for interpretations and details of wording to prior translations, especially Holstenius' Porphyry, Colson's Philo, The Revised Standard Version, The New English Bible, and Conybeare's Philostratus, and to the standard lexicons and works of reference. No work of scholarship can be complete without an expression of thanks for the works of earlier scholars.

PART ONE

I. PERSONAGES AND PERSONALITIES

OUR THEME will be the genesis, fortunes, and consequences of an ancient type of biographical writing called aretalogy. The various connotations of the word in antiquity we shall glance at in another connection; for the present we may define it as a formal account of the remarkable career of an impressive teacher that was used as a basis for moral instruction. The preternatural gifts of the teacher often included power to work wonders; often his teaching brought him the hostility of a tyrant, whom he confronted with courage and at whose hands he suffered martyrdom. Often the circumstances of his birth or his death involve elements of the miraculous. The teacher may have been convinced of his mission and his preternatural endowment; or he may have been an earnest reformer profoundly concerned for the spiritual improvement of his fellow men and pretending to occult powers in order to make his teaching acceptable; or he may have been an impostor interested only in reputation and gain. The men who made the formulation of his career the basis and authority for their doctrine may have been devoted disciples committed to propagating the teachings of the master, or they may themselves have been conscientious teachers who attributed their own insights to some suitable figure and elaborated his career with preternatural embellishments in order to give credit to the doctrine they wished to propagate, or they may have been charlatans who exploited a fabrication to facilitate their own chicanery.

Throughout the history of the phenomenon there have been people who welcomed, believed in, and defended the sanctity of an aretalogy, and have been others who scoffed. Men are naturally grateful to eminent leaders or benefactors and desire to ensure their continuing support or inspiration; but men also grow indifferent or sceptical, and unless there is something like an organized cult to perpetuate his memory, the eminent figure of one generation falls into oblivion in the next. The roll of individuals deemed worthy of veneration varies, therefore, in length and composition from age to age. In credulous or in authoritarian societies the list is apt to be long and to include persons who contributed to the establishment, maintenance, and justification of the authoritarianism. In ratior.alistic or in democratic societies the list is apt to be much reduced; the human shortcomings of the large figures are not glossed over, and there is a feeling that society rather than its leaders is responsible for advances : if the particular individual associated with a given movement had not come forward, some other must soon have done so.

In our generation the traditional roster of movers and shakers credited with altering the course of human history has been whittled down to a puny handful, an Alexander or a Mohammed, and even here what we are shown are the clay feet and the sustaining armature provided by interested parties to keep the figure erect. But the armatures have their own independent interest. For the effect exerted upon the course of history the authorized image of the hero is more important than his historical personality. It is upon the image rather than the person that reverence is bestowed, whether formally in an organized cult or informally in popular tradition, and it is the cult, formal or informal, that ensures the survival of the image.

As a preliminary to an enquiry into literary images of a particular kind of personage we must consider modes of literary treatment of personages generally. These differ in different literatures, and since the early history of aretalogy and its pioneers are Greek, we must begin by examining the Greek paradigms. What kinds of personages engaged the interest of Greek writers? What qualities did they celebrate? How narrowly was personality characterized? When did the personage come to overshadow the story in which he figured, or in other words, when did biography become an independent genre, and what were its canons of veracity? How important, to begin with, is the individual?

Until the last quarter of the fifth century B.C. we encounter a strange ambivalence. On the one hand there is a remarkable drive for assertion of individuality, in literature as in life. The highest ambition of great personages is to become a subject of song for later generations, and singers and their audiences were very ready to accord great personages the renown they earned. On the other hand there is reticence or indifference, curious by later standards, to the human personalities of the great personages so highly regarded. It is sometimes said that commonplace traits are ignored because the personage is idealized; as often a better explanation is that the ideal is personified.

In the epic we do get glimpses into the individual personalities of the heroic personages, as when Achilles receives Agamemnon's ambassadors or Athena reminds Diomedes of his father or Briseis speaks of Patroclus' kindliness after his death, but these are touches to make the central ideal more effective. When Hector is dragged behind Achilles' chariot, we are shown his beautiful hair fouled in the dust, and we recognize the truth of the picture : Hector must indeed have had such hair, and from the beginning of the poem, but the detail is noticed by the poet only when it is relevant to the essential Hector.

Aeschylus shows greater indifference to nonessential detail. The large figures of the *Oresteia* are exhibited not in the round but only frontally with only such traits as are significant for the crucial conflicts in which they are involved. Of Agamemnon we are told only enough to know that he is the kind of man who might have been general at Troy and have earned the hatred of a woman like Clytemnestra, and of Clytemnestra we are told only enough to know that she might have accepted Aegisthus as lover and have murdered a man like Agamemnon. Orestes, whose guilt or innocence is the central theme of the trilogy, is almost wholly without character and merely a lay figure to illustrate the solution of an abstract problem.

The point is that the classics who set the tone for Greek literature were poets; the difference between their created personages and those of familiar flesh and blood is the difference between high poetry and prose. Poetry is organic, stylized, creative; prose is representative, descriptive, constructive. The difference is implicit in Aristotle's dictum that poetry is more philosophical than prose, or in the remark that Sophocles showed men as they should be whereas Euripides represented them as they are. Representing, describing, and constructing a wholly credible character in a novel does not necessarily argue lesser creative power in the prose writer; it is only that the poet's creativity is of a different order and hence can be indifferent to prosaic verisimilitude. Aeschylus' recognition scene in the *Choephoroi* is poetically just, and Euripides' ridicule of it in his *Electra* is prosaically just.

Greek plastic art offers an illuminating analogy, even in the point of chronology. The pediment sculptures of the temple of Zeus at Olympia, as Charles Seltman has pointed out, are like the tragedies of Aeschylus, those of the Parthenon like the history of Thucydides. The personages of Aeschylus are pure creations, independent of the specimens of humanity found in the world of the senses. Even the costumes they wore upon the stage, like the exalted language they intoned, were unlike anything in the ordinary experience of the audience. So the sculptures of the same period, stylized and colored in disregard of literal verisimilitude, were independent of familiar types; they were new creations, not merely idealizations of ordinary humanity. The specimens which the prose artist depicts, whether in language or in stone, may indeed be selected and even posed, but they are not new creations.

If we carry the analogy a generation further, we can see that the statues of Praxiteles are like the illusive rhetoric of the orators. In both media there is less concern with the subject matter than with the impressions it can be made to give. These new artists do not create, in the sense that Aeschylus or the sculptor of Olympia created; they distort familiar experience to produce calculated effects. Eventually the distortions might assume the proportions of caricature, without, however, reaching the dignity of new creation.

The true poets, whatever their medium, produced no portraits and no biography. When portraits and biographies came to be made, they were influenced—as indeed their subjects must have been—by the ideals of the poets. This influence is conspicuous in the type of literature that is our concern, and we must therefore look more closely at a particular aspect of the poetic ideal and then see how it affected the character of prose biography in general.

If the personages of epic and tragedy were fresh creations, they must nevertheless have reflected and in turn influenced the ideals of the community out of which they grew and to which they were addressed. A significant trait common to them all is a relentless drive for individual excellence and for the fame that excellence would win. This is clearly the motivation of the Homeric hero, whose elders enjoined him when he went forth into the world "always to be excellent, always to prove superior to all others." Achilles, who is the beau ideal of the *Iliad,* had been given the choice, and had deliberately preferred a short and glorious life to a long and obscure one. To serve his glory when it is put into question, he prays for the defeat of his own side and withholds help from his comrades in their desperate · need. Less individualistic societies must have condemned such conduct, but Achilles is not censured for it; on the contrary, he remains a model for the heroic code.

The model was respected by later poets who dealt with the heroic figures of saga and especially by Sophocles, whom we shall deal with more fully when we come to examine the concept of the hero. Perhaps because Homer was so central in education, the drive for individual excellence and distinction that his poems inculcate permeated and conditioned all of Athenian life. Inherently aristocratic as it seems, the code was adapted to the egalitarianism of the democracy, which would indeed have been impossible without a strong sense of individual worth. Even such things as dramatic and musical compositions were produced in prize competitions with fame as the principal reward.

Even writers of the fourth century who are suspicious of heroic poetry seem to accept the Homeric code without question, as a

handful of quotations will show. In his *Evagoras* (3) Isocrates
says : "We shall find that ambitious and high-souled men . . .
choose a glorious death in preference to life and are more jealous
of their reputations than of their existence, shrinking from
nothing in order to leave behind a remembrance of themselves
that shall never die." In Plato's *Symposium* (208 CE) Socrates
quotes Diotima as saying : "Think only of the ambition of men
and you will wonder at the senselessness of their ways, unless you
consider how they are stirred by the love of an immortality of
fame. They are ready to run all risks, greater far than they would
have run for their children, and to spend money and undergo any
sort of toil, and even to die, for the sake of leaving behind them a
name that shall be eternal." And in the *Apology* (28 c) Socrates
cites the example of Achilles, who knowingly courted certain
death in order to assert his honor; not death or anything else
should deter a man from doing what becomes him to do.

But these same authors are also pioneers in the writing of
biography of historical figures. Isocrates' *Evagoras* and the
Agesilaus of Xenophon which imitates it are indeed not so much
biography as panegyric, concerned, like epic, to glorify the individual excellence of their subjects. It may be, as C. M. Bowra
has suggested, that epic itself developed out of panegyric and
lament. The Song of Deborah in Judg. 5, which glorifies Jael for
her slaying of Sisera, and David's lament for Saul and Jonathan
in II Sam. 1 are the kind of thing out of which epic may well have
grown. But they, like epic, are poetry. Isocrates chose prose on
principle and was fully aware of its differences from poetry. His
Evagoras is therefore descriptive and constructive rather than
creative, and though his form is almost as rigidly stylized as
poetry and he omits discreditable episodes, he does present sufficient characteristic detail for a credible personality to emerge.

Xenophon's *Agesilaus* is very like the *Evagoras,* but it is more
outspokenly didactic and so a nearer approach to the particular
species of biography that is our main concern. It is good to know
such a career as Agesilaus', Xenophon implies, in order to understand contemporary history and to appreciate a sterling leader
as he deserves; but it is also good to cherish such an embodiment

of an ideal as a permanent guide and inspiration to proper political and personal conduct. Such a motivation is even more obvious in the *Cyropedia,* which deals not with a contemporary but with an almost legendary figure out of the remote past. Here Xenophon is almost wholly indifferent to history; what he is concerned to present is the perfect ideal of a gentleman and soldier, and what he has written is virtually a hagiography for a cult—as we shall see the true aretalogies are. But in order to make his paradigm serviceable—as Castiglione and numerous other authors of prescriptions for the ideal courtier or prince found it to be—Xenophon included a mass of personal detail. We know all that we could wish to know about Cyrus' personal habits, tastes, opinions, and principles in all the encounters of life. The *Cyropedia* is not only a general exhortation to nobility but a specific prescription for rules of etiquette.

II. THE HERO AND HIS CULT

THE CYRUS OF THE *Cyropedia* is a superlative human being who deserves high respect and emulation, but he makes no claim to preternatural endowment to raise him above the limits of ordinary humanity, and so he cannot properly become the object of a cult. For the subjects of true aretalogies preternatural gifts are claimed, and to understand the development of the genre and its significance we must see what precedents Greek experience can show for human beings (not gods) achieving a cult. Of the several phenomena that may have contributed to the conception of the preternaturally endowed leader, the most obviously relevant is the institution of heroization, to which we now turn.

In its proper usage the term "hero" carries a meaning both wider and more specific than our use of it to designate the principal personage in a work of fiction or in a battle. The most obvious distinction between the usages is that whereas the hero of a play or novel or battle is usually a living man, the hero in the technical sense must be dead; it is as much a paradox to speak of a brave warrior during his lifetime as a hero as it is to speak of a good man during his lifetime as a saint. Hero denotes preternatural potency of some sort associated with a dead man. Originally, in its technical sense, the word meant little more than ghost, and the offerings made at a *hērōon* were intended to ward off the harmful interference with the living of which the ghost might be capable. As with other ritualistic observances, the meaning attached to hero cults was gradually refined, at least in circles represented by formal literature. In literature only persons who had wrought or suffered in some extraordinary way and had

10

thereby significantly enlarged the scope of humanity are dealt with as heroes, and the cults offered them are intended not to appease their hostility but to assert their potency and to evoke their aid or inspiration in the field of their own achievement.

The earliest presentations of heroes in literature are of course Homer's, and the great exemplar is Achilles. Irregular as most of Achilles' conduct may be by civilized standards, and indifferent as he may be to the needs of his community, he yet serves it well by carrying the limits of human possibilities forward. His enrichment of humanity earns him his heroic status. The most Homeric of the tragic poets, as the ancients saw, was Sophocles, a number of whose plays can be described as demonstrations that a personage recognized as a hero did in fact deserve that status. Such an approach can be most illuminating, as Cedric Whitman has shown, in the two Oedipus plays, the *Antigone,* the *Trachinians,* and especially the *Ajax.*

Ajax is exhibited as a self-centered brute, inconsiderate of his wife and of his crew, who are wholly dependent upon him. At the opening of the play we are expressly shown that the goddess Athena herself disapproves of his headstrong truculence. But the decision to allow his body burial, taken at the end of the play, is a sign manifest that his quality is acknowledged and that he deserved the status of hero, which he in fact held. If society needs the kind of service that only an Ajax can supply, it must be willing to take his faults into the bargain. And so with Antigone. She is warped and recalcitrant and a little in love with martyrdom, but it is a useful thing for the rest of us to see a young woman sacrificing her all for what she conceives to be a religious duty. In these and other of Sophocles' plays the chorus and lesser characters counsel prudence, which is the course ordinary humanity must pursue. It is by ignoring prudential considerations and pursuing his independent course that the large personage achieves heroization.

The potency of most of the heroes celebrated in literature falls, as is to be expected, in the field of warfare or other strenuous activity, but poets and physicians and other creative pioneers might also be heroized; Sophocles himself was, though apparently not for his poetry. In another connection we shall examine the question of poetic inspiration as against independent creativity, and we shall find that views on the subject held by individuals are consistent with their general outlook on the validity of the supernatural. But even those poets who believed themselves inspired expressed pride in the poetry they wrote, not in the fact of their inspiration. The prophets of the Old Testament, by contrast, were avowed vehicles for revelation of the divine will—which must in any case have found some instrument to make itself known. The tragic poets who were their Greek analogues were, as the Greek sense of *poiētēs* indicates, makers; what they produced was individually theirs, and they received prizes and public honors for the excellence they had manifested. The memory of the prophet might be honored for his having been a chosen vessel; the memory of the tragic poet was honored for his own achievement. The one suggests sainthood, the other heroism.

The histories of the two categories show useful analogies, and we shall find them affecting one another and in some cases merging; but in essence they are distinct. To attribute heroism to a saint or saintliness to a hero, as in such expressions as "saintly warrior" or "hero of the spirit," is effective rhetoric, but of the figure called oxymoron, where the effect rests upon an essential paradox. Actually the business of the saint and the business of the hero are so far removed from one another that each may be economically defined in terms of opposition to the other. Because heroes are celebrated in memorable literature, or because they are by nature self-assertive where saints are by nature self-effacing, or simply because the climate of our age is secular, it is easier for most of us to recall a list of heroes than of saints. Literature and the popular imagination often surround the man of action with a mystique, seldom the saintly man with physical prowess. The mystique is a vital factor in survival; without it and its reflection in great literature heroes fall into oblivion.

It is quite probable that the great personages of early Israelite history also once enjoyed something like the status of Greek heroes, but as monotheism with its corollaries of a single authority and a central sanctuary asserted itself, the independent stature of early heroes would inevitably be diminished. We can see the process at work. The patriarchs in Genesis, it is true, remain thoroughly secular in outlook and behavior, but these were so firmly planted in popular memory that they could not be omitted and the redactors could do little to spiritualize them. Moses was undoubtedly a great organizer and leader, but the organization, like the Law it was intended to preserve, was given to him ready made. The judges are clearly heroes, but they are presented as instruments, manipulated rather than inspired, to promote the cause of true religion. And so with the kings : their prowess as conquerors or administrators is admirable only if they submitted to divine will; a successful but Baal-worshiping king like Omri is dismissed in a sentence.

The personalities of the prophets are more fully and firmly delineated than those of the kings, possibly because the redactors of the Bible favored the prophetic rather than the royalist party, so that on the basis of their utterances and their style imaginative modern critics can draw plausible portraits of individual prophets, each with his own characteristics. But their utterances are not represented as being generated in the minds of the prophets. Style and content might suggest an original thinker and powerful artist, but always there is the disclaimer of originality and art in the cachet "thus saith the Lord." Always, in kings and prophets alike, it is the transcendent deity who is steadily in control, and the humans who execute his designs are agents, not principals. Their choice is only as between a prescribed good and a forbidden evil, in a word, between obedience and disobedience; but mere obedience, even when it extends to works of supererogation, is not enough to earn a place among those whose independent spiritual creativity and energy is commemorated for significant enrichment of humanity. Among the Greeks not obedience but independence, which of necessity must often rebel against obedience, was the criterion for distinction. Under a paramount authority the only kind of distinction accessible to the individual is that which promotes the interests of the authority.

Warriors fight the battles of the Lord as prophets teach his, not their, doctrine. A warrior or prophet who fought or taught outside the authoritative structure could have no standing. Neither rebel nor conformist could rise high enough above the accepted level to be conceived of as possessing special potency.

But the special potency with which the Greeks endowed chosen individuals was conferred upon them only after death. To preserve the principle of equality the Athenian democracy was also reluctant to acknowledge preternatural endowment in the living. The institution of ostracism was specifically devised to prevent a cult of personality from taking root; when Athenians grew uneasy at hearing Aristides always called "the just," they ostracized him. If any Athenian was personally responsible for the victory over the Persians, which was Athens' most splendid achievement and the beginning of its career of greatness, it was Themistocles, and Themistocles died a pensioner of the Great King. If any Athenian was responsible for his city's glory in the latter half of the fifth century, which was its golden age, it was Pericles, and Pericles was stripped of office. Modern democracies are much more solicitous of their immortals.

Greek determination to keep notables within human dimensions finds illustration in the pages of Plutarch, who belongs, to be sure, to a later century but who out of conviction adhered to the continuing stream of Greek thought in such matters. Plutarch is careful not to attribute preternatural potency to any of the Greek worthies whose lives he writes, and particularly so in the case of those to whom such potency was in fact attributed. Alexander was adored as a god in his lifetime and in Plutarch's day was revered as a divine personage even by some of the peoples he had conquered; and yet Plutarch pointedly emphasizes Alexander's human failings and discounts his claims to supernatural origins or direction. Lycurgus was reputed to have received directions for instituting the Spartan polity directly from Apollo at Delphi, and a man so conservative in his piety as Plutarch might well be expected to be at least noncommittal about the legend. Instead he starts his life of Lycurgus with expressions

of grave doubt about the veracity of the traditional accounts of
Lycurgus and indeed about his very existence.

Independence cannot be more emphatically asserted than by
voluntary submission to death. Even suicide is countenanced in
the pagan tradition, and in some cases even recommended; in
any system that places complete authority in a supreme external
power, it must be counted a sin. The classical prose passages cited
above declare expressly that the high-souled man encounters
death cheerfully for glory's sake, and we have seen that death,
usually under remarkable circumstances, is a prerequisite to
heroization. The self-willed death of Achilles or the suicide of
Ajax is the decisive factor in confirming their heroic status. When
the death serves the spiritual welfare of the generality, when it is
for the sake of religion or of a patriotism that amounts to religion, we approach the genus of martyrdom that is an important
factor in the writings we shall presently consider. Curiously, it is
the females, the heroines, who make the transition to the later
mode. Sophocles' Antigone, as we have seen, invites death in the
service of religion. She may be too inarticulate and too hard to
engage the full measure of our sympathy, but that is not true of
the Iphigenia who is immolated in Euripides' *Iphigenia at Aulis*
who comforts her mother in a speech that seems to be an echo
of actual martyrdoms (1368 ff.) :

> Hear, mother, the thought that occurred to me as I pondered the thing.
> I am resolved to die. And I will do it gloriously. I have put all mean
> thoughts out of my heart. Come, see it with me, mother, see how right
> I am. The whole might of Hellas depends on me. Upon me depends
> the passage of the ships over the sea, and the overthrow of the
> Phrygians. With me it rests to prevent the barbarians from carrying
> our women off from happy Hellas in the future, should they attempt
> such a thing. All these things I shall achieve by my death, and my
> name, as the liberator of Hellas, shall be blessed. Indeed, it behooves
> me not to be too fond of life; you bore me for the common good of
> all the Hellenes, not for yourself alone.

Because Iphigenia is an ordinary girl, not impelled to her selfless act or assured of reward by reason of preternatural endowment, her heroism is the more appealing. Her voluntary death for
the sake of the common good makes her story a transition from

the general category of heroizations to the special class of aretalogy. But the very circumstance that makes her story so appealing prevents the transition from being complete. For a true aretalogy we desiderate a subject who is, to be sure, human but who can make a claim to preternatural potency by miraculous works or by the circumstances surrounding his death. Frequently the circumstances surrounding his birth are also remarkable, but only in retrospect, after he has proven his status. This he is compelled to do, often by confronting and outfacing some tyrant; always there is disbelief and resistance that he must overcome. Are there Greek precedents for assertion of preternatural potency against powerful opposition?

III. PATTERNS OF ACHIEVEMENT:
DIONYSUS, HERACLES, THESEUS

THE EFFECTIVE CATALYST for aretalogy, it will be maintained in a subsequent chapter, is the Platonic image of Socrates. The image is never articulated into a systematic biography, to be sure, but must be assembled from traits reported in diverse treatises; nevertheless the scattered details do combine into a consistent picture that is probably Plato's own creation and that certainly influenced subsequent pictures of great teachers. The consequences of the Platonic image we shall look at in due course; our present object is to examine its antecedents. Specifically, what existing models might have supplied suggestions or details for such an image as Plato created?

One model, perhaps the most obvious, we have seen. Whether in the heroic age or under the democracy the institution of heroization accustomed the public to special recognition of eminence. Any outstanding figure who enlarged the boundaries of the human potential might, as has been observed, attain commemoration as a hero; and though Socrates was not formally heroized, the existence of the institution would be suggestive to anyone who desired to endow Socrates with special status and make such status acceptable to a public.

But the excellence of the subject of aretalogy is more narrowly defined than the excellence of other heroes. In the first place, he is consistently and intentionally benevolent and free from the stark passions so often inseparable from the ordinary hero's virtues; his benefits are conferred by design, not as a by-product of his own wilfulness. These benefits are of a spiritual, not material, order; his is a cure of souls, and his teaching, by example as well as by precept, is continuous. The capacities he brings to his task transcend the ordinary; his doing and his suffering are preternatural. Frequently his election is signalized by extraordinary circumstances surrounding his birth; sometimes divine paternity is claimed for him. The circumstances surrounding his death are no less remarkable; he is somehow transfigured, or he receives other marks of divine approbation. Frequently he is made to confront some worldly potentate who charges him with wizardry or subversiveness, but he succeeds in outfacing the tyrant and in demonstrating the power of his personality and his teaching.

If the developed image of the aretalogists is a conscious creation, it is legitimate, and it may prove illuminating to seek for the germs out of which one or another of these metaheroic traits received its character. Our search for antecedents should move among the race of men, however preternaturally endowed, not among gods, for the essence of the saint is his mortality. But in polytheism divinity is not so absolute as in monotheism. There are gradations of rank, and hence the possibility of promotion. In the Hellenistic age kings could assume divinity, though the gesture can have had little spiritual meaning to their subjects. But in the formative age when belief in the gods was more vital, certain gods who were benefactors of mankind were thought to have achieved their divinity. These, in particular Dionysus and Heracles, may well have contributed to the image of the holy teacher. They were not originally Olympians but of questionable origin, they enriched the spiritual store of mankind notably, they were long denied recognition, and they served as paradigms of attainment through struggle.

Toward the end of the fourth century B.C. Euhemerus taught that even the Olympians had advanced to their divine status from human origins. In his *Sacred Composition* he declared that in the temple of Zeus on the island of Panchaia in the Indian Sea he had seen large golden pillars on which were inscribed the acts of Uranus, Kronos, and Zeus. (The word for "acts", *praxeis,* is the regular term for the deeds of a holy teacher.) The notion that the gods were originally human had doubtless been adumbrated in earlier speculation; Euhemerus' fiction purports to document the theory that the gods whom men worshipped had originally been benevolent kings and conquerors for whose extraordinary benefactions mankind had shown gratitude by making them the objects of worship. In the case of certain deities whom he does not name, Asclepius for example, Euhemerus' explanation is almost certainly right. In any case, both before and after Euhemerus the earthly vicissitudes of certain deities afforded mankind a sort of pattern and inspiration that the greater and remoter Olympians could never provide. Most useful for our present purposes are Dionysus, who was a relative late-comer to Olympian society, and Heracles, whom even Herodotus considered a mortal.

All of our ancient stories about Dionysus show him as first despised and then cherished or asserting his power. The oldest is in Homer (*Iliad* 6.129ff.) :

> Know that I will not fight against any god of the heaven,
> since even the son of Dryas, Lykourgos the powerful, did not
> live long; he who tried to fight with the gods of the bright sky,
> who once drove the fosterers of rapturous Dionysos
> headlong down the sacred Nyseian hill, and all of them
> shed and scattered their wands on the ground, stricken with an ox-goad
> by murderous Lykourgos, while Dionysos in terror
> dived into the salt surf, and Thetis took him to her bosom,
> frightened, with the strong shivers upon him at the man's blustering.
> But the gods who live at their ease were angered with Lykourgos,
> and the son of Kronos struck him to blindness, nor did he live long
> afterwards, since he was hated by all the immortals.

(tr. RICHMOND LATTIMORE)

Not Zeus-nurtured princes alone but ordinary piratical sailors failed to recognize Dionysus' divinity. In the ancient Hymn to Dionysus (*Homeric Hymns* 7) we read how Tyrsenian pirates mistook him for an elegant youth and kidnapped him as an easy and profitable prey. "They sought to bind him with rude bonds, but the bonds would not hold him, and the withes fell away from his hands and feet; and he sat with a smile in his dark eyes." Presently he caused grapevines to spread along the sails and ivy to twine about the mast, and then transformed himself into a roaring lion, so that the frightened sailors jumped overboard but were mercifully saved by being changed into dolphins. This episode is repeatedly echoed, with variations, in later literature and art; it is the subject of the sculptural decoration on the choragic monument of Lysicrates (344 B.C.) that still stands in Athens.

But the fullest image of Dionysus rejected and then asserting himself in power is that in Euripides' magnificent *Bacchae*. The play has been diligently and profitably mined by students of religion for details of Dionysiac beliefs and cult, but it has also exercised students of drama, who have proposed interpretations poles apart. Some have seen in the recognition of the religious factor in life the aged Euripides' devout recantation of his youthful criticism of the gods; others see the picture of Dionysus' heartlessness a consistent step forward in Euripides' alleged rationalism. To consider the play as a tract, either pro or con, is a mistake; but its profounder meanings, which lie elsewhere, are not our present concern. What is obvious to any reader of the play in any age is that an unknown figure whose claims to divinity were rejected by the constituted authorities of the state did in the event prove that he was indeed a powerful god, to the measureless discomfiture of the constituted authorities. In later ages spokesmen for a deity not recognized by the constituted authorities, not excluding Christians, regularly cited the example of the *Bacchae* to show the danger of despising an unknown god.

It is clear enough that Dionysus might be a paradigm for the persecuted spiritual figure who discomfits the secular authority, but is it proper to reckon him among the antecedents of aretalogies of *human* figures? We may argue that it is, on the basis of the peculiar and familiar history of his own and his cult's transformation. He stood apart from the Olympians, and it was known that his origins were alien and therefore humble and that he had won such esteem as to acquire a share in Delphi with Apollo himself. It was known that his cult originally involved practices abhorrent to Greeks—frantic dancing, rending and devouring certain animals raw, even human sacrifice; but the orgiastic elements had been reduced to more decorous observances. The fact that the progression toward civilized Hellenic norms was felt—no such development is perceptible in the case of the genuine Olympians—made it easier to measure Dionysus by a human yardstick, as Orpheus (with whom Dionysus came to be associated) and similar figures are measured.

But more important in the present context are the new functions attributed to Dionysus. Originally a power of fertility, he came to be associated more narrowly with wine and then with the release, intellectual and spiritual as well as physical, that wine symbolizes. And his case for mankind is not limited to the highborn, as Apollo's so often was, but is dispensed freely to all who will receive it. Here is the conclusion of one of the beautiful odes in praise of him in the *Bacchae* (416ff.) :

> Our deity, Zeus's son, rejoices in festivals. He loves goddess Peace, who brings prosperity and cherishes youth. To rich and poor he gives in equal measure the blessed joy of wine. But he hates the man who has no taste for such things—to live a life of happy days and sweet and happy nights, in wisdom to keep his mind and heart aloof from overbusy men. Whatever the majority, the simple folk, believe and follow, that way will I accept.

Making life tolerable by teaching the wisdom that dispels care and sweetens existence is by no means the sum of the ethical teaching associated with Dionysus. Where Athenians were most aware of his presence and potency was at the festival of the Great Dionysia, and the central activity in that festival was attendance at the theater, which was on ground consecrated to Dionysus and presided over by his priest. It may be that the performances originally related more directly to the career of the god, so that when the subjects shifted, some conservatives are said to have objected, "What has this to do with Dionysus?" But whatever the subject, the presentation was in fact an act of worship of Dionysus and somehow accountable to him. And it is needless to point out that the most widely disseminated as well as the profoundest ethical doctrine available to the Athenians was that which they received in the dramas presented in the theater of Dionysus.

Conceiving of him as in some sense a teacher and in some sense self-made is still not enough to reduce him to the human level. The trouble is, paradoxically, that his rise and his functions came to him too easily; there was nothing like a strenuous effort required to demonstrate preternatural qualities, or preternatural courage required to confront his would-be persecutors. It is only in humans that preternatural capacities are striking and therefore an effective device for giving their doctrines credit. Nevertheless, for an artist in the process of creating an image, as we assume Plato created the image of Socrates, it is not unreasonable to imagine that the figure of Dionysus and Euripides' play may have made some contribution.

About Heracles' availability and suitability as a pattern there can be no question, for he was definitely known to be a hero, not a god, and he was actually revered by Cynics and Stoics as the prime example of a man raised above ordinary humanity by his services to mankind. According to the myth the celebrated labors that he performed for Eurystheus were not voluntary but imposed upon him by the ill-will of Hera, who, because she could find no strength other than Heracles' own capable of crushing Heracles, afflicted him with a fit of madness during which he killed his own children; but by the fifth century, on the evidence of the tragic poets, Heracles had been transformed into the great benefactor of mankind who devoted his life to cleansing the world of monsters (easily allegorized) that afflicted it, then mastered even himself when he found that he had slaughtered his own children during his tyranically inflicted insanity, and finally was assumed into heaven.

Actually the configuration of Heracles in classical and later literature is, as might be expected, a composite of several strands. Quite probably there had been a real Heracles, who ruled at Tiryns and won high esteem for extraordinary prowess or service. But Herodotus (2.43) realized that the Argive hero could not be identical with the god called Heracles in Egypt. An oriental strand is suggested by the story of Heracles' ignominious servitude to the Lydian queen Omphale and by the existence of a temple identified as his in Carthaginian Cadiz. Within Greece the various adventures ascribed to him derive from disparate sources, but all of them, from his strangling of the serpents in his cradle to his incineration on Mount Oeta and his transmission of his symbolic bow to Philoctetes, were shaped into a reasonably consistent totality. Here is Heracles' own summary of his career, before the final act, as conceived by Euripides (*Heracles* 1266ff.) :

> While I was still at suck, Hera set her snakes
> with gorgon eyes to slither in my crib
> and strangle me. And when I grew older
> and a belt of muscle bound my body—
> why recite all those labors I endured?
> All those wars I fought, those beasts I slew,
> those lions and triple-bodied Typhons,
> giants, and four-legged Centaur hordes!
> I killed the hydra, that hound whose heads
> grew back as soon as lopped. My countless labors done,
> I descended down among the sullen dead
> to do Eurystheus' bidding and bring to light
> the triple-headed hound who guards the gates of hell.
> And now my last worst labor has been done:
> I slew my children and crowned my house with grief.

(tr. WILLIAM ARROWSMITH)

With the sympathetic support of Theseus, Heracles scorns suicide and determines to continue his career. The end is depicted at the close of Sophocles' *Trachinians,* where Heracles, realizing that the prophecy of Zeus is now fulfilled, orders his son to place him upon the funeral pyre while he is yet alive. When he appears as *deus ex machina* at the close of Sophocles' *Philoctetes,* he declares that he has won "deathless glory" (the word, significantly, is *aretē*) by enduring his many labors to the end. His very presence serves to remind Philoctetes that the bow he had used in the service of mankind must not be put to unworthy or selfish use. What the later Stoics made of Heracles appears in Seneca's version of the pyre scene in his *Hercules Oetaeus.* The report of Heracles' last moments there (1618–1757) comes to this : Heracles undergoes a "passion" on a pyre in order to become a savior of mankind; this is to be followed by a "resurrection" and an "apotheosis"; Alcmena waits at the foot of the pyre; Heracles speaks to his father in heaven and hears his reply : "Lo! my father summons me, and opens his heaven : Father, I come." In this connection it is interesting to note that the chief items in Heracles' career are traditionally spoken of as the *Praxeis,* or Acts, and the lesser items as the *Parerga,* or incidentals. That the image of Heracles influenced later histories of teachers and benefactors of mankind there can be no doubt, for he himself was celebrated as an exemplar.

How attractive the image of Heracles was can be seen from its palpable influence upon that of Athens' own favorite hero, Theseus. The deeds especially associated with Theseus—his slaying of the Minotaur, which relieved Athens of the terrible tribute of young lives exacted by Crete, and his union of the separate Attic communities to form a single Athenian state—are important and direct benefits that do not require allegorization and were undertaken as such, not under constraint of a Hera or a Eurystheus. But even his suppression of antisocial monsters and brigands, such as Sinis or Procrustes, events that may have been inspired by the Heracles legend, are also self-willed and not imposed from without as a punishment. In the tragic poets Theseus regularly represents Athenian ideals at their noblest. It is he who helps broken Heracles, defends persecuted Oedipus, embodies the principles of chivalry and succor for the afflicted. But Theseus too suffered an unjust and violent death and then received the homage he merited. He was killed by King Lycomedes when he was in exile at Scyros, but eventually his bones were brought back to Athens by Cimon, and a hero-shrine was built to contain them.

Theseus is a hero, as Achilles or Ajax was a hero, but the quality of the services attributed to him are a much nearer approach to those celebrated in later aretalogies, and many of the facets of the holy teacher's career are present at least in germ in the career of a Theseus. Always in the aretalogies the circumstances surrounding death are extraordinary; frequently martyrdom is involved, and sometimes transfiguration. Finally, the memory of the holy teacher, as of the hero, received a particular kind of observance. But the kind of observance bestowed on the subjects of aretalogies differed from that originally paid to heroes, and it will be useful to notice the relationship between the two.

To hold their beloved or honored dead in memory is natural to all men, but their motives are not always the same. Observances may be intended to benefit the dead, as when perquisites of the living are bestowed upon them as funerary offerings, or prayers or acts of charity are devoted to the welfare of their souls; or they may be intended to benefit the living, as when among primitive peoples offerings are meant to appease the dead and so prevent them from returning to injure the living, or simply out of a desire to continue the satisfactions of an affectionate attachment so far as loyalty to its memory can avail to preserve it, or for the inspiration to excellence which a remembered and esteemed model can afford. Except where special religious beliefs obtain, the latter motivation is the one most commonly recognized among enlightened peoples, though the others may be subsumed in it; we observe the birthdays of Washington and Lincoln not for their benefit but for ours. In the case of heroes it is clear that originally observances bestowed upon them were simply a means of quieting their ghosts, but soon the motives of affection and then of inspiration entered in, and these latter were fixed in the consciousness of the people by the character of the festivities ordained for such a hero as Theseus. The institution of a specific day made celebrating the memory of the benefactor a solemn duty. It is this spirit and mode of commemoration that the writers of the developed aretalogies hoped to secure. The whole object of their enterprise, real or alleged, was inspiration, and when they were concerned for the perpetuation of a cult they stipulated certain days as obligatory for solemn observance.

Looking backward from the vantage point of the developed aretalogy we can see how lineaments of the configuration of Dionysus or Heracles or Theseus may have contributed germs to its growth, but it is hard to imagine these germs developing into the end product without an intervening catalyst to fructify them and give them shape, and this catalyst may well have been the Platonic image of Socrates. The great obstacle to positing a connection between the three figures and Socrates is their remoteness in age and therefore in stature; it took little imagination to assimilate a fourth- or third-century figure to Socrates, but it would take a great leap of the imagination to assimilate a contemporary to Heracles or Theseus.

There were indeed personages in the Greek tradition much closer to Socrates in kind or in time who may have helped bridge the leap. Orpheus, Pythagoras, and Empedocles, whom we shall look at more closely in another chapter, were all teachers of spiritual doctrine, and though claims of preternatural potency were made for all of them, they were themselves definitely not divine; the latter two were only a century removed from Socrates in time. And not only these avowed promulgators of special doctrine but also great poets whose teaching was more general were believed to have been inspired. Unlike the mysterious teachers named, the poets, except for their inspiration, behaved like ordinary men in the common encounters of life and so were a step nearer to Socrates, and hence possibly a fertile source for traits in the Socratic image. We ourselves think of inspiration mainly in a metaphorical sense, and it will therefore be useful to consider what it may have meant to the ancients.

IV. THE INSPIRATION OF POETS

THE RATIONALISM upon which the modern world prides itself was a concomitant if not a result of the humanist revival. The humanists and their successors set a high and perhaps exaggerated value upon all the intellectual and artistic productions of classical antiquity, but more fruitful than the models of form that the classics provided was the underlying assumption that characterizes so many of them—the thoroughly rationalist doctrine that man is the measure of all things. Modern appreciations of the Greek experience naturally emphasize its humanism, and it may well be that rationalism is the most significant and the most admirable facet of Greek thought.

But it was certainly not the sole or for any considerable stretch of time the dominant facet. Very near the surface enlightenment and repeatedly breaking through and suffusing its hard brightness are darker or richer tints, sometimes crude and primitive, sometimes soaring to the noblest fancies the mind of man has conceived. The tension between the humanist and the spiritual strands is not limited to particular periods when the one or the other held the upper hand but is discernible throughout the course of Greek history. The one strand is represented by Homer, the Ionian physicists and Hippocrates, the Sophists, Euripides, the Epicureans; and the other strand by Hesiod and Pindar, Pythagoras and Empedocles, the towering figure of Plato, and to a degree the Stoics. Back of the latter group stands the enigmatic figure of Orpheus, tantalizing in its amorphous outlines and Protean manifestations, difficult to grasp in any particular manifestation and yet exercising a pervasive influence over the

whole course of Greek thought. The two strands come into conflict at many points; the issue between them that is of particular
relevance to our present purpose is that whereas the rationalist
tendency must be suspicious of preternaturally potent personalities, the more mystical view might provide a seedbed for
the cult of personalities.

The best information on how a given people remote from ourselves conceived of their world and of their relations to it is to be
found in the books they wrote, and not so much in systematic
and scholarly analyses and expositions as in their creative literature, what the Greeks would call poetry, whether written in prose
or verse. For the Greeks the evidence of their creative literature
carries great weight, not so much because it is full and far-ranging
and artistic as because it is serious. The concept of mere belles-
lettres, of art for art's sake, did not arise until the Hellenistic age,
when poets had no real audience but were pensioners of the
Ptolemies and wrote to impress one another. In the Classical
period the poet looked upon himself and was looked upon as
a responsible teacher. He made his work as beautiful as possible,
as cabinetmakers and stonemasons did also; but to fashion a
beautiful poem that did not instruct and edify would have seemed
as absurd as fashioning a beautiful chair that could not be sat in.
And he was more directly controlled by his audience than poets
usually have been; if he wrote drama, for example, his work had
to be accepted for presentation by an elected magistrate, and his
success depended on the approval of the people acting through a
panel of its own representatives.

If the poet is an authorized teacher, what is the basis of his
authority? From the point of view of the audience it should be
the same as the basis of other authority they accept. In the
Athenian democracy sovereignty was conceived of as residing in
the people, and the officials, chosen by lot or for special com-
petence for limited terms, were agents to whom the sovereign
people delegated specific tasks. In this sense the poets were agents
of the people and derived their authority to teach from the
people. To follow the political analogy, in a polity where the
ruler, not the people, was sovereign, doctrine promulgated by the

poet as agent of the sovereign would derive its authority from the sovereign. But of whatever sovereignty, popular or personal, he might be agent, the poet must be presumed to possess special insights and a special gift for communicating them. Is he himself responsible for his utterances, or is he a chosen mouthpiece for inspiration from some external source? The determination of this point is crucial for our central question.

It is usual for classical poets, and for their successors who follow classical norms, to invoke the aid of the Muses or to speak of themselves as servants of Apollo or otherwise to acknowledge the reality of supernatural assistance. In late and derivative poets who regarded Greek practices as canonical, reliance on supernatural inspiration is nothing more than a conventional pretense and even intended to be recognized as such by informed readers. And yet even in authors far removed from the Greeks the conventional phraseology may express genuine conviction, else John Milton would not have taken pains to specify the special character of the Muse he invokes (*Paradise Lost* 1.6ff.):

> Sing, Heavenly Muse, that on the secret top
> Of Oreb, or of Sinai, didst inspire
> That shepherd who first taught the chosen seed
> In the beginning how the heavens and earth
> Rose out of chaos.

Milton's particular pieties were his own, but the pious attitude of which they are an expression is not confined to a particular age and surely obtained, in a more literal conception than Milton's, among the Greeks who first spoke of poetic inspiration. The survival of gestures and formulas as mere convention is in itself proof that they once actually meant what they purport to mean.

To discover how far the notion of divine inspiration was meaningful we must consider first the attitudes of the poets—Homer, who is somewhat ambivalent; Hesiod and Pindar, who apparently believe themselves inspired; and the lyric poets, who insist on their independence—and then the explicitly stated position of Plato. It may be, of course, that the process of conventionalizing had already proceeded some distance even in the earliest poets we have, for they were not the first of their kind but already the product of an antecedent poetic tradition. Homer in particular is in many respects in advance of fifth-century poets in his treatment of myth; many of his views seem to show purposeful opposition to and "correction" of rival views. It may be that his invocations to the Muses too are cynical. Within the poems they occur most typically at the opening of some listing where the poet is in particular need not of inspiration but of memory. The fullest such invocation is prefixed to the Catalogue in *Iliad* 2.484ff. :

> Tell me now, you Muses who have your homes on Olympos,
> For you, who are goddesses, are there, and you know all things,
> And we have heard only the rumor of it and know nothing.
> Who then of those were the chiefmen and the lords of the Danaans?
> I could not tell over the multitude of them nor name them,
> Not if I had ten tongues and ten mouths, not if I had
> a voice never to be broken and a heart of bronze within me,
> not unless the Muses of Olympia, daughters
> of Zeus of the aegis, remembered all those who came beneath Ilion.

Perhaps little more than the gift of good memory, so essential for the oral poet, is intended by the credentials of the bard Demodocus, of whom it is said (*Odyssey* 8.63) that "the Muse had greatly loved him and had given him good and ill : she took away his eyesight but gave him delightful song." In the opening of the *Iliad,* and of certain major sections within long poems, we do have what looks like an appeal for inspiration as well as memory. The first words of the *Iliad,* in the Greek order, are "The wrath sing goddess." For moderns the translation of the late W. H. D. Rouse is correct : "An angry man, that is my story," for "sing goddess" means no more to us than a declaration of the subject of a long and serious work. It is very doubtful that Homer intended it to mean more to his original audiences. We can see the process of reduction in meaning of such expressions in the epithets "charming" and "enchanting" applied to the productions of the bard. We ourselves use these words in utter oblivion of their original and literal meanings, and they are used with similar oblivion in Homer.

But before such expressions were reduced to metaphor, they must have reflected a belief that an actual magical power had been communicated by a divine patron. Hesiod clearly believed that he had been given a physical rod as a manifest symbol of such power. The Muses, he says (*Theogony* 29–35),

> A branch of laurel gave, which they had plucked,
> To be my scepter; and they breathed a song
> In music on my soul and bade me set
> Things past and things to be to that high strain.
> Also they bade me sing the race of gods,
> Themselves, at first and last, ever remembering.

Hesiod's belief in his divine mission is consistent with his religious outlook generally. He has a fall of man, brought on by the importunate curiosity of a woman, very like that in Genesis, and a system of rewards and punishments in the hands of Zeus, who is informed of men's misdeeds by thirty thousand watchers whose business it is to observe men's behavior.

Hesiod represents the dour mainland tradition, whereas Homer represents Ionian enlightenment, and it is interesting to note that the lyric poets of the eastern Mediterranean not only pointedly fail to invoke divine inspiration but insist on their own independence to the point of flouting conservative tradition. Typical of the attitude is Archilochus, who can blandly record his indifference to the prime article in the warrior's code :

> Some Thracian strutteth with my shield;
> For, being somewhat flurried
> I left it in a wayside bush,
> When from the field I hurried;
> A right good targe, but I got off.
> The deuce may take the shield;
> I'll get another just as good
> When next I go afield.
>
> (tr. PAUL SHOREY)

Even the Athenian Solon introduces his fine lines on *eunomia*, or good order, not with an acknowledgment of external assistance but with the phrase, "This it is that my heart biddeth me tell the Athenians."

Pindar is as deeply convinced of the poet's supernatural endowment and of his own election to the high office of poet as is Hesiod, and his case is more interesting because he lived in the bright light of the fifth century and is in many ways the most Greek of poets. Repeatedly he emphasizes the antitheses between genius (*phya*) and craftsmanship (*technē*), between the man who knows by nature and the man who learns (*Olympian* 2.94, 9.100; *Nemean* 3.40). "To me," he says with simple assurance (*paean* 7b), "the Muses have handed on this immortal task." It is by virtue of his office that Pindar can confer immortality on the subjects of his epinician odes—such as Homer had conferred on Ajax (*Isthmian* 4.37). In Pindar too his view of inspiration is consistent with his religious outlook generally. His extended picture of the Elysian Fields, the haven of the blessed (*Olympian* 2), is a sufficient proof of his affinities with the Orphic cult, and we shall find that Orpheus himself is the prime model for the holy teacher who is celebrated in aretalogies.

The author chiefly responsible for crystallizing and propagating the doctrine of inspiration is Plato, who makes it explicit on the lips of Socrates. In the *Apology* Socrates tells of his efforts to disprove the statement of the Pythia to the effect that no one was wiser than Socrates. Conversation with men in several fields proved that he and they alike were ignorant, but that whereas they were not aware of their ignorance, he was, so that in that particular he might be called the wiser . Then he went to the poets, of whom he had high expectations :

> I took up their poems, those which I thought they had taken most pains to perfect, and questioned them as to what they meant, and I hoped to learn something from them at the same time. Well, gentlemen, I am ashamed to tell you the truth; but I must. Almost all the bystanders, with hardly an exception, one might say, had something better to say than the composers had about their own compositions. I discovered, then, very soon about the poets that no wisdom enabled them to compose as they did, but natural genius and inspiration; like the diviners and those who chant oracles, who say many fine things but do not understand anything of what they say. The poets appeared to me to be in much the same case.

In the *Ion* Socrates explains that inspiration works upon the

rhapsode like a magnet upon an iron ring, which can then trans-
mit its magnetism to a chain of rings :

> So that the Muse not only inspires people herself, but through these
> inspired ones others are inspired and dangle in a string. In fact all the
> good poets who make epic poems use no art at all, but they are in-
> spired and possessed when they utter all these beautiful poems, and
> so are the good lyric poets; they are not in their right mind when they
> make their beautiful songs, but they are like Corybants out of their
> wits dancing about. As soon as they mount on their harmony and
> rhythm, they become frantic and possessed; just as the Bacchant
> women, possessed and out of their senses, draw milk and honey out
> of the rivers, so the soul of these honey-singers does just the same. . . .
> For the poet is an airy thing, a winged and a holy thing; and he can-
> not make poetry until he becomes inspired and goes out of his senses
> and no mind is left in him; so long as he keeps possession of this, no
> man is able to make poetry and chant oracles.

So in the *Phaedrus* we read : "Whoever knocks at the door
of poetry without the Muses' incitement, persuaded that by art
alone he will be a sufficient poet, fails of perfection, and
the work of the sober is forthwith eclipsed by the work of the
frenzied." Benjamin Jowett, whose translations of Plato were
long esteemed as something like the authorized version, doubted
the authenticity of the *Ion,* one suspects because he found it difficult to conceive of a pagan holding a doctrine of inspiration. A
similar prejudice is responsible for making Socrates say, at the
end of the *Symposium,* that the man who writes tragedies can
write comedies also. What Socrates does say is that if a man
writes tragedies "by craftsmanship" (*technē*), he should be able
to write comedies "by craftsmanship" also. But men who wrote
tragedies did not in fact write comedies also; therefore something
beyond craftsmanship must be required, and that something is
inspiration.

No later pagan, unless he were specifically echoing Plato,
spoke of poetic inspiration in such unequivocal terms. In his
Rhetoric (1408B), it is true, Aristotle says *entheon gar hē poiēsis,*
"poetry is divinely inspired" : but in the *Poetics* (1455A) he
offers alternatives : "Poetry implies either a happy gift of nature
(*euphuia*) or ecstasy (*manikē*)." The whole of the *Poetics,* as

most of subsequent criticism, really rests on the former alternative.

In setting forth the potency of poetic inspiration Plato repeatedly employs the analogy of religious materials uttered in a state of possession. It is a plausible surmise that the analogy stems from an original identity. The Latin *vates* or the English *bard* connotes religious teaching as well as poetry, and we have noticed that classical Greek poets were recognized as responsible teachers on ethics and morality. Perhaps it was only a process of democratic secularization that introduced the formal cleavage between the two functions, so that what Plato was doing, in effect, was attempting to restore the original unity, and by corollary, the authority of the poet-prophet.

It is in order to certify that the doctrines of the subjects of aretalogy possess the authority of inspiration that they are credited with preternatural potency. But there are degrees in the potency attributed to them corresponding to classes of aretalogy. Those associated with Neopythagoreanism or with Neoplatonist thaumaturgy are credited with capacities and acts outside the natural bounds of humanity. Those that derive more directly from the Platonic image of Socrates, like that image itself, do not greatly transcend the limits of the credible but do in every case exhibit some voucher of divine approbation and support. Socrates several times went into a rapt state in which he was oblivious to his surroundings, and he spoke of a detached *daimonion* within him that advised him against wrong choices in moments of indecision but apparently did not offer positive counsel. This *daimonion*, it is fair to say, is not an invention of Plato's, for Xenophon also mentions it. But Xenophon does not make it a voucher for inspiration to the degree that Plato does. In the light of his general views on the subject it is not remarkable that Plato should represent Socrates as inspired. But the image Plato wished to construct required a more vital association with the supernatural than the somewhat faded doctrine of poetic inspiration could afford. For this construction certain figures of former generations, whose function, like Socrates', was teaching, whose memory was still green, and who were believed to have had direct connections with the supernatural may well have offered inspiration and suggestion. To these we must now turn.

V. FROM ORPHEUS TO EMPEDOCLES

THE INSTITUTION OF HEROIZATION, we have seen, provided a climate in which the memory of a holy teacher might receive reverent consideration; the attainment of recognition by certain deities who worked for the improvement of the human condition might have supplied a paradigm for the teacher's struggle; and belief in the inspiration of the poet's message had wide if not universal currency. All of these factors may well have contributed to the image of Socrates, but it is of interest to inquire whether they may have been brought together to some degree before Plato to adumbrate that image.

Socrates marks an epoch in the history of philosophy as his image does in the history of aretalogy; there were philosophers before Socrates, and some of them are reported to have behaved in ways at least as odd. The actual Socrates, therefore, however strange his conduct or novel his doctrine, belonged in a tradition, and a contrived image of Socrates would be likely to exploit that tradition, choosing traits from one source or another to produce the effect desired. The predecessors of Socrates are grouped together under the designation of pre-Socratics, which includes teachers of quite different outlook. The principal ones are the so-called Ionian physicists like Anaximander and Anaximenes and the atomists like Democritus and Leucippus, all definitely rationalist; but the term is also applied to mystics like Pythagoras and to men like Empedocles who were at once mystic and rationalist. With the physicists and their congeners we shall have little concern, for the Platonic Socrates deliberately turned away from them. The others have left a perceptible precipitate in the writings of Plato. In the background of all of them and of Plato himself looms the figure of Orpheus and the institutions and beliefs of Orphism, and it is to these matters that we must now direct our attention.

Enthusiastic appreciation of Orphism a generation ago made of it a full-blown religion with a founder, scriptures, creed, ritual, and something like an ecclesiastical organization. The enthusiasm was promoted, if not generated, by admirers of the classics who were made uncomfortable by crudities in other manifestations of religion in Greece and therefore eager to discover a structure into which ideas more acceptable to modern norms could be projected. So firmly entrenched was the conception of Orphism as an established religion that men like Arnold Toynbee (in Vol. 5 of his *A Study of History*) could speak of the "historic Orphic Church." Excess in one direction was answered by excess in the other; a series of critical scholars, including the great Wilamowitz, complained that the elaborate structure was founded mainly on dubious hypotheses.

There was, to be sure, no Orphic Church; to posit one is anachronism. That some features of the creed ascribed to the Orphics are in apparent contradiction to others is no great matter, for recognized religions exhibit similar inconsistencies; more significant, perhaps, is the circumstance that no individual is ever spoken of as an Orphic. But the allusions collected in Otto Kern's *Orphicorum Fragmenta* (1922), even after they are subjected to the searching criticism of Ivan Linforth's *The Arts of Orpheus* (1941), do indicate that a reasonably consistent attitude distinguishable from other attitudes prevalent in Greece is specifically associated with Orphism in a number of passages and may reasonably be associated with Orphism in other passages where the connection is not made explicit.

If we may not speak of an Orphic religion, therefore, in our sense of "a religion," we may speak of it as a movement, as Martin Nilsson, our most eminent authority on Greek religion, speaks of it. If our extant Orphic literature is late and spurious, if the lost Orphic books listed by Clement of Alexandria are mainly pseudepigraphical, they yet point to a very strong likelihood that a genuine Orphic literature did exist. There can be little doubt that the cosmogony by which the chorus justifies the primacy of birds in Aristophanes (*Birds* 685ff.) is a parody of Orphic doctrine. The Hippolytus of Euripides' play may not be an Orphic, as has often been alleged, because it is hard to reconcile a devoted huntsman with vegetarianism, but his father Theseus thought he had grounds for reviling him as one (lines 952ff.) :

> "*You* are temperate and uncontaminatèd by evil? Your high claims will never convince me; I won't be such a fool as to attribute to the gods such a lack of discernment. Go then and brag, cry up your vegetarian diet like a quack. Hold Orpheus your master, rant away, revere the vaporings of your many screeds."

What a rationalist knew of devotees of Orphism, then, was that they pretended to special purity, followed a vegetarian diet, paid special reverence to Orpheus as their master, and regarded his writings as sacred.

It is clear that the Orphics possessed a characteristic cosmogony and anthropogony, adapted from elsewhere, it may be, but associated in the popular mind with their movement. It is also clear that they avoided the use of meat and of wool; when Herodotus (2.81) says that the Egyptians allowed no wool to be taken into their temples or buried with them, he notes that "here their practice resembles the rites called Orphic and Bacchic." But the salient teachings of Orphism have to do with ethics and eschatology. These rest upon the dualism of body and soul, with the notion that the one is good and enduring and the other transitory and evil, and that one should be suppressed in the interest of the other. Perhaps it was because physical bodies are unclean that Orphics avoided slaughter and eating of flesh; more likely it was because of a belief in transmigration of souls. The corollary of the dichotomy between soul and body is a system of rewards and punishments in an after life. The motivation for proper conduct, including ritual purifications, was to ensure a desirable lot in a future existence. The system was capable of high spirituality, but it also involved elements of crudeness, and it was susceptible of abuse in the hands of self-seeking priests and charlatans.

Of more concern in our present context is the individual regarded as the founder of Orphism and believed to have promulgated its doctrines in poems that he sang. Whether Orpheus was a real personage or mythical or merely the projection of the Orphic sect—all of these views have been maintained—is of no real consequence, as it is of no real consequence whether the Lycurgus who established the Spartan system was historical or an invention; whether real or imagined, our sources speak of him as a man. His date would be two generations before the Trojan War, for he is regularly represented as participating in the Argonautic expedition, and his place of origin is Thrace. Always, among the Argonauts and elsewhere, he is represented as a singer, with lyre in hand; Aeschylus and Euripides say that he could attract trees and beasts and even stones by his music and could charm whomever he would. He is said to have descended to the underworld to recover his wife Eurydice, who had been bitten to death by a snake. His power survived his death; he was killed and dismembered by a band of Thracian maenads, but his severed head floated on to Lesbos, singing as it went.

An hypothesis which fits all the traits ascribed to Orpheus, suggested by the Swiss scholar K. Meuli and elaborated in E. R. Dodds's *The Greeks and the Irrational,* is that Orpheus was a shaman. Shamanism was prevalent in Thrace, and other mysterious Thracian figures known to the Greeks, Abaris and Aristeas, were clearly shamans. Dodds summarizes his arguments as follows (p. 147):

> Orpheus' home is in Thrace, and in Thrace he is the worshipper or companion of a god whom the Greeks identified with Apollo. He combines the professions of poet, magician, religious teacher, and oracle-giver. Like certain legendary shamans in Siberia, he can by his music summon birds and beasts to listen to him. Like shamans everywhere, he pays a visit to the underworld, and his motive is one very common among shamans—to recover a stolen soul. Finally, his magical self lives on as a singing head, which continues to give oracles for many years after his death. That too suggests the North: such mantic heads appear in Norse mythology and in Irish tradition. I conclude that Orpheus is a Thracian figure of much the same character as Zalmoxis—a mythical shaman or prototype of shamans.

Some of these traits Orpheus shares with other figures, and it is therefore pertinent to ask why he in particular became the central figure in a religious movement. The Thracian Abaris, Herodotus (4.36) tells us, "is said to have gone with his arrow all round the world without once eating"; in Siberia souls are still said to ride on arrows. Later writers preserve the tradition that he banished pestilences, predicted earthquakes, and composed religious poems. Of Aristeas, Herodotus (4.13–15) tells even more wonderful stories : he travelled through the north in a trance; he was seen dead in a fuller's shop in Proconnesus, was simultaneously seen on the road to Cyzicus, and seven years later reappeared in Proconnesus, where he wrote a poem and again disappeared; and many years later he appeared to the Metapontines in Italy and bade them set up an altar to Apollo, saying that Apollo had once visited their country, with himself in attendance in the shape of a crow. Hermotimus of Clazomenae was similarly able to travel and observe far-off events while his apparently dead body remained at home. Stories like these were familiar enough in fifth-century Athens for Sophocles to allude to them without citing names : when Orestes in the *Electra* (62ff.) is troubled by the possible omen in feigning his own death, he consoles himself with the reflection, "Often before now have I seen wise men die in vain report, and then, when they return home, they are held in more abiding honor."

But Orpheus was held in higher and more abiding honor than the others. Even in the sixth century the epithet "of renowned name" (*onomaklyton* : Ibycus, frg. 17) was applied to him. The several references to him in Plato (*e.g., Symposium* 179D; *Republic* 10, 620A) sound as if a real person, not a mythological figure, were spoken of. When Isocrates (*Busiris* 11.38) objects to blasphemous things said of the gods by the poets, he says that Orpheus was particularly liable to the charge and so died by being pulled to pieces. Others of his class, as we noticed, also composed poems, but none attained such high fame as a singer as Orpheus. Many passages praise his singing for its specifically magic power, but sometimes it is the quality of the singing, rather than wizardry, that seems to receive the greater emphasis. So in the *Alcestis* (357ff.) Admetus wishes he possessed "the tongue and tunefulness" of Orpheus so that he might charm Persephone and her husband and so bring Alcestis back. Here, of course, the object of the desired skill is still for a purpose like Orpheus' own, but in the *Medea* Jason says, "Let me not possess gold in my house nor the power of singing more beautifully than Orpheus unless it makes me famous." If Orpheus shared his wonder-working powers with others, then, it was as a singer that he was most eminent. Among Greeks of all periods, we must remember, a high reputation as a singer implied not virtuoso performance but superlative content. Connected with the gift of song, that others possessed, is one distinction that others did not, and that is the reputation for having introduced secret mysteries. This is alluded to as early as Herodotus but made most specific in Euripides' *Rhesus* 943f.

The reason that Orpheus, and not others of his class, was honored for his spiritual gifts and by critical minds may be the quite simple fact that his doctrine was spiritually superior, or lent itself to spiritual elaboration. The latter is the more probable alternative, and we may surmise that Orpheus' high reputation was further enhanced in order to give higher authority to the doctrine attributed to him. Whether he was historical or a myth quickened into life, it is clear that the personality of Orpheus was an object of esteem amounting to reverence, and that this esteem served to document the validity of teachings ascribed to him. It is highly probable that he was the first such figure in the western tradition, for the antecedent religious atmosphere, whether Cretan or Achaean, did not lend itself to such development; in any case he is the first such known to western tradition. Socrates, as we have observed, however extraordinary he may have been, was not so extraordinary as Plato portrayed him, and Plato enhanced Socrates' personality in order to give greater authority to the teachings ascribed to Socrates. Plato was as aware as any modern that well-intentioned people might manipulate religious sentiments for a desirable end, as the *Laws* amply shows, and he was as capable of analyzing the history of the Orpheus myth as any modern. To say that he consciously took the Orpheus complex as his model for fashioning his own holy teacher is to indulge in fantasy, though it is not beyond the range of possibility.

But we need not insist that Plato had a single model for his enterprise. Between Orpheus and Socrates there were other teachers for whom special sanctity was claimed. Pythagoras, in particular, was a more tangible figure, was credited with a more sophisticated and better articulated doctrine, and so was nearer to Plato in outlook as well as in time. Indeed Pythagoras himself became the subject of a legend that both borrowed from and contributed to the Socratic legend and ultimately swallowed and sophisticated and better articulated doctrine, and so was nearer gorean legend ultimately assumed will be presented in the latter part of this book. What concerns us at present are the aspects of Pythagoras and Pythagoreanism that may have helped shape Plato's portrait of Socrates.

Our extant biographies of Pythagoras date to the third and fourth centuries A.D. and are so heavily incrusted with legend that the historical Pythagoras is hard to isolate. Indeed, some extreme critics have thought him a syndicate rather than an individual, and some have regarded him as a newcomer from India and his name as a hellenization of the Sanskrit *pitta gurū,* or Father Teacher. But there is no sufficient reason to doubt the tradition that he was one man and a Greek, the son of Mnesarchus of Samos, and that about 531 B.C. he emigrated thence to Croton, in southern Italy. In regard to the doctrine attributed to Pythagoras, there is again great uncertainty. Many scholars are convinced that the mathematical and musical contributions attributed to him are not in fact his but for various reasons came to be associated with his name late in the fifth century.

But what concerns us is Pythagoras' ethical and spiritual teachings, and here there can be little doubt that they are his own. According to these teachings the soul is a fallen divinity incarcerated in the body as in a tomb and condemned to a cycle of reincarnation as man, animal, or plant. This explains Pythagorean abstention from animal food and even from certain vegetables. The soul can be released from the cycle by the cultivation of purity, which may involve study of natural science; study thus becomes a religious duty. It is this aspect of Pythagorean teaching that opened the way for attributing mathematical and other sciences to him. As important as his doctrine is the society Pythagoras established to preserve and promulgate it. The society was a closed body, apparently graded into divisions of "auditors" and "students" and subject to a very strict communal discipline. The spiritual exercises were directed to the achievement of purity and entailed silence, constant self-scrutiny ("where did I go astray, what have I done, what that I should have done have I failed to do"), and the observance of certain ancient precepts that were given a symbolic meaning.

It is obvious that Pythagoras was a highly gifted personality who deserved the respect given him; but even if he had not been, it was inevitable that a religious society should endow its founder with special sanctity, and increasingly so as the foundation receded into the past. There were of course mockers, in comedy New and Old and among hard rationalists. Contemporaries of Plato who were not in sympathy with Platonism took a critical view of Pythagoreanism also. Here, for example, is a comment of Isocrates (*Busiris* 28) :

> On a visit to Egypt Pythagoras became a student of the religion of the people, and was first to bring to the Greeks all philosophy, and more conspicuously than others he interested himself in sacrifices and in ceremonial purity, since he believed that even if he should gain thereby no greater reward from the gods, among men, at any rate, his reputation would be greatly enhanced. And this indeed happened to him. For so greatly did he surpass others in reputation that all the younger men desired to be his pupils, and their elders were more pleased to see their sons staying in his company than attending to their private affairs. And these reports we cannot disbelieve; for even now persons who profess to be followers of his teaching are more admired when silent than are those who have the greatest renown for eloquence.

The very tone of the pejorative remarks in this passage suggests a polemical attitude : Isocrates sets himself to belittle Pythagoras as a self-seeker because the generality of people tended to set too high a value upon him. Other and earlier authors speak of Pythagoras with varying degrees of respect; the list includes such names as Xenophanes and Heraclitus, Herodotus and Ion of Chios, Empedocles, and in particular Plato. In a number of other authors who do not mention Pythagoras by name the influence of Pythagoreanism is perceptible. The most telling case is Pindar. His praises of *ponos* (toil) and his conception of "harmony" are plausibly thought to derive from Pythagoreanism, as does much of his religious posture generally "It is not mine to wonder," he says (*Pythian* 10.48). "When the gods appoint it, nothing is too strange." But the largest and clearest precipitate of Pythagoreanism is in Plato, who is also the most effective agent for spreading aspects of the doctrine.

Plato's relationship to Pythagoras is different from his relationship to Orpheus. Citations of Orpheus are of an almost purely literary nature, which is to say mainly decorative. Pythagoras is cited as an authority whom the writer accepts, and often his doctrine is presented without his name being mentioned. Materials in dialogues as diverse as the *Republic* (especially in the vision of Er) and the *Timaeus* are clearly adaptations of Pythagoreanism. Perhaps there is some connection between the concern for mathematics attributed to Pythagoras and the large place that subject occupied in the teaching of the Academy, even if the direction of the movement is toward rather than from Pythagoreanism. Most striking, perhaps, is the very organization of the Academy and Plato's insistence (in the *Seventh Epistle*) that doctrine was to be assimilated not out of books but only by long-continued and intimate contact with the master. The later schools of philosophy were all organized as cults, with the teacher as the responsible leader; that apparently was the only means of effecting a corporate existence capable of transmitting property and placing it under the legal control of the head. Even the Museum at Alexandria was organized as a cult of the Muses. Even Epicurus received the honors appropriate to the head of a school; for example, his birthday continued to be celebrated. So far as we can see, the pre-Socratics (with the obvious exception of the Hippocratics) had no such organization. If the Academy was a pioneer in this respect, it may be that Plato was consciously adopting an admired Pythagorean institution. The position of

Pythagoras in the institution he could not well claim for himself (or for any contemporary) and so made Socrates his surrogate; that he thought a peculiar efficacy should inhere in the head of a school we can see from the autobiographical *Seventh Epistle*.

But any derivation* of Platonic matter from Pythagorean is subject to the important qualification that the influence may actually have operated in the reverse direction, for the image of Pythagoras that prevailed at the turn of the fifth and fourth centuries was undoubtedly colored by contemporary philosophic (including Platonic) thought. It is not improbable that philosophers who attributed to Pythagoras doctrine that was not his were quite aware of what they were doing; surely thinkers interested in the progress of speculation, as Plato was, must have known that Pythagoras was used as a convenient vehicle for contriving, giving authority to, and propagating a particular complex of ideas. If the Platonic image of Socrates is a creation for a similar purpose, then no personality in antecedent history could have been so suggestive and so perfect a model. The fact that Pythagoras himself subsequently became the subject of the mass of hagiological writing—of which a specimen will be presented in the latter part of this book—shows how outstandingly appropriate for the purpose his image was. Plato did not adopt the model, as later writers did, but mastered and adapted it, and it is a mark of his own high originality and artistry that he did so. His own creation is more consistent and more credible, and therefore more edifying and inspiring.

There remains one other figure in the pre-Socratic group of whom it is possible to conceive that his traits contributed to the developed image of the holy teacher, and that is Empedocles of Agrigentum. In view of the sharp distinction rationalist ages draw between wonder-working and philosophy, Empedocles is a puzzling phenomenon; it is hard to believe that the acute, clearheaded, and original thinker who wrote the poem *On Nature* (of which about 350 lines are extant) should also have written *On Purifications* (of which only about a hundred lines are extant); but there can be no doubt that he did in fact write both

poems. If Orpheus is possibly merely a hypostatization, and
Pythagoras dim and shadowy, there can be no doubt of the
historicity of Empedocles and of the outlines of his career. He was
born of an aristocratic family in Acragas in Sicily about 493 B.C.
and lived for sixty years, so that Socrates was nearly forty when
Empedocles died. As a young man he championed democracy at
Acragas, was offered and refused the kingship, was subsequently
exiled and went to the Peloponnesus, where he recited his
Purifications at Olympia. He visited the panhellenic colony of
Thurii in 443 B.C., shortly after it was founded by Pericles. There
are various miraculous stories of his death, either by translation
or in the crater of Etna.

Empedocles was philosopher, scientist, poet, orator, statesman,
and at the same time mystagogue, miracle worker, healer, and
claimant to divine honors. For his high attainments in philosophy
we have the unimpeachable evidence of the best ancient critics
as well as his own writings; much of his doctrine is incorporated
in Aristotle. His eminence as a literary artist is suggested by the
fact that his pupil Gorgias is reputed to be the founder of artistic
Greek prose style. But stories of his preternatural capacities were
also much publicized. He is said to have stayed the winds by
his magic, to have restored a dead woman to life, to have vanished
bodily from the mortal world and to have become a god. These
specific tales may be later embroidery supplied by the credulous;
what is of particular interest is that in this case we know that
Empedocles himself fashioned his legend and started it on its
way. He himself declared that he could teach his pupils to stay
the winds and revive the dead, he himself declared that he was
no longer mortal but an immortal god, and he himself described
the throngs who came to him in search of occult knowledge and
magical cures.

We cannot, as some have essayed to do, divide Empedocles
into two and say that he started either as a magician or as a philosopher and was then converted to the other, for the claims to
wonder-working are found not in *Purifications* but in *On Nature*.
Nor can we say that his object was to synthesize the two, for there
is only juxtaposition and no attempt at synthesis. The point is

that the functions which are differentiated amongst ourselves became so after the time of Empedocles; in his day there was no incongruity in a single preternaturally endowed individual practising various arts that were at one in requiring special spiritual endowment. Perhaps the apparent incongruities in the traditional career of Pythagoras or even of Orpheus are to be similarly explained (as E. R. Dodds believes they are); perhaps these personages too themselves designed the shape of the legend in which they are swathed.

In all three of the teachers we have glanced at here we can see that the element of the miraculous, though it persisted as such and was even elaborated, was at the same time allegorized or otherwise endowed with rich spiritual meaning. The process is surest in the case of Orpheus; the association of lofty spiritual doctrine with so shadowy a personality suggests a large degree of conscious manipulation. In the case of Pythagoras we know that he himself gave spiritual meaning to primitive tabus, as his devotees centuries later were to give spiritual meaning to neutral acts of his own. We can see the process at its clearest, in a later stage of thought, in Plutarch's *Isis and Osiris,* where rites essentially barbaric are given a purer (and quite alien) significance. Where there was no central authority to enforce continued observance of outworn ritual, and indeed no single set of observances exclusively binding, the next logical step would be to promote the spirituality at which the interpretation aimed without the tabus out of which they had been alleged to derive. What could give the spiritual doctrine a focus and authority was the personality and career of the teacher who promulgated it. Empedocles went beyond both Orpheus and Pythagoras in deliberately shaping his career to provide focus and authority and perhaps scope for allegorical expansion in a desirable direction. If his predecessors are considered in this light, we can see that Socrates is in a direct line of succession, with the miraculous elements suppressed, in keeping with the tastes of a sophisticated age, the spiritual emphasized, and enough of the preternatural gifts left to produce a figure that could serve as a focus and examples. But if it was natural for the image of a Socrates to appear in succession to his predecessors, his coming into being required the services of a midwife, to use the figure Plato puts into Socrates' mouth, and the midwife, it would seem, was Plato.

VI. THE IMAGE OF SOCRATES

AS SURELY AS THE FIGURE OF ACHILLES is the paradigm for heroic epic, so surely is Socrates the paradigm for aretalogy. He is manifestly the point of departure for the development of the genre after his time, but he is also the culmination of antecedent development. It is likely that the historical Achilles (assuming there was one) was both more and less than Homer's image of him, but even if he was exactly as the image represents him, without it he could never have served posterity as a paradigm. Nor could Socrates have served posterity except through the image Plato fashioned. It is not, strictly speaking, a developed aretalogy that Plato presents; that is to say, he does not provide a single systematic account of a career that can be used as a sacred text. Indeed, Plato's treatment made it impossible for others to elaborate the image plausibly or to reduce it to a sacred text. But the whole image, full and consistent and unmistakable, is presupposed in every Platonic dialogue which contributes to it. Undoubtedly the historical Socrates was an extraordinarily gifted and devoted teacher, and his image does undoubtedly reflect the historical figure, but the image clearly transcends the man, and the image is the conscious product of Plato's art.

Because of Plato, and only Plato, Socrates' position in the tradition of western civilization is unique. Other fifth-century Greeks have won admiration bordering on adulation for high achievement in various fields, but only Socrates is completely without flaw; the perfect image leaves no opening for impugning his wisdom or temperance or courage or whole-hearted devotion to his mission. We might expect that a dim figure out of the im-

49

perfectly recorded past, an Orpheus or Pythagoras or even Empedocles, might be idealized, but Socrates lived in the bright and merciless light of a century that could ostracize Aristides, deny prizes to Sophocles, throw Pericles out of office. Perhaps the nearest approach to Plato's idealization of Socrates is Thucydides' idealization of Pericles; some critics have thought that Thucydides' main motive in writing his history was to glorify Pericles. But Thucydides never claimed for Pericles the kind of potency that Plato suggests for Socrates, and on the basis of Thucydides' own history the world has accepted Pericles as a far-seeing but not preternaturally gifted or wholly successful states-man. Only in the case of Socrates has the idealized image effaced the reality.

What makes Plato's share in the idealization obvious is the existence of parallel accounts of Socrates that are less reverent. Plato's reports are indeed the fullest : the larger part of his exten-sive writings purports to be an exposition of Socrates' thought. But there are other witnesses. We have in addition the quite ex-tensive *Memorabilia* of Xenophon, who was roughly a contem-porary of Plato and also a pupil of Socrates, and a few pages of the Socratic dialogues of a third contemporary and pupil, Aeschinus of Sphettus. All of these were written after the death of Socrates, which must obviously have placed his entire career in a new perspective, especially for his admirers. In the *Clouds* of Aristophanes, Socrates is the central figure, and the boot is on a different foot, for it was produced in 423, when Socrates was not yet fifty and therefore in the prime of his career but not yet shielded by the extraordinary eminence later bestowed upon him. Nor was Aristophanes' comedy the only caricature of Socrates. Also in 423 a comic Socrates figured in a play of Amipsias and two years later in one of Eupolis. These poets, it must be remembered, were dealing with a personality that was familiar to them and also, perhaps more important, to their audiences.

The caricature, certainly Aristophanes' and presumably the others' also, is of course grossly unfair : Socrates did not meddle with natural science or receive pay for his teaching, as the *Clouds* alleges he did : the most carping critic could not question his probity. The very absurdity of the charges and the topsy-turvy carnival atmosphere of the festival eliminated the possibility of rancor; in the *Symposium,* of which the fictive date is a decade after the presentation of the *Clouds,* Plato represents Aristophanes and Socrates as consorting on the friendliest of terms. And yet it is plain that Aristophanes' large audience was not outraged by the frivolous treatment of a saint, and in the *Apology,* which Socrates is presumed to have pronounced at his defense twenty-five years later, the point is made that the caricature had seriously prejudiced the public against Socrates. To some degree, then, the caricature is a significant corrective to later idealization.

If we discount the evidence of Aristophanes as malicious or motivated by a desire to amuse at any price, we still have Xenophon, who treats Socrates with reverence, to be sure, but represents him as a kind of cracker-barrel sage, with no hint of the soaring spirit we encounter in the pages of Plato. Xenophon was indeed a simple and a practical man, but he was not a fool, and only a fool could reduce the Platonic Socrates to the Xenophontic. Probably Socrates was in fact more than the utilitarian sage Xenophon represents him to be, as he was more than the logician he proves to be in Aristotle. Probably there was basis in fact for the saintly and intellectual qualities Plato attributes to him, and the highly developed doctrines Plato puts into his mouth may be legitimate implications of actual Socratic utterances. We need not expect that a mind like Xenophon's should elaborate the implications or even perceive them, but we might expect that he would at least echo some of the utterances Plato represents as having been characteristic of Socrates.

Really to know where the truth lies, as between Plato's Socrates and Xenophon's, we should have his actual words or a public record of his deeds, but Socrates wrote nothing and was not, like Pericles, a statesman. The image is therefore not subject to correction on the basis of his own works. Aristophanes also deals harshly with Euripides, but we have Euripides' own plays to read, so that the caricature tells us more of Aristophanes than it does of Euripides. Isocrates wrote an encomium of Evagoras and Xenophon of Agesilaus, but the praise of these statesmen carries its own corrective. Of Socrates we know, or think we know, much more than of those others—what he looked like, how he dressed and walked and talked, and most of all, what he thought and taught.

The entry under "Socrates" in a handbook would run something like this : Socrates was a strikingly ugly man, trained as a stone carver, who went about Athens, in a peculiar waddling gait, humbly dressed and shoeless, asking questions and provoking discussions chiefly on ethical problems. He was followed and admired by a group composed for the most part of upper-class youths. He might be spoken of as a Sophist by a comic poet, but he differed from the Sophists obviously in that he took no regular pupils and received no pay. He believed in his own mission to question people, chiefly to the end of convincing them that an unexamined life is not worth living. Sometimes he went into a sort of trance while pondering a thought. In his discourse he habitually employed homely images drawn from the daily life of artisans, but he was not cowed by persons of superior wealth or social position. The upshot of his doctrine was that the world of our senses lacks reality and that man must aspire to union with true goodness and beauty, which are beyond the sensible world. In 399 B.C., at the age of seventy, he was tried and condemned to death on the charge of disbelieving in the gods of the state and persuading others to his disbelief.

Actually the only significant datum in the inventory which is beyond dispute is that Socrates was condemned to death in 399 B.C. and accepted his penalty when he might have evaded it. The magnanimity of this act no one can belittle; it is enough to purify and enhance even a questionable career, and it is certainly enough to sanctify a Socrates. For Plato it clearly marked a decisive turn, as he himself records in his autobiographical *Seventh Epistle*. For him it undoubtedly crystallized the image of Socrates that fills the early dialogues. It must be remembered that Plato was Socrates' junior by forty years, so that it was only during the last years of Socrates' life that Plato could know and follow him. All the dialogues were of course written after Socrates' death. In Plato himself we see the process of idealization of which a series of busts of Socrates arranged chronologically provides ocular demonstration. The earliest are simply of a rather clownish but grave-faced laborer, but as the series proceeds the face is refined, though its lineaments are still recognizable, until at the end the eyes look upward into space and the lips are open in an expression of rapture.

However wise and saintly the historical Socrates may have been, it is clear that the image is an idealization and clear also that Plato is the chief agent in the process. All of Plato's earlier dialogues, and the more plainly in the degree of their earliness, are as much concerned with the personality of Socrates as with his teachings. His pre-eminence in reason, his devotion to his mission, his selfless concern for the spiritual welfare of his fellow men, the purity of his life, even his social gifts, are made prominent. The *Apology,* quite possibly the earliest of the Socratic pieces, is concerned with the man and his personal program, not his doctrines. Here he is made to present, without coyness or swagger or unction, his own concept of his mission to sting men, like a gadfly, to self-examination and to serve as midwife to their travail with ideas. The *Apology* also illustrates the devotion of his disciples to Socrates and the surprisingly large proportion of his jurors who were willing to acquit him. Again, in the short early dialogues, which are mainly concerned with questioning common misconceptions of such abstract nouns as "piety" or "friendship," it is the man as defined by his program, not the abstract doctrine, that is being presented. In the great central group—*Protagoras, Gorgias, Symposium, Republic*—the proportion of doctrinal content is larger, but the doctrine requires the personality of Socrates to make it plausible. The moral significance of education may emerge from the rather piratical dialectic in the *Protagoras,* but the argument takes on special meaning from Socrates' wise and tender treatment of the eager and youthful disciple who is enamored of Protagoras' reputation. That it is a worse thing for a man to inflict than to receive an injury and that a good man is incapable of being injured is the kind of doctrine which absolutely requires that its promulgator be a saint, as Socrates is pictured in the *Gorgias*; on the lips of a lesser man it would be nothing more than a rhetorical paradox. A great weight of individual prestige must similarly be built up to enable a man to enunciate the grand scheme of the *Republic,* and the occasional playfulness of the tone only emphasizes the stature of the individual who enunciates it. People too earth-bound to recognize such stature, like Thrasymachus in Book I, can only find the whole proceeding absurd. And only from a man whose special stature was recognized could the vision of Er be accepted as other than an old wives' tale.

In the *Symposium* more than in other dialogues the individuality of Socrates is underscored. It is not a trivial matter, for establishing the character of Socrates, that he could be welcome at a party of the fashionable wits of Athens, could get himself respectably groomed for the occasion, and engage in banter with his fellow guests without compromising his spiritual ascendancy one whit. We hear incidentally of his absolute bravery in battle and his disregard of self in the service of a friend, of his extraordinary physical vitality that enabled him to stand all night pondering some thought while his fellow soldiers bivouacked around him to watch the spectacle, of how he could lose himself in some doorway in a trance and so make himself late for his appointment until he had thought through whatever was on his mind. The subject of the *Symposium* is love, and love had been conceived of, in the series of speeches praising it, in a range from gross homosexuality to romantic attachment, to a cosmic principle of attraction and repulsion, to Socrates' own concept (which he says he learned from Diotima, the wise woman of Mantinea) of an ascent to union with the highest goodness and beauty. It is a soaring concept, too lofty for ordinary flesh and blood, and Socrates' audience, both those at Agathon's banquet and the countless others who read of him in Plato, must inevitably defend their own humbler status by suspecting that the ugly man who talked so fine might himself follow a much lower kind of love : what of the notorious intimacy with Alcibiades? Alcibiades, flown with wine and bedecked with ribbons, crashes into the party without knowing what had gone before. Alcibiades is the most sought-after young man in Athens and at the very height of his glory; he had already been given the command of the Syracusan expedition but not yet become involved in the scandal of the mutilated Hermae. Only Alcibiades, and Alcibiades drunk, could tell the story of his attempted seduction of Socrates and its utter failure, and could thus demonstrate that Socrates' life was as lofty as his professions and that he had in fact attained the vision of the true good.

But it is in the *Phaedo* that Socrates comes nearest to being translated to a higher order of being. In prison, during the hours preceding his death, Socrates discourses to his devoted followers on the most timely and timeless of all questions, the immortality of the soul. The *Phaedo* is the most spiritual and the most eloquent of all dialogues; the account of Socrates' last moments is surely the second most compelling passion in all literature. If Plato's object was to inculcate a belief in immortality, there are of course sound practical reasons for giving the spokesman of the doctrine extraordinary prestige. In such an issue it is the personality of the teacher rather than the cogency of his arguments that is most persuasive. Most readers of the *Phaedo* share the experience of Cicero, who wrote (*Tusculan Disputations* 1.74) : "While I am reading the book, I agree, but somehow, when I lay the book down and myself reflect on the immortality of the soul, that agreement disperses." The use of the myth is itself a confession that logical arguments could not suffice, and only a man of Socrates' status could make myth serve the ends of rational argument.

But the saintliness with which Socrates is endowed in the *Phaedo* seems more than a mere device to promote belief in the immortality of the soul. If belief is being inculcated, it is belief in Socrates, not in immortality. Only an occasional reader of the *Phaedo* could rehearse its arguments for immortality years or months after he had laid the book down; the saintliness of Socrates he can never forget. It is his image of Socrates rather than any specific doctrine that Plato wished to crystallize and perpetuate. From the tenor of all his writing it is clear that Plato believed that the welfare of society depended upon leadership by specially endowed and dedicated men. Ordinary men following a prescribed code would not do. Indeed, Plato conceived of his own effectiveness as teacher in much the same way; in the auto-biographical *Seventh Epistle* he tells us that no one could claim to have apprehended his teachings merely from study of his writings : long personal contact with a master spirit is essential.

In the centuries after Plato the images of certain saintly figures who, like Socrates, had selflessly devoted themselves to the spiritual improvement of the community and· had accepted the suffering, sometimes the martyrdom, these efforts entailed, played a considerable role in the development of religious ideas and practices. In some cases the image may have masked a character negligible or dishonest, and the men who created and exploited the image may have done so for selfish motives; but in some cases, surely, the man behind the image was a devoted teacher whose disciples embroidered his career in good faith into a kind of hagiology that they then used for moral edification. Whatever the motivation, there can be little doubt that the prime model for the spiritual hero was Socrates, and less that the pattern for the literary formulation of his passion was the *Phaedo*. When we come to deal with certain later teachers and the stories of their careers, we shall see how these were influenced by the configuration Plato gave to the personality of Socrates and the record of his life and death.

Plato merits high eminence both as artist and as teacher; no other philosopher in the European tradition has made such effective use of art for communicating doctrine. His greatest creation and his most effective vehicle for teaching is the image of Socrates. If he made use of existing materials for his creation, so also did Homer and Shakespeare. And just as the creations of Homer and Shakespeare established patterns for their successors to emulate, so also did Plato's. We are now ready to look at the work of these successors, and first at the form they established and followed.

VII. THE LITERARY GENRE

POSTERITY FELICITATED ACHILLES on having a Homer to herald his prowess, and more than one Latin general carried a poet in his train to celebrate his achievements. But except as *dramatis personae* in a literary work, or unless their prowess was in the service of a religious ideal, warrior heroes tend to fall into oblivion. With innovators in the realm of the spirit it is otherwise. Their doctrines, adapted, it may be, to later tastes and needs, could have permanent validity, and hence the pioneers themselves could continue to be directly useful, not merely as inspiring examples. Spiritual and ethical doctrine, moreover, involves the personality of the teacher in a way that mathematical or metaphysical doctrine does not. Scientific principles once communicated have no dependence upon the ingenious mind that conceived them; ethical doctrine frequently depends upon an *ipse dixit*. Full loyalty to a system includes knowledge of the teacher who promulgated it.

Aside from credal considerations there is a natural desire, shared by peoples of various levels of sophistication, to know the personalities responsible for significant cultural innovations. So Edward Gibbon justifies the publication of the *Memoirs of his Life and Writings* (ca. 1789): "I may judge from the experience both of past and of the present times, that the public are always curious to know the men who have left behind them any image of their minds : the most scanty accounts of such men are compiled with diligence and perused with eagerness." The curiosity, the diligence, and the eagerness are multiplied in the case of minds whose images are continually operative, of richly endowed

57

pioneers of the spirit who have by their personal careers altered
the course of history, or what amounts to almost the same thing,
have been believed to have altered it, and have in consequence
been accorded esteem approaching reverence. The career itself
might serve as an instrument of moral instruction, and it could
most effectively be applied to such use if it were reduced to
literary form, with the virtues of the subject enhanced and his
failings minimized. So reduced to writing, it constitutes an
aretalogy, the species of literature we are concerned with here.

The clearest adumbration of the species we have so far encountered is the Platonic image of Socrates, which exploits and
combines elements present in antecedent literary images. But in
Plato the aretalogy is clearly a means and only incidentally an
end in itself. It is as if his work as a whole premised an aretalogy—
which he had himself created but not reduced to literary form as
such. In the earlier dialogues Socrates' conversations provide
shading and color for a silhouette precisely as dialogue gives
depth and subtlety to characters a novelist creates. But even in
the earlier dialogues, and of course in the later, when Socrates
recedes from view, Plato's paramount concern is with the doctrine, which becomes increasingly detachable from the image.
Nevertheless, the image as established possesses its own independent value for ethical instruction and might be employed by
later teachers to illustrate and enforce doctrine quite different
from Plato's. It is the aretalogy of Socrates implied, or even premised, in Plato that doubtless became the model for an
independent literary genre.

If we seek to construct a genealogy for the genre, we should
identify it as a species of biography, which is in turn a species
of history. To the rationalist mind each member in this succession
marks a decline in factual reliability. In the Hellenistic age, and
probably as a result of the teaching of Isocrates, historiography
departed from strict objectivity in several directions. It attempted
to engage attention by sensational devices appropriate to drama
and expatiated on the fortunes and psychological reactions of
participants in historical conjunctures; it centered interest upon
large personages, almost to the degree that the history served to

illustrate the career of such personages; and it sought to propagate particular outlooks and inculcate particular loyalties. If these tendencies mark a decline from scientific impartiality, they do result in work that is more attractive to ordinary readers, more edifying and more patriotic, as can be seen in the Roman history of Livy, the fullest flowering of Hellenistic historiography.

Partiality and edification may be a flaw in history; in biography they are almost inevitable. Biography is colored by eulogy, of which it is doubtless an outgrowth, and no man is on his oath when commemorating the dead. "See if that's Paw," the perplexed widow whispered to her son when she found it hard to recognize the sterling character she heard eulogized. If it was not Paw, it might conceivably have been someone else; the peculiarity of aretalogy is that its hero could not conceivably have been anyone else. For us the difficulty arises when what is in fact aretalogy purports to be biography. A notable case in this kind is Eusebius' *Life of Constantine the Great,* to which Eusebius appends as a voucher that he had the supernatural elements from the lips of Constantine himself, late in Constantine's life, that he would not have credited the story from any other informant, but that he did credit it from the lips of Constantine. Gibbon notes the shrieking discrepancy between Constantine's career and Eusebius' account, and on the basis of the discrepancy the eminent Jakob Burckhardt characterizes Eusebius as the foremost conscious liar in history.

By nineteenth-century standards of scientific historiography Burckhardt's characterization is not unreasonable; but Eusebius was following a literary tradition that made room for gradations in truth. For prose narrative (*diegesis, narratio*), defined as "discourse of things that happened or might have happened," three categories of fidelity to fact are distinguished : *alēthēs historia* ("true history") for what is literally true; *pseudēs historia* ("false history") for what is wholly imaginary; and *plasmata* or *hos genomena,* "fiction" or "as might happen." In the first two categories no reader could be in doubt as to the quality of belief expected; the first is to be accepted as a purely factual account, like a chronicle; the second as a complete fantasy, intended only to amuse. In the third category the quality of truth depends upon the art and conscience of the writer, and its correct apprehension depends upon the literary experience of the reader. It was expected that the *plasma* should have a core of actual history, that its imaginative expansion should preserve historical verisimilitude, and that it should be morally edifying. Departure from strict fact in writing of this kind is therefore not simple deception, but it may be disingenuous if an author is aware that a naïve audience is likely to receive his *plasma* as *alēthēs historia*. Even without the systematic categorization intelligent readers are cognizant of the gradations. We cherish little George Washington's "Father, I cannot lie; I did it with my little hatchet," even though we dismiss Parson Weems as a pious fraud. Eusebius' audiences have stopped at pious.

After so elaborate a preamble it is something of an anticlimax to have to acknowledge that we have no complete text surviving from the past specifically labelled aretalogy, and indeed that the word is hardly recognized in our standard dictionaries; but there can be no reasonable doubt that the thing and its name once had currency. We know that the careers of holy men were given literary form in order to serve as a basis for moral instruction because vestiges and adaptations of such works are recognizable in certain biographical and other writings that have in fact survived. And we can infer the existence of the word with assurance from the meaning of *aretalogus* in Latin and of *aretas legein* in Greek.

In sophisticated Roman authors *aretalogus* signifies a professional reciter of wordy and incredible stories. So when Augustus entertained friends at dinner, Suetonius tells us (*Augustus* 74): "He introduced music and actors and even strolling players from the circus and especially *aretalogi*." We learn a little more about what cultured Romans thought of *aretalogi* from a passage in Juvenal's Egyptian satire (15.13ff.): "When Ulysses told a tale like this (scil. of cannibalism) over the dinner table to the amazed Alcinoüs, he stirred some to wrath, some perhaps to laughter, as a lying *aretalogus*." The passage goes on to list the impossibilities in Ulysses' narrative and then adds: "Did he deem Phaeacian people so devoid of brains? . . . The Ithacan's tale was all his own with none to bear him witness." For his own tale Juvenal specifies a precise time and place. We shall see that Ulysses' narrative is elsewhere cited as a typical aretalogy by those who depreciate the form, and that the aretalogist usually supplied assurances of veracity, mock or real, in the form of oaths, witnesses, or date.

But even in the Romans there are hints that aretalogies could be serious. So Porphyry, glossing the name Crispinus in Horace (*Sermones* 1.1.20), says: "Plotius Crispinus was a student of philosophy; he also wrote poems, but so voluble (*tam garrule*) that he was called an *aretalogus*." The interesting point here is that a student of philosophy could also be an *aretalogus*. In his *On Poetry* (24, Jensen) Philodemus of Gadara, who may have been Horace's teacher and was himself a writer of Cynic diatribes, equates the aretalogist with the writer of mimes; the mime, in the Hellenistic age, was a serious study of morals, and writers of mimes were in fact called "biologists," or students of life. We learn more of the serious aspect of the aretalogist from the Bobbio Scholia in the Juvenal passage "*Aretalogi* tell of miraculous deeds, which is to say *virtutes* [=*aretas*]." This is in keeping with the meaning of the word attested from the fourth century B.C. down: originally an aretalogist was a kind of evangelist who proved the stature of a deity or holy man by reciting his miraculous works. So a slave in Terence (*Adelphi* 535, based on Menander) says: "I shall make him think you a god; I shall recite your *virtutes*." The original sense of the word is shown by the usage of the Septuagint, where "to speak the wonders of God" is regularly rendered by *aretas legein*, literally "to speak the virtues." *Aretalogus,* then, is "one who (professionally) speaks the wondrous deeds of a deity or a divinely gifted human," and *aretalogia* is the discourse he composes.

It is clear that the derogatory sense the Romans attached to *aretalogus* was the development of a rationalist and aristocratic society, when many who set themselves up as religious teachers might in fact have been charlatans and mountebanks whose main appeal was to the mob. We shall find that the Greek Lucian was even more outspoken and more serious in his condemnation of religious charlatans and specified a number of them by name. But surely the impostors could not have flourished if there were not also honest men who felt themselves called to improve the moral health of their fellows and who spent themselves generously in their efforts to do so, and the meaning of aretalogy could not have been debased unless it had once possessed a dignity that could be exploited.

It is obvious that the potency claimed for the subject of an aretalogy was not always of the same order but varied according to the nature of his own career, the level of the audience to which the aretalogy might be addressed, and the general religious climate that fostered its growth. A sophisticated environment might curtail the supernatural aspects of a figure too deeply rooted in the popular imagination to be dismissed and which could still be morally profitable without the extravagant claims made for it. To court a credulous and thirsty following, on the other hand, a quite human and unpretentious teacher might be raised to virtually divine potency. The appeal of the teacher kept within human limitations is based mainly on intellectual conviction; the teacher for whom supernatural claims are made asks for something like religious conversion. A significant difference between the two types is in their prospects for survival. Rationally communicated doctrine tends to be assimilated into the anonymous texture of general thought and outlook; there is much greater likelihood of survival for a personality individualized and sustained by a religious legend. Where such a legend takes shape, the doctrine is a function of the personality, rather than the reverse, and in course of time may be refined and extended to a point where the original teacher would find it unrecognizable. The personality survives because those who cherish the legend constitute something like an organized cult, with leaders concerned for its propagation and its adaptation to new climates and new conditions. The two strands do interact upon one another : mystics are endowed with rational doctrine and rational thinkers with a mystique.

The prime example of the vicissitudes and the longevity of a legend built about a teacher is that associated with Pythagoras, which will be exhibited at length in a later chapter. Our extant versions of his biography, reverently set forth by Diogenes Laërtius, Porphyry, and especially Iamblichus, date to the third and fourth centuries A.D., which shows that the legend continued to function for over a millennium. The figure of Pythagoras continued central though the legend underwent changes. Before the fourth century B.C. Pythagoras came to be credited, surely apocryphally, with a body of mathematical and musical doctrine, and during the first Christian century the legend was again refined and embellished. But in the long course of its history it also affected other legends and bodies of doctrine. At one end of the span it is a significant ingredient in the teachings of Plato and in his image of Socrates, and at the other it affected the way of life and the doctrines of the Essenes. Its continuing effects, dissociated from the name of Pythagoras, are perceptible in Christianity and Judaism and Islam.

The prime example of the earthly teacher is the image of Socrates as fashioned by Plato. The image includes traits supplied by the Pythagorean complex, but it does not clothe Socrates with the divine aura of Pythagoras. In consequence it was rather the pattern of the Socratic image than the personality of Socrates himself that persisted over the centuries. Teachers and reformers whose personalities and programs were quite un-Socratic are represented as doing and suffering according to the pattern Plato sketched out for Socrates. In this sense the Platonic Socrates is the source for all subsequent aretalogies, pagan and Christian.

It is in large part because they were swallowed up by new and more viable orthodoxies, the rationalist type by the secular philosophies of the Hellenistic age and the mystical by new religious movements, that the older aretalogies have all but disappeared. Vestiges of them may be traced in systems that adapted and absorbed them, and in some degree in the writings of hostile critics who ridiculed them. If in the competition of religions paganism had prevailed, we might have had to deduce our notions of Chris-

tianity from the attacks of Celsus; as it is, we conjecture what
Celsus' attacks must have been like from the refutation of Origen.
Similarly we can get some sense of the claims made by and for
religious teachers whom he distrusted from the ridicule heaped
upon them by Lucian of Samosata.

Perhaps because he was himself a Hellenized Syrian of the
second century A.D., Lucian has what amounts to a romantic
reverence for the rationalism of classical Athens. His satires of
precious imitators of classical forms, pretentious teachers of
philosophy, and hypocritical teachers of religion are merciless.
In *How to Write History* he takes the measure of empty writers
who aped the manners of Herodotus and Thucydides. In the
Hermotimos and other pieces he derides the hypocritical and
self-seeking teachers of philosophy. In the *True History* he
parodies the writers of Utopias, most of whom set forth programs
of reform. And in a number of pieces, most notably *Alexander the
False Seer,* he ridicules pretenders to occult powers.

From the circumstances that Alexander's teacher was an associate of Apollonius of Tyana and that Alexander himself
claimed affinity with Pythagoras, it is clear that he was a teacher
of the same type as Apollonius. Alexander's career, as told by
Lucian in an epistle addressed to Celsus, is a kind of reverse
aretalogy. Though his birth was humble and known to be such
by his fellow townsmen, he claimed descent from Perseus and
connection with Apollo. He was handsome, intelligent, and mag-
netic; all who encountered him were convinced that he was good
and kindly and honest, whereas he was in fact a cunning liar,
trickster, perjurer. His devices included burying inscribed tablets
that foretold his advent, and arranging to have them discovered,
and sealing a newly hatched serpent in a large egg and then fore-
telling its discovery, and subsequently draping about his neck
a large tame serpent that he claimed was the divinity miraculously
grown adult. He charged enormous fees for oracles that he issued
in ambiguous or unintelligible form, and he exploited private
matter communicated to him for purposes of blackmail. Sometimes he affected possession and foamed at the mouth. He knew
that the prime motivations of men are hope and fear, and he

consciously set about exploiting these motives. He got along well enough with Platonists, Stoics, and Pythagoreans, but was at constant war with the Epicureans. Those who questioned his genuineness he declared were possessed by demons. He had foretold that he would die by a thunderbolt at the age of one hundred and fifty. Actually he died before he was seventy and was exposed as a fraud when the doctors found that they had to remove his toupee to treat his head.

On Lucian's evidence Alexander was quite clearly an impostor, but the Peregrinus of whom Lucian writes in a similar vein may have been a sincere seeker and teacher of truth; the worst motive Lucian can ascribe to him is love of notoriety. Peregrinus went through many adventures, including a conversion to Christianity. When his Christianity was discredited because he ate forbidden meats, he reverted to Cynicism and practised Cynic austerities. He closed his life by immolating himself on a pyre.

These two pieces are more or less biographical in form, and if the same matter were reported in a reverent rather than cynical tone, they could be described as aretalogies. A third piece, on a character called Demonax, is a biography of a man who is good and wise but without supernatural pretensions. The fact that Demonax's real virtues were those to which the others only pretended, that he served his followers out of genuine kindliness and not to gain reputation, and that he avoided any kind of claim to supernatural endowment, make the *Demonax* a criticism of the teachers whose careers were made the basis of a cult. When death was near and he was asked his wishes about burial, he said, "Do not trouble; scent will summon my undertakers." And when his friends said it was indecent for so great a man to be left to birds and dogs, he said, "There is no harm in making oneself useful in death to anything that lives." The Athenians did give Demonax a public funeral and honored the stone seat on which he used to rest when he was tired, but they did not make Demonax a cult figure.

These specimens from Lucian illustrate the two directions in which Plato's image of Socrates may have influenced later writers. Alexander and Peregrinus are clearly stages towards Philostratus'

Apollonius of Tyana and Iamblichus' Pythagoras. Demonax, who has several traits drawn from the image of Socrates, illustrates the rationalist influence. The philosophic implications of the image become part of the general philosophic legacy or (more noticeably) provide a pattern for the historians' accounts of significant and sympathetic characters. When later historians, a Livy or a Tacitus, wish to paint a great-spirited Roman, they borrow pattern or colors from the Hellenistic biographies of the preternaturally endowed benefactor and teacher.

VIII. THE STOICS

EVEN BEFORE the regrettable copies of the Socratic image had come into the world for the Lucians to ridicule, there were some, like the Peripatetic Aristoxenus, who demurred at the image itself. As the fourth century wore on, the unity of learning was broken up by compartmentalization, so that specialists at the extremes could invite ridicule. Plato himself, in one significant respect, may be thought of as continuing in the course set by Empedocles. His intellectual horizons are very different, and it is impossible to imagine him writing either *On Nature* or *Purifications*; and yet, considering his mathematics on the one hand and his myths on the other, Plato too is in the tradition of the single teacher who combines what we may call scientific and spiritual interests. If we wish to separate the strands we may conceive of the scientific element as being carried forward by Aristotle and the Peripatetics and eventually by the Alexandrian Museum and Library, and the spiritual by the Hellenistic schools, mainly the Epicurean and Stoic.

In the spiritual element, which is our concern, we have noticed a division between the rational and the mystical, though neither strand is untouched by the other. Of the two major Hellenistic schools the more thoroughly rationalist and the earlier was the Epicurean. The initial impulse of Epicureanism seems to have been determined opposition to Platonism. Its doctrines were definitely antireligious, in the ordinary view of religious, but despite the truculent materialism of its atomic theory and its consistent exclusion of all supernatural intervention in human affairs, Epicureanism is still basically a spiritual movement. The title of

Lucretius' magnificent poetic manifesto of Epicureanism is plainly an echo of Empedocles' *On Nature,* but Lucretius preaches his materialist doctrine with the zeal of an evangelist. Even more paradoxical, and of particular interest in the present context, is the fact that Epicurus himself was the object of reverent homage such as was bestowed on none of the other Hellenistic founders of schools. For half a millennium he was revered as the personality who had released mankind from the bondage of ignorance, and his birthday was observed with religious devotion. The paradox is not unexampled. The Buddha opposed oppressive antecedent beliefs on essentially rational grounds—and himself became an object of worship.

But the more influential strand of spiritual teaching in the Hellenistic world was carried by the Stoics, who derived not from Plato but (at least according to the succession they later regularized) from Socrates himself, by way of Diogenes of Sinope and Diogenes' model Antisthenes. Antisthenes, described by Xenophon as one of the most devoted followers of Socrates, is the founder of the Cynic movement—not school—for the Cynics were never organized into a school. His teaching was mainly ethical, and not unlike Socrates' : happiness is based on virtue, pleasures are specious and make for happiness only if they are the result of toil. Odysseus is superior to Ajax as wisdom is superior to brute strength. Unlike Socrates, Antisthenes was a prolific writer and produced dialogues, interpretations of Homer (of which the Odysseus–Ajax comparison is an example), and fictional speeches. Remarks attributed to Antisthenes have the same ring as those attributed to Diogenes. For example, he derided pride in Attic birth by remarking that snails and locusts could claim the same distinction; and when he was applauded by a set of rascals, he said, "I am much afraid I have done something wrong."

The first Cynic properly so called (from the surname *Kyon,* "Dog," given him for his shamelessness) was Diogenes of Sinope. Diogenes was clearly influenced by Antisthenes, though probably not a pupil of his. The essence of Diogenes' teaching is that self-sufficiency can be attained by limiting one's needs to the demands of nature, which can be satisfied cheaply and easily. It was by demonstrating in his personal behavior his belief that nothing natural can be indecent that he acquired his surname. Usages or institutions that depend only on convention are unnatural, vitiate self-sufficiency, and should be disregarded. His lessons Diogenes taught by his own pointedly unconventional behavior and by paradoxical sayings that showed the absurdity of the mores he derided. He was undoubtedly picturesque in speech and in conduct, and many of the anecdotes told of him and of the pointed sayings attributed to him are doubtless true, but a single lifetime, even his own very long one, is not sufficient to make room for all of them. Soon after his death he became a figure of legend to whom any "cynic" deed or saying could be ascribed, and this took place in dialogues and novels written around him. His actual teaching, like his life, is obscured by the tendency of the Stoics to attribute their own theory to Diogenes and so place them in the Socratic tradition, for Diogenes' master Antisthenes was a Socratic, and his pupil Crates was the teacher of Zeno.

To a greater degree than any other, Cynic teaching is more effectively communicated by example than by precept. The shortest way to condemn conventional standards is to say, when asked where in Greece good men are to be found, "Men nowhere, boys in Sparta." The best way to prove that the appurtenances of civilization are useless is not to argue the point but to throw your cup away and lap water out of a brook like a dog. The most convincing demonstration of the emptiness of conventional values of rank and ambition is not to maintain that Alexander is only flesh and blood and that political favor is vanity, but to ask the great Alexander, when he offers a favor, to stand out of your light. The figure to whom such demonstrations are attributed impresses his personality upon the popular imagination as no creator of a cosmogony or a logic can do. And for later teachers who propagate the master's teaching, it is far more effective to picture what he would do in a given situation than what he would say. What the master did or was alleged to have done gives greater credit to what he said or was alleged to have said.

Less sophisticated ages attended to what Orpheus or Abaris or Aristeas did, and what they did may have been consciously exploited by themselves or by others to give credit to what they were reported to have said. In a more gullible age sincere Neoplatonists performed the hocus-pocus of their thaumaturgy (as we read in Firmicus Maternus' *Matheseos*) to give credit to their genuinely spiritual teaching. We can see how Diogenes could acquire and retain his extraordinary celebrity; but we can also see why, though many writers—Seneca and Dio Chrysostom and others—use his career as texts for sermons, that career was never raised to an aretalogy. The missing ingredient is love. All that we know of Diogenes suggests the gnashing malcontent who would not have debased the current coinage (his own figure of his activity) if his own currency had been up to accepted standards. The most philanthropic of his utterances would appear to be the reply to the man who asked of what city he was; Diogenes said he belonged to no city but was a cosmopolite, or citizen of the world. On Stoic lips this would have been a gallant assertion of the ecumenical ideal based on the equality of all men. On Diogenes' lips it was the ragged exile's expression of furious contempt for the cherished citizenship that he could not share. His teaching, in a word, was too negative to be made the subject of aretalogy.

What Diogenes did out of scorn for his fellow men his disciple Crates did out of love. Crates distributed his wealth and separated himself from his well-born family in order to benefit his fellow men. He was called the "door opener," for all doors flew open at his coming to welcome his instruction. In his case it was perhaps his want of assertiveness that hindered his fame, or perhaps it was because his efforts were swallowed up in those of his more original and more forceful disciple, Zeno, who was the founder of the Stoic school. Zeno's doctrine was essentially revolutionary, for it disregarded existing social stratifications and governmental organizations and set up new criteria for excellence and a new dignity for individual man, however humble or exalted his position, as a part of the divine intelligence with which he would one day be reunited. Such a doctrine is as much an evangel as a philosophy, and it was natural for its founder to receive a kind of regard different from that paid to philosophers. Zeno possibly, and some of his important successors as head of the Stoic school certainly, were of Semitic origin, and his unworldliness and thirst for righteousness are sometimes attributed to that circumstance. Needlessly, for antecedent Greek experience has shown teachers both of unworldliness and of righteousness. It may be that the doctrine held a particular appeal for the East; on the other hand, Epicureanism was the official philosophy of the Seleucid court.

It is something of a paradox that so far as tangible evidence shows, Epicurus enjoyed a higher esteem and for a longer period than did Zeno. He was spoken of in terms of mingled awe and affection, his devotees carried his picture about with them, his career was rehearsed for precept and example, and his birthday was solemnly celebrated until the end of antiquity. It is incredible that Zeno did not receive similar regard, for every Stoic sage (and Zeno was the prime exemplar) was regarded with reverence. On the other hand, though many unflattering things are said of Zeno, our sources show that Epicurus was the object of more persistent and virulent vilification. The explanation of the simultaneous survival of extravagant praise and extravagant blame throws light on our particular subject.

The source of much of our information (or more accurately, gossip) concerning these and other leaders of the Hellenistic schools was the intense rivalry, based frequently on unworthy motives, that created animosities between the schools. There is much evidence, particularly in the satire of Lucian, to suggest that the principal concern of many teachers was to inculcate an exclusive loyalty to their own schools, for which the main instrument was vilification of rival schools. This explains the denigration of certain teachers that we find in the pages of Diogenes Laërtius, and it explains too the extravagant praise he also reports. To ensure sectarian devotion it was not enough to represent the master merely as a towering intellect; he must also have performed wonderful works, and if the circumstances of his life lent themselves to such adornment, he must have faced the persecution of a tyrant, have met martyrdom gloriously, perhaps even have appeared to his followers after his death.

It is true that the pattern in all its details is found only in such a work as Philostratus' *Life of Apollonius of Tyana* (summarized in a later chapter of this book), late in date and belonging rather to the Pythagorean than the Socratic tradition. But data in Diogenes Laërtius' biographical sketches, especially concerning the deaths of his subjects and especially in the case of Stoics, seem to be drawn from aretalogies rather than ordinary biographies. From Lucian and other satirists we can see that the ability to work wonders was claimed by or for many teachers who were the objects of special reverence. These fragments and vestiges of aretalogies we shall consider in another connection; for the present we shall look at a group of writings that are partial or embryonic aretalogies in the Socratic tradition. The fullest picture of a teacher confronting a sovereign and suffering martyrdom is that of the philosophic Eleazar recounted in IV Maccabees. Another picture of a similar confrontation, with the saint bearing off the victory but without martyrdom and told rather as an edifying tale than as history, occurs in Dio Chrysostom's *Hunters of Euboea*. The fullest story of a life devoted to human betterment, a martyr's death, and a transfiguration is that of the Spartan Cleomenes. Cleomenes himself was, to be sure, not a philosopher but a king; his career was said to have been shaped by a Stoic teacher, however, and the record of his career, assimilated to Stoic ideals, was used by Stoic teachers for edification. Cleomenes lived in the later part of the third century B.C., and the Stoic teacher said to have guided him was Sphairos of Borysthenes, a disciple of Zeno himself. Though the extant version of Cleomenes' story is as late as Plutarch, the story itself is the earliest in our list; we therefore turn to Cleomenes.

IX. CLEOMENES, THE HUNTERS OF EUBOEA; ROMANCES

SO DRAMATIC is the received story of the reforming kings of Sparta in the latter half of the third century B.C., and so obviously a text for Stoic preachment, that its historicity may well be suspected. There have been students who doubted that Cleomenes was as noble a character as he is depicted, that his program had anything to do with Stoicism, that the Stoic Sphairos was ever his mentor, and indeed that early Stoicism was as revolutionary as has been assumed. Others (the present writer among them) have believed that the story as presented is substantially true. But in fact, except to historians who must know what really took place, the degree of historical truth in such a story is of interest only as a footnote; the important thing is that the story obtained currency and worked its effects in its present shape. From the point of view of the development of aretalogy an unadorned report of a doctrinaire's career is less significant than one that makes a heroic doctrinaire out of a character historically neutral.

What is most appealing in the early Stoic ideal is not its logic or its physics but its ethics, of which it is not too much to say that it grew out of a thirst for righteousness. All men possess dignity as portions of the divine, and in the all-inclusive brotherhood of man differences of rank or geography would sink into insignificance. The new ecumenical society must have been envisioned in Zeno's own social program, set forth in his (lost) *Republic,* and would involve the dissolution of existing polities. But Zeno's successors in the Stoic tradition saw that such a revolutionary program could not be realized at a stroke (though Alexander the Great, after his first successes, seems to have striven consciously

for a spiritual union of diverse peoples) and addressed themselves
to a kind of gradualism, seeking to effect their ends by degrees
through influencing the powers that were. If the hard realities of
existing political institutions and powers could not be made perfect in the twinkling of an eye, progress could be achieved in one
corner or another and a single enclave might even be made to
approximate the ultimate ideal.

The first example we have of a Stoic teacher attempting to
guide a sovereign in paths of reform is Sphairos of Borysthenes,
who belongs to the first generation of Zeno's disciples. If
Cleomenes was indeed Sphairos' secular arm to the degree
scholars have surmised, then Cleomenes is an important link,
practical if not doctrinal, in the Stoic chain; his career, as set
forth by Plutarch, is in effect an aretalogy for Stoicism. The Lives
of Cleomenes and his predecessor Agis are combined with those
of their Roman analogues (whose Stoic mentor was Blossius of
Cumae) into a single group. For his Greek pair Plutarch drew
heavily upon the account of Phylarchus (late third century
B.C.); none of Plutarch's other biographies makes such large
use of a single source. But Phylarchus, who is thus our ultimate
source, does not have a high reputation for reliability. He is often
cited as an example of the "pathetic'" school of historians, which
favored melodramatic effects over accuracy, and his tendency
towards sensationalism is severely reprehended by the sober
Polybius, who insisted that history must be "pragmatic." Moreover, Phylarchus was a devoted admirer of Cleomenes, and his
account is therefore strongly partisan. On the other hand
Plutarch, who was discriminating in his use of sources and not
sympathetic to revolution or to Stoicism, thought Phylarchus'
account worth transcribing, and critical modern historians like
the late W. W. Tarn accept it as essentially true. But for our
purposes, as has been observed, the truth of the story is a minor
consideration. It is the more remarkable, if the story is untrue,
that it could have taken shape and received acceptance so soon
after the events it purports to describe.

To appreciate the significance of Cleomenes' career we must
look briefly at conditions in Sparta in the third century B.C. and

at Cleomenes' own antecedents. In the old Spartan system, called Lycurgan, equality (but only among the Spartiate caste) was ensured by the absence of private property. Prohibition of coinage in precious metals and strict sumptuary regulations prevented the accumulation of wealth. The Spartiates were under military discipline from childhood on. Their contributions to the military mess, which preserved their status, were drawn from the produce of land allotments worked by the Helots. The allotments could not be sold or hypothecated or otherwise alienated. The system was undermined when one Epitadeus, of unknown date, passed a law that enabled holders of allotments to mortgage them, so that by the middle of the third century most of the land was concentrated in the hands of a tiny minority of possessors, mostly women, and there were only seven hundred Spartiates left who were able to maintain their status. Sparta had fallen low indeed from its ancient power as well as its ancient simplicity, and there was need for a vigorous hand to put things right.

Agis IV, who became king of Sparta in 244 B.C., before he was twenty, was an idealist possessed by a passion to restore Sparta to its pristine glory. The obvious means for doing so was to restore the Lycurgan system, and this Agis set himself to do. But it is clear that the system which was Agis' pattern was not that originally attributed to Lycurgus nor indeed any that had actually been followed. What was called the Lycurgan system in the third century, the pattern of which is set forth in great detail in Plutarch's *Life of Lycurgus,* is an artificial construction of contemporary Stoics, based indeed on traditional Spartan socialism and simplicity but elaborated in such detail as to make it impossible to conceive that it was ever actually applied. Agis' aim was to provide allotments for the landless in order that equality and the common meals might be restored. He proposed to divide the land nearer Sparta into 4,500 lots for Spartiates, and the remoter districts into 15,000 lots for the *Perioeci.* The Lycurgan system, as described in Plutarch's *Life of Lycurgus,* provided for 4,000 lots for Spartiates and 30,000 for the *Perioeci.* The similarity of these ratios is clearly not fortuitous.

To make a redistribution of land possible and useful to the new holders it was necessary that it be relieved of the heavy mortgages encumbering it. Agis' own sincerity is demonstrated by the fact that he freely distributed his own holdings, free of encumbrances, and induced the wealthy women of his family (in whose hands, as we have noticed, there was likely to be a great accumulation of property) and some of the young nobles who became his devoted followers to do likewise. But some of the propertied class, Agis' own uncle Agesilaus at their head, were less idealistic. Their extensive holdings were laden with heavy mortgages, whose cancellation would be very profitable to them. To promote the execution of half of Agis' program they simulated interest in the reform project as a whole. First they displaced the ephors with men of their own group and so were able to effect the banishment of the older, reactionary king, Leonidas. Then they proceeded to cancel debts; the bonfire upon which the mortgage deeds were burned Agesilaus cynically declared was the holiest blaze he had seen. But with the cancellation of debts reform stopped. The distribution of land was postponed on one pretext or another, and distrust of Agis was thus aroused among his followers. Then Agesilaus and his followers contrived that Agis go north to war, and they then displaced with their own creatures the ephors devoted to his cause and recalled Leonidas. When Agis returned, he took sanctuary in the Temple of the Brazen House, whence he was treacherously lured and finally murdered.

In order to secure the property to which Agis' young widow was heir, Leonidas caused her to be married to his very young son Cleomenes. But the gentle and beautiful Agiatis had no hatred for her boy husband, whom she knew to be innocent of any intentional wrong toward her, and rather filled him with enthusiasm for the improvement of Sparta's lot according to the plans of Agis. But the chief agent in educating Cleomenes to his reforming mission was the Stoic Sphairos. Among Sphairos' writings, as listed by Diogenes Laërtius, there occur such significant titles as "Of Kingship," "Of the Spartan Constitution," "Of Lycurgus and Socrates." It is clear from these titles as from the career of the Spartan kings that Sphairos had a considered program for action, but it is also clear that he imparted to his pupils a religious zeal for implementing the program.

Cleomenes was as dedicated as Agis had been, perhaps even more earnest and intense, but also maturer and more practical. His ambitions for a regimented Sparta, if not for himself, were larger and more carefully thought out. After he had matured his plans through a decade of kingship, he provoked a war with the Achaean League in order to make an opportunity for his revolution. He took an occasion to leave the citizen troops in camp at a distance from Sparta, hurried home with the mercenaries he had engaged, turned the ephors out of office, and exiled eighty of his more powerful opponents; in accomplishing this revolution only fourteen lives were lost. Cleomenes proceeded to cancel debts and distribute land in accordance with the plans of Agis, setting aside eighty lots for the men he had exiled. As a result of the new allotments and consequent enfranchisements Cleomenes was able to put some fifteen thousand Spartiates into the field as compared with the traditional Spartan six thousand. He restored the old education and the rigorous discipline in food and clothing. "His alone of all the Greek or royal armies," the *Life* records, "had no stage players, no jugglers, no dancing or singing women attending it, but was free from all sorts of looseness, wantonness, and festivity; the young men being for the most part at their exercises, and the old men giving them lessons."

The regenerated Sparta might have continued indefinitely, or as long as Rome could endure it, if Cleomenes had been content to forego larger ambitions. But Sparta's new military strength made Cleomenes a third factor (with Antigonus Doson of Macedonia and Aratus, the leading spirit of the Achaean League) in the politics of Greece. To control the grasping Macedonian, Aratus should have combined with Cleomenes, but Cleomenes' communistic tendencies, that had actually been widely heralded among the disinherited of the Peloponnesus, prevented such a combination. The disinherited favored Cleomenes; Aratus with the propertied classes naturally turned to Antigonus. Even so, Cleomenes might have succeeded if it had not become apparent that his social reformation was intended for Sparta only and was calculated to produce a Sparta so strong that it could resume its traditional hegemony in the Peloponnesus. In the Battle of Sellasia (222 B.C.) Cleomenes was defeated by Antigonus with Macedonian and League troops and with the connivance of an associate whom he had trusted.

Before Sellasia, Ptolemy of Egypt, who was interested in checking consolidation of Greek power, had promised Cleomenes help, but on condition that he send his mother, Cratesiclea, and his children as hostages. Cratesiclea insisted on going for Sparta's sake, despite Cleomenes' embarrassment at suggesting the move; and when she later suspected that his policy might be swayed by concern for her safety, she admonished him to do "what was fitting and advantageous for Sparta, and not, because of one old woman and a little boy, be ever in fear of Ptolemy." Now Cleomenes resolved to go to Egypt to procure help for liberating Sparta.

At the island of Aigialia, en route to Africa, one of his friends, Therycion by name, proposed suicide as a worthier alternative to supplicating an Egyptian. Cleomenes countered with the claim of duty : "A self-inflicted death ought to be not flight from action but an action in itself; it is as shameful to die as it is to live for one's self alone." Therycion went aside to the beach and there killed himself. His death left the company numbering thirteen, Cleomenes and twelve followers. Of these the most attractive and energetic was Panteus.

In Egypt Cleomenes was disillusioned by the dissolute and feckless court, and presently, when a pretended friend reported his impatience to the king, he and his company were put under virtual house arrest. When he got wind of the king's intention to put him to death, he resolved upon a sortie to liberate the Egyptians as well as his own company. How he carried his resolution out is told in the concluding section of Plutarch's *Life*, here somewhat abbreviated :

Ptolemy had gone to visit Canopus. Cleomenes spread a report that the king had liberated him, and because the king regularly sent presents and a banquet to people about to be released from imprisonment, Cleomenes' friends sent him these things, and so deceived the guards, who thought the king had sent them. Cleomenes shared the provisions with the guards and then feasted with his friends, wearing garlands on his head. It is said that he started his enterprise sooner than he had intended because a slave who knew the plan had spent the night outside with his mistress, and he was afraid that it would become known. At noon, then, when the guards were sleeping off their wine, he put on his tunic, opened the seam over his right shoulder, and with sword drawn sprang forth, accompanied by his friends similarly equipped, being thirteen in all. Hippitas, who was lame, joined the first onset with all his might, but when he saw that he slowed the others, he asked them to kill him and not ruin the enterprise by waiting for a man who was useless. It happened that an Alexandrian was leading a horse past the door; they seized it, mounted Hippitas upon it and dashed through the narrow streets summoning the crowds to freedom. These were brave enough, apparently, to praise and admire Cleomenes' daring, but not one had the heart to follow and help him.

Ptolemy son of Chrysermus, who was coming out of the palace, three of the company fell upon and killed. Another Ptolemy, who was commandant of the city, drove towards them in a chariot; they rushed upon him, scattered his servants and his guards, pulled him from the chariot, and killed him. Next they went to the citadel, to break open the prison and free its many prisoners. But the guards effectively barred the way, and Cleomenes, foiled in the attempt, roamed through the city; no one joined him, but all fled in panic. Cleomenes gave the attempt up and said to his friends, "No wonder that men who run away from freedom are ruled by women," and then bade them die in a manner worthy of himself and of their record. Hippitas was first struck down, by his own request, by one of the younger men, then each of the others, calm and unafraid, killed himself, all except Panteus, whom the king asked to wait until he and the others were dead then kill himself. When all the rest were lying prostrate on the ground, Panteus went to each in turn and pricked him with a dagger to see whether he were still alive. When he pricked Cleomenes' ankle, he saw his face twitch, so he kissed him and sat down beside him, and at the end he embraced the dead body and then killed himself.

The report of Cleomenes' death spread. Cratesiclea, noble as her spirit was, was overwhelmed, and wailed, embracing Cleomenes' children. The elder broke away and threw himself from the roof; he was badly hurt but did not die, and was taken up crying because he was prevented from dying.

When Ptolemy heard what had happened, he ordered that the body of Cleomenes should be flayed and hung up, and that his children, his mother, and the women with her should be killed. When

Cratesiclea was led to her execution, the wife of Panteus took her hand, held her robe up for her, and gave her encouragement. Cratesiclea was unfrightened and asked only that she might die before the children. At the place of execution the children were first killed before Cratesiclea's eyes, and then she herself was killed, saying only, "Children, where have you gone?" Then Panteus' wife, who was a magnificent figure of a woman, girded up her robe and attended to each of the dying women quietly and calmly, and laid them out for burial. Finally, when all the others were cared for, she composed herself, with her dress lowered at the neck, and allowed none but the executioner to come near or look at her. She died bravely, and needed no one to straighten or cover her body.

A few days later those who watched at the crucified body of Cleomenes saw a huge serpent coiled about the head and covering the face so that no carnivorous bird could light upon it. Awe and fear seized upon the king in consequence, and thus gave the women a basis for various purificatory rites, for the man who had been taken away had been beloved of the gods and preternaturally endowed. The Alexandrians visited the site frequently to worship, and hailed Cleomenes as a hero and a child of the gods.

Eventually cleverer heads stopped the practice and offered an explanation for the phenomenon. Just as putrefying oxen breed bees, horses wasps, and asses in a similar state beetles, so human bodies, they said, produce serpents when the lymph about the marrow collects and coagulates. It was because they noticed this phenomenon that the ancients associated serpents rather than other animals with heroes.

The rationalizing explanation may have served to put an end to an incipient cult, as it was intended to do, but it does not alter the fact that crucified Cleomenes had actually become the object of a cult. It is true that he died in an attempt at violent insurrection, and true too that his whole career was devoted to patriotic concern for Sparta rather than to unworldly doctrine. He was, after all, king of Sparta, and the historian, even a Phylarchus, must deal with the political and military aspects of his career. But the Stoics had fused the ideal of a regenerated Sparta with their own idealistic program, so that a martyr for their cause could be pictured as a martyr for Sparta, and historians would naturally seize upon the latter aspect. What we do have is the picture of a man of self-abnegating devotion, whose good faith and kindliness as well as his high dedication are stressed throughout his career, being driven to an ignominious death by an unseeing tyrant and then being justified by some particular mark of divine solicitude and approval, which causes people to recognize his superior status and offer him reverent regard.

The picture of a dedicated man of the spirit who is persecuted by an oppressive secular authority and yet somehow receives marks of approval we shall encounter in several aspects. The parallel of the model of social justice whose humble integrity similarly prevails over entrenched reaction, but with no preternatural support or claims, is less common but perhaps more obviously a development of the Cleomenes pattern. The derivation seems more likely when the story is told by a professed preacher of Cynic doctrine—as Dio Chrysostom in his later phase was— and when presented as an edifying parable rather than as literal history.

The story in question is that commonly called "The Hunters of Euboea" and is part of the *Seventh Oration* of Dio Chrysostom. A shipwrecked traveler, chilled and destitute on a desolate shore, is hailed by a roughly dressed hunter who offers to escort him to the simple hut where he will provide food and warmth. On their way to the hut the hunter tells the story of his life :

> There are two of us, stranger, who live in the same place. Each is married to the sister of the other, and we have children, both boys and girls. We live by hunting for the most part, but we work a bit of land, too. The place is not really ours; we neither inherited nor bought it. Our fathers were free men, indeed, but just as poor as we. They were herdsmen, and kept cattle for a rich man who lived on this island. This man owned many herds of horses and cows, many sheep, many fine fields, many other valuables, and all these hills. When he died, his property was confiscated—people say the emperor did him in for his property. His herds were immediately driven off to be butchered, and with them our own few head of cattle. Nobody paid our wages. For the time we could only stay where we had been keeping the cattle. We had built huts and a wooden corral for the calves. It was not very big or very sturdy, but a makeshift for the summer.

The two men gradually improved their steading and eked out a simple living, until one was summoned to the city to answer a charge of nonpayment of tax. At the trial, which is held in a

crowded theater, the guileless simplicity of the child of nature
makes the heated eloquence of the sophisticated prosecutor look
ridiculous. A friendlier speaker arose to say that people who cultivated deserted land should be rewarded rather than penalized,
and charged that the officials who oppressed such honest citizens
had themselves plowed up the gymnasium and were grazing their
cattle in the public square. When the defendant is called upon to
rebut the charges, he gives a careful inventory of his small stock
of vegetables and meat and then says :

> That is what we have. If you want all of it we will give it you for the
> asking: you don't have to seize it from us as if we were foreigners or
> wicked folk unwilling to give it up. We too, mark you, are citizens
> of this city, as my father used to say. Once when he came here, there
> was a distribution of cash bonuses to citizens, and he got his with the
> rest. Our children, too, we are raising to be your fellow citizens, and
> if you are ever in need, they will help you, against robbers or enemies.
> Now, of course, there is peace; but if such an emergency should arise,
> you will pray for more like us to show up. Don't imagine that this
> speaker here will ever fight for you; he can scold, of course, like
> a woman. We will give you a share of meat and hides when we catch
> any game: just send someone to fetch them. If you bid us pull our
> huts down, we shall pull them down if they harm you. But then give
> us housing here: else how can we endure the winter? There are plenty
> of houses inside your walls that no one lives in; one of them will be
> enough for us. But if we do not live here, if we do not add to the con-
> gestion of so many people living in the same spot, does that make us
> candidates for resettlement?
>
> Now that ungodly and wicked business of shipwrecks he brazenly
> spoke of—I almost forgot to mention it, though it should have been
> my first point—could any of you possibly believe it? . . . Heaven
> forbid that I should ever get profit or gain from people's misfortune!
> No, I have received no benefits whatever from shipwrecks, but have
> often pitied their mariners when they came my way. I have received
> them in my hut, have given them food and drink, helped them in any
> other way I could, and escorted them back to civilization. But which
> of them would bear me witness now? It was not for testimonials or
> gratitude that I helped those people—I never even knew where they
> came from. I only hope that none of you is ever involved in that kind
> of experience.

The bread which the hunter had cast upon the waters comes
back to him :

While I was making my speech, a man in the audience arose, and I thought to myself, "There was another of the same ilk, doubtless ready to lie about me." But this is what he said: "Gentlemen, I have long been of two minds about this man. I could not believe he was the man I thought, but now I am positive that he is. It would be criminal, or worse, sinful, not to declare what I know and render payment in mere words for the substantial acts of kindness I experienced. I am, as you are aware, a citizen," he continued, and pointing to his neighbor, who then also rose from his seat, said, "and so is this man. Two years ago it happened that we were sailing in Socles' boat. The boat was wrecked off Caphereus, with the loss of all but very few of its passengers. Of these some were taken in by purple fishers, for they had money in their purses. But we were stripped bare when we were cast up, and so walked along a track hoping to find some shepherds' or cowherds' shelter. We might have died of hunger and thirst, but after a struggle got to some huts, where we stopped and called for help. This man came up and brought us in and kindled a slow fire, which he increased by degrees. He himself rubbed one of us down and his wife the other—with lard, for they had no oil. Finally they poured warm water over us until they brought us round; we had been numb with cold. Then they made us lie down, covered us with what they had, and put wheat loaves before us to eat. They themselves ate parched millet, and they gave us wine to drink while they themselves drank water. Venison was plentiful, both roasted and boiled. The next day we wanted to leave, but they kept us for three days. Then they saw us down to the plain, and when we left, they gave us meat and a very fine skin for each of us. When he noticed that my health was still delicate from my recent exposure, he put a little tunic on me that he took off his daughter; she wrapped another rag round herself. When we got to a village, I gave the tunic back. Next after the gods, then, it is due to this man that we have survived."

The people had listened to the man's speech with pleasure, and they applauded me. Now I recollected the incident. I called out, "Hello, Sotades!" I went up and kissed him and the other man. When I did so, the people laughed heartily, and then I realized that in the cities people do not kiss one another.

The hunter is of course roundly applauded, given a dinner in the city hall, and left in peace for the future. Virtue had prevailed, and its vindication had edified the hunter's audience and through them Dio's. Persons in positions of authority have been admonished to eschew self-seeking and to abate the rigor of legal enactments in the face of manifest righteousness; humbler auditors have received a lesson in the virtues of industry and fortitude, in the satisfactions of a frugal life close to nature, and in the duty of assisting the distressed, which is not only good and pleasing in itself but even brings a reward; all are improved by the glimpses of an Arcadian Eden.

But though the didactic aim of the tale is more obvious than Cleomenes', its lesson is less compelling and less demanding. The basic difference between the two is that the "Hunters" is palpably a fiction, serious in purpose, it is true, and skillfully wrought, but intended to convince rather than to convert. The Cleomenes story is, or purports to be, a veracious account of an actual king— a king who spent himself for an ideal, suffered persecution at the hands of a wicked sovereign, and received marks of divine approbation after his death. We move from the realm of literature to the realm of religion. The hunter is an appealing example, Cleomenes is himself a figure of power.

Because it lacks the requisite religious attributes, specifically the motifs of death and transfiguration, the "Hunters" can be called aretalogy only in a figurative sense; and yet it does exploit and illustrate certain characteristics of aretalogy proper. The central figure is a superlatively good man sorely tried, he is confronted by a suspicious and unsympathetic ruler, and he does win over, in a public spectacle, an audience that had been indifferent or hostile. Where he misses the pattern is that instead of suffering martyrdom, he goes home to a farm now prosperous, where he will live happy ever after. It happens that this is precisely the pattern of our extant Greek romances, that on the surface have nothing to do with aretalogy but that may be purposeful adaptations of the form calculated to inculcate a kindred doctrine.

The plots of the romances are easy to reduce to a formula. A young couple of high birth and superlative virtue are separated after their marriage or are prevented from marrying by some external force. In their efforts to be united, establish their true identity, and recover their proper status, they wander over many lands, suffer shipwreck and kidnaping by pirates and brigands, and resist incessant attacks on their virtue. In a spectacular scene at the end, regularly in the presence of a large concourse that is won over and exults in their salvation, their identity is acknowledged, their virtue vindicated, and they are assured of a happy life ever after. One obvious moral in this pattern is that piety receives its proper reward, nor is this as banal as it may seem, for the world of the romances is governed by the unpredictable goddess Fortuna, and the assurance that there is indeed a connection between a man's conduct and his fate is as necessary as it is unexpected.

But there are other recurrent motifs in the romances that may have a deeper religious significance. In each of them the steadfast hero is tormented almost to death, even crucified or about to be crucified, and then providentially delivered. Also in each there are one or more instances of the motif that has been called "premature burial." The victim is ostensibly dead, and his body is formally disposed of, or else under some pressing crisis he is thrust living into an underground chamber with little expectation that he will emerge safe; but subsequently he does in either case emerge safe into the light of day. The thwarted execution and the apparent resurrection enhance the stature of the intended victim.

The recurrence of these motifs and the uniformity of the pattern make the four extant romances of the type seem much alike; when the books have been laid down, it is not easy for a cursory reader to sort them out. General sameness within a literary genre is a familiar enough phenomenon in Greco-Roman antiquity; one thinks of the Plautine adaptations of New Comedy, that are equally difficult for a cursory reader to sort out. But in the case of the romances there may be a different explanation, as Carl Kerényi has suggested in his *Griechisch-orientalische Romanliteratur in religionsgeschichtlicher Beleuchtung* (1927). The romances, according to Kerényi, do not merely seem to be but are in fact telling an identical story, and the story they are telling is the sacred myth of a particular cult (Kerényi suggests a cult of Isis) in which the unacknowledged deity is humiliated, afflicted, tormented, even executed and buried, and then has his true identity unexpectedly demonstrated and asserts himself in glory.

The theory cannot indeed be proved, but it does possess a certain plausibility. A major obstacle to accepting the romances as purposeful retelling of a sacred myth, to a modern reader, is the effectiveness of the disguise : the stories as told are so adequate as entertainment that the reader is not encouraged to probe for hidden meanings. Here certain observations may be in place. If the stories are in fact religious propaganda, contemporary audiences would be readier than modern ones to recognize polysemous levels and to grasp allegorical or otherwise concealed meanings. Furthermore, as we shall see was done with the life of Apollonius of Tyana, one means of conferring respectability upon a subliterary or exotic cult was to put its sacred myth into currently fashionable literary form. Kerényi's hypothesis that the romances are religious propaganda, in effect aretalogies, is therefore not outside the bounds of possibility.

But even if we reject the hypothesis, we may go so far as to agree that although the whole purpose of the romances is entertainment, the outlines of their plot and much of their incident may well have been adopted from cult myth. For the survival of originally religious forms as belles-lettres after the religious meaning had faded, we have ample analogies in the literature of late antiquity. Virtually all classical art forms originally had some religious function or association and were retained for their esthetic value long after the religious implications came to be forgotten or ignored. In the sense that Lycophron's *Alexandra* is a tragedy, or Callimachus' *Hymns* are in any real sense hymns, or even Apollonius' *Argonautica* is an epic, the romances are aretalogies. Beneath their surface ornament we can detect the soberer outlines of an instrument of spiritual instruction, and even in its denatured guise the instrument is still effective. Such moral doctrine as the romances do contain, chiefly in the matter of approved modes of conduct between the sexes, they have communicated to audiences multiplied manyfold through the masses of creative literature in several languages that they helped to shape. Even when it is emasculated, aretalogy has proved to be a prime instrument of propaganda.

X. MARTYRDOMS

A SHIP'S CAPTAIN who by sailing into a gale had endangered the life of King Xerxes and caused the death of a number of his nobles had his head struck off by the king's orders, Herodotus (8.118) tells us, but only after he had been presented with a gold crown. Apparently only a man entitled to a crown could be worthy of a great king's attention. Something of the same logic is involved in the practice of Greek tragedy. In the *Bacchae* of Euripides, the best classical example of the kind of literature that concerns us here, Dionysus, who speaks for the new religion that King Pentheus suspects and abhors, is in fact Pentheus' own cousin. It is in keeping with the proprieties of Greek tragedy that the victim of a fall should be of comparable station with its agent; a moral tale has greater impact if its characters are great personages. To make the victim humble and despised and then represent him glorified while his persecutor is crushed to earth is, from the viewpoint of classical taste, a move in the direction of melodrama. When the heroic figures of tragedy give way to ordinary types, as in the later Euripides or in New Comedy or in the romances glanced at in the preceding chapter, the tendency towards melodrama is easily perceptible.

An important factor in giving the Cleomenes story its force is the circumstance that Cleomenes himself was of blood royal, and it is by no means atypical that the holy men who are victims of tyranny should be of noble status or have claims of nobility proffered for them. In the case of Cleomenes it was not an opposing king but a segment of the populace that experienced the first effects of the hero's moral victory. In the case of the *Bacchae*

Pentheus himself is made to feel Dionysus' power. The latter pattern is the normal one for aretalogy. It is almost a corollary of the equality of status that the king himself, not merely an unsophisticated and hence susceptible audience, is capable of being so affected by the steadfastness of an opponent he respects that he undergoes something like conversion.

Eleazar, the figure we shall consider next, was indeed not a king but an aged and highly revered priest who presumably held the highest dignity among the people to whom his martyrdom was addressed, whom the oppressing king respected as a philosopher, and who was capable of conversing with the king on terms of virtual equality. The story of Eleazar's martyrdom is told quite briefly in II Maccabees and much more fully and with greater sophistication and artistry in IV Maccabees. Both books were composed in Greek and follow Greek modes of structure and expression. It is clear that the account in IV Maccabees derives from no independent tradition but is based exclusively on the account in II Maccabees. The additional detail and the difference of approach in IV Maccabees are therefore the author's own. It is then of interest to observe that the direction of the new treatment is to conform Eleazar's utterances and bearing to those of Socrates and hence to bring the whole closer to the contours of an aretalogy.

The earlier and shorter version of the story, told in II Maccabees 6:18–31, runs as follows:

Eleazar, one of the leading scribes, a man of advanced age and a fine appearance, was being forced to open his mouth and eat pork. But he, welcoming a glorious death in preference to a life of pollution, went up of his own accord to the torture wheel, setting an example of how those should come forward who are steadfast enough to refuse food that it is wrong to taste even for the natural love of life. Those who were in charge of that unlawful sacrificial meal, because of their long-standing acquaintance with the man, took him aside and privately urged him to bring meat provided by himself, which he could properly make use of, and pretend that he was eating the meat of the sacrifice, as the king had ordered, so that by doing this he might escape the death penalty, and on account of his lifelong friendship with them be kindly treated. But he, making a high resolve, worthy of his years and the dignity of his age and the hoary hair which he reached with such distinction, and his admirable life even from his childhood, and still more of the holy and divine legislation, declared himself in accord with these, telling them to send him down to Hades at once.

"For," said he, "it does not become our time of life to pretend, and so lead many young people to suppose that Eleazar when ninety years old has gone over to heathenism, and to be led astray through me, because of my pretense for the sake of this short and insignificant life, while I defile and disgrace my old age. For even if for the present I escape the punishment of men, yet whether I live or die I shall not escape the hands of the Almighty. Therefore by manfully giving up my life now, I will prove myself worthy of my great age, and leave to the young a noble example of how to die willingly and nobly for the sacred and holy laws."

With these words he went straight to the torture wheel, while those who so shortly before had felt kindly toward him became hostile to him, because the words he had uttered were in their opinion mere madness. As he was about to die under the strokes, he said with a groan,

"The Lord, in his holy knowledge, knows that, though I might have escaped death, I endure dreadful pains in my body from being flogged; but in my heart I am glad to suffer this, because I fear him."

Here the oppressor is not a personalized tyrant but almost an impersonal force, and Eleazar's fortitude is a victory over human weakness, almost like an athlete working alone against a record, rather than a contest. The tyrant does eventually recant, but not as a result of the martyrdom (9 : 16–17):

The holy sanctuary, which before he had plundered, he would adorn with the finest offerings, and he would give back all the sacred dishes many times over, and the expenses incident to the sacrifices he would supply from his own revenues; and in addition to this, he would become a Jew and visit every inhabited place to proclaim the power of God.

All that the story aims at, in the context of the history of the whole war, is to show that the basis of the war was religion and to demonstrate the temper of the combatants. We should expect a different kind of treatment in a work in which the story was central, as it is in IV Maccabees.

Even here, ostensibly, it is brought in only as an illustration of the philosophical principle that is the stated subject of the book : "religious reason is sovereign over the emotions." Indeed, the alternative and more accurate title of the work is "On the

Sovereignty of Reason." When the story begins, with chapter 5, the stage is carefully set : the tyrant and his counsellors are seated upon a lofty place, and men at arms and presumably a concourse of spectators are present. The king begins by adducing arguments to prove that Eleazar's position is philosophically untenable, and Eleazar counters with other arguments in rebuttal. It is a mark of our author's art, as of Eleazar's steadfastness, that the king is willing to connive at a subterfuge to save the priest's life, and that aside from the cogency of philosophical arguments and the availability of legalistic loopholes, Eleazar, like Socrates, is moved by his responsibility to his previous career, that must not be stultified by an ultimate weakness. As in the case of Socrates too, and unlike the direct Pythagorean succession, there are no supernatural interventions at the end. The king is not browbeaten into submission by some divine manifestation, nor is there any indication other than his own utter conviction that Eleazar has won divine approval. But the king himself, to say nothing of Eleazar's own following, is much impressed by the martyrdom of Eleazar and of Hannah and her seven sons, and profits by the example. "For the tyrant Antiochus, taking as a model the course of their virtue and their constancy under torture, advertised their endurance as a pattern to his own soldiers : he thus got them noble and courageous for infantry battle and for siege, and he ravaged and vanquished all his enemies" (4:23–24).

In itself the story of Eleazar may be only an imperfect example of aretalogy, but it is an important monument in the history of the genre because on the one hand it is so palpably influenced by the image of Socrates and on the other it is so palpably the prototype for a long series of subsequent martyrdoms. The parallel with Socrates is unmistakable. Like Socrates, Eleazar is an old man revered as a teacher by his own devoted followers and for that reason suspected by the authorities, who regarded his teaching as subversive. The setting is made to approximate a law court (as it is not in the short version in II Maccabees), and in his defense Eleazar, like Socrates, persists in adhering to his own teachings, which he is certain are more wholesome for the community as a whole than those the authorities would impose. Like Socrates too he disdains purchasing a necessarily brief extension of life at the price of betraying the long career that had preceded. At the close of the *Apology* Socrates introduces other-worldly considerations. He speculates on the possibility of encountering true judges in the world to come—Minos and Aeacus and Rhadamanthus—and of consorting with such sages as Orpheus and Musaeus, Hesiod and Homer. His concluding sentence is : "The hour of departure has arrived, and we go our ways—I to die, and you to live. Which is better God only knows." Eleazar does not require a *daimonion* to reassure him that his course is right, for he possesses the Law, nor does he speculate on his fate after death. His concluding words are a prayer for his people (IV Maccabees 6:27–29) : "Thou knowest, God, that though I might have saved myself, I die in fiery torment for the sake of the Law. Be merciful to thy people, and let my punishment be sufficient for their sake. Make my blood an expiation for them, and take my life as a ransom for theirs."

The particular Platonic treatise that would seem to have been present to the mind of the author of IV Maccabees is the *Gorgias*. Here Socrates refutes the Sophist Callicles, who maintains the justice of capricious tyranny on the grounds that justice is the power of the strong, employing the argument that the laws of morality are only convention (*nomos* means both "law" and "convention"), whereas the true criterion of morality is "nature" (*physis*), which is notoriously red in tooth and claw. The position of Eleazar—and of our author—generally is very like that of Socrates, as a few excerpts from the *Gorgias* will show. Socrates presents two paradoxes : "If it is necessary either to do or to suffer wrong, it is better to suffer than to do it" (469c); and "The wrongdoer is worse off if he is not punished than if he is" (472E). Callicles objects that the tyrant can nevertheless subject his victim to torture; but Socrates insists that "any wrong whatsoever done me or mine is worse and more shameful to the wrongdoer than to me the wronged" (508E). There is an "art of providing so that we suffer no wrong" (510A), and that is by "avoiding any unjust word or deed in regard to either men or gods" (522CD). The important thing is for a man to persevere in his own true values and to retain his control despite the assaults of immediate fear and interest. "The temperate man, being just and brave and pious, is the perfection of the good man, and a good man fares well however he fares and is blessed and happy, while the wicked man or evildoer is wretched" (507B). True judgment will take place in the future when men are stripped of their bodies, which confuse judgment in this life, and their bare souls can be examined (523). This must be kept in mind in shaping our conduct. "No man fears the mere act of dying, except he be utterly irrational and unmanly; doing wrong is what one fears : for to arrive in the nether world bearing one's soul fraught with a heap of misdeeds is the uttermost of all evils" (522E). And here is Socrates' conclusion : "Let us therefore take as our guide the doctrine now disclosed, which indicates to us that this way of life is best—to live and die in the practice alike of justice and of all other virtue. This, then, let us follow, and to this invite everyone else; not that to which you trust yourself and invite me, for it is nothing worth, Callicles" (527E). If the *Gorgias* was not our author's specific source, it is quite clear that Platonism in general was, for his doctrine is consistently Platonic; and no one could attempt to dramatize Platonic doctrine without remembering the image of Socrates. Perhaps the best evidence that Platonism and the image of Socrates shaped the image of Eleazar is that the account in II Maccabees, which was certainly our author's sole source for the story, suggests neither Platonism nor Socrates.

If Socrates was indeed the model for Eleazar, then he can be said to be the model for the long series of Christian martyrdoms that were palpably influenced by the story of Eleazar. During the early centuries of the Roman empire when devout Christians were being persecuted by the state authorities, IV Maccabees provided the one obvious paradigm for inculcating steadfastness under torture, for the position of the Christian victims vis-à-vis the persecuting emperors was precisely analogous. Eleazar had only to make a token recantation and Antiochus would have relented, and so would Roman governors have relented if the Christians on trial had recanted. This is clear from Trajan's rescript, addressed to Pliny as governor of Bithynia, which is our earliest official evidence for Rome's attitude towards Christians. Here are Trajan's words (Pliny 10.97) :

> No search should be made for these people; when they are denounced and found guilty, they must be punished; with the restriction, however, that when the party denies himself to be a Christian, and shall give proof that he is not (that is, by adoring our gods), he shall be pardoned on the ground of repentance, even though he may have formerly incurred suspicion.

This remained the official attitude during the persecutions of the succeeding centuries, until the edict of Constantine made Christianity a lawful religion. Like Eleazar before Antiochus, any Christian might save himself by publicly recanting his Christianity; and it was Eleazar that Christian teachers had in mind when they held the Maccabeans up as models of fortitude and perseverance.

The earliest literary account of a martyrdom we have is that of Polycarp, dated in the second century. (Polycarp, it is worth noting, was also a nonagenarian.) The description of the constancy of the martyrs in the *Martyrdom of Polycarp* (ch. 2), and especially of the reasoning that gave them courage, is remarkably reminiscent of IV Maccabees :

> All the martyrdoms, then, were blessed and noble which took place according to the will of God. For it becomes us who profess greater piety than others to ascribe the authority over all things to God. And truly, who can fail to admire their nobleness of mind and their patience, with that love towards their Lord which they displayed? who, when they were so torn with scourges that the frame of their bodies, even to the very inward veins and arteries, was laid open, still patiently endured, while even those that stood by pitied and bewailed them. But they reached such a pitch of magnanimity, that not one of them let a sigh or a groan escape them; thus proving to us all that those holy martyrs of Christ, at the very time when they suffered such torments, were absent from the body, or rather that the Lord then stood by them and communed with them. And looking to the grace of Christ, they despised all the torments of this world, redeeming themselves from eternal punishment by a single hour. For this reason the fire of their savage executioners appeared cool to them. For they kept before their view escape from that fire which is eternal and never shall be quenched, and looked forward with the eyes of their heart to those good things which are laid up for such as endure.

This martyrdom set the tone for subsequent works of the same nature; if IV Maccabees influenced one, it influenced all. The paradigm of Eleazar is invoked by both Cyprian and Origen in their *Exhortations to Martyrdom,* and it is echoed in Ambrose, Augustine, and others. The elegant style as well as the substance of IV Maccabees influenced the writers of the golden age of patristic oratory. Gregory Nazianzen's *Oration on the Maccabees* and John Chrysostom's four homilies on the Maccabean martyrs make large use of it. Gregory actually uses the word "proto-martyr" in speaking of Eleazar. Ambrose, who was the chief Latin Father to make large use of the Greeks and so the principal channel through which Greek influence reached the West, makes patent use of IV Maccabees in two treatises, *De officiis minoribus* and *De Jacob et vita beata* : the latter is virtually a transcript of our book. Augustine (*City of God* 18.36) says that the Books of the Maccabees were received and preserved by the Church "on account of the extreme and wonderful suffering of the martyrs told therein."

A martyrdom is in effect an aretalogy, and if it gives largest place to the holy man's heroism under persecution and his glorious death, that is because the death is after all the crown of the career. The object of the literary aretalogy was to serve as a hagiographa for a cult, and so it was with the martyrdoms. The martyrs were revered not only as paradigms but for their continuing preternatural power and their relics were cherished as a source for such power. Possession of the relics of martyrs was sometimes warmly disputed. In the Middle Ages there was rivalry over the possession of the Maccabean relics between Rome and Cologne; they are now reputed to be in a convent in Cologne.

Martyrdom implies a minority devoted to spiritual beliefs that the representatives of the dominant majority disapprove and seek to suppress. In view of the nature of our religious traditions it is natural that the martyrs of whom we know should be mainly Christian, but there were others also, and some pagan. Our best evidence for their existence comes from some dozen bits of papyri, mostly discovered and identified since 1893, which have been called as a group *Acta Alexandrinorum* or *The Acts of the Pagan Martyrs*. The separate documents purport to be transcripts of quasi-judicial proceedings in which some stalwart Alexandrian defending Hellenic tradition against Roman or Jewish encroachments defies a Roman emperor, sometimes of the first century, and is martyred in consequence. Scholarly opinion no longer holds that these documents are actual court records nor yet that they are parts of a single fictional work or even of a single compilation of works of the same class. They do indeed have a more or less common form and a common anti-Roman or antisemitic tenor, and they may well have been based on actual events. But the form had apparently become a literary genre, whose object it was to communicate a particular moral lesson, specifically that Hellenic integrity must be preserved against the encroachments of barbarian dilution at all costs.

What is of special interest, since the *Acta* are not a single work, is that so many disparate writers adopted the same form. Evidently, then, the pattern was well established. Even when an account of a striking and meaningful death had not been written to conform to the pattern, it was apt to be incorporated into an anthology of such deaths.

The cause for which the Alexandrians celebrated in the Acta died was not what we should describe as religious, though it did involve loyalty to cherished tradition. Loyalty to republican ideals brought death to a number of Romans, especially when the principate first began to show its absolute character, and several have their names recorded, especially in the pages of Tacitus. It is natural for a new tyranny to be resisted, natural that a sympathetic historian should record the victims' names, and even natural that he should make his account detailed and moving and hence that it should resemble such avowed martyrdoms as those of the Pagan Martyrs. But in some instances it seems not improbable that Tacitus was consciously following the established pattern. The accounts of the deaths of Petronius and Seneca might suggest such a pattern, that of the death of Cremutius

Cordus does so more clearly. Here is the passage in Tacitus (*Annals* 4.34–35) :

> In the year of the consulship of Cossus and Agrippa, Cremutius Cordus was arraigned . . . ; the emperor listened with an angry frown to his defense, which Cremutius, resolved to give up his life, began thus:
> "It is my words, Senators, which are condemned, so innocent am I of any guilty act; yet these do not touch the emperor or the emperor's mother, who are alone comprehended under the law of treason. I am said to have praised Brutus and Cassius, whose careers many have described and no one mentioned without eulogy. Titus Livius, pre-eminently famous for eloquence and truthfulness, extolled Pompey in such a panegyric that Augustus called him a Pompeian, and yet this was no obstacle to their friendship. . . . The poems which we read of Bibaculus and Catullus are crammed with invectives on the Caesars. Yet the Divine Julius, the Divine Augustus themselves bore all this and let it pass, whether in forbearance or in wisdom I cannot easily say. Assuredly what is despised is soon forgotten; when you resent a thing, you seem to recognize it. . . . To every man posterity gives his due honor, and if a fatal sentence hangs over me, there will be those who will remember me as well as Cassius and Brutus."
> He then left the Senate and ended his life by starvation. His books, so the Senators decreed, were to be burnt by the aediles; but some copies were left that were concealed and afterwards published. And so one is all the more inclined to laugh at the stupidity of men who suppose that the despotism of the present can actually efface the remembrances of the next generation. On the contrary, the persecution of genius fosters its influence; foreign tyrants and all who have imitated their oppression have merely procured infamy for themselves and glory for their victims.

It was doubtless because of the example of aretalogy proper that instances of heroic death, historical or otherwise, to assert some spiritual principle, came to be collected as an edifying type of literature. Descriptions of such deaths in historical or biographical compilations must often have been drawn from collections of *teleutai*, or *exitus clarorum virorum*. Particularly cherished were the saintly figures who spoke their minds before the powerful of the earth. A telling example is the Indian gymnosophist called Calanus, who conversed with Alexander the Great and whose story is rehearsed or alluded to in a dozen different

authors. Here (from Philo, *Quod omnis probus liber* 14) is the
letter that Calanus is said to have written when Alexander
threatened to compel him to accompany him to Greece :

> Calanus to Alexander. Your friends urge you to apply violence and
> compulsion to the philosophers of India. These friends, however, have
> never even in their dreams seen what we do. Bodies you will transport
> from place to place, but souls you will not compel to do what they
> will not do, any more than force bricks or sticks to talk. Fire causes
> the greatest trouble and ruin to living bodies: we are superior to this,
> we burn ourselves alive. There is no king, no ruler, who will compel
> us to do what we do not freely wish to do. We are not like those philo-
> sophers of the Greeks who practice words for a festal assembly. With
> us deeds accord with words and words with deeds. Deeds pass swiftly
> and words have short-lived power; virtues secure to us blessedness and
> freedom.

And here is Calanus' death, as told in Plutarch's *Life* of
Alexander :

> Calanus, who had suffered for a little while from intestinal disorder,
> asked that a funeral pyre might be prepared for him. To this he came
> on horseback, and after offering prayers, sprinkling himself, and cast-
> ing some of his hair upon the pyre, he ascended it, greeting the Mace-
> donians who were present, and exhorting them to make that day one of
> pleasure and revelry with the king, whom, he declared, he should soon
> see in Babylon. After thus speaking, he lay down and covered his head,
> nor did he move as the fire approached him, but continued to lie in
> the same posture as at first, and so sacrificed himself acceptably.

Arrian (*Anabasis* 7.3) tells the story of the death more fully,
declares that the story is vouched for by reliable authorities, and
points to its usefulness to "those who are desirous of learning
how steadfast and immovable a thing the human mind is in regard to what it wishes to accomplish."

PART TWO

XI. "LIVES"

SO FAR we have considered the genesis and nature of aretalogy and some manifestations of its initial impulses. Let us now complete this study by presentation of four works in which the influence of the aretalogical tradition is particularly clear : the lives of Pythagoras, Moses, Jesus, and Apollonius of Tyana. Of these, the life of Pythagoras was the first to have been recast as an aretalogy, and we therefore place it first, although the forms in which it has been preserved are latest of all. Pythagoras may have thought himself something more than man, and some of his immediate followers may have believed him a god, but the aretalogical development of the stories about him seems to have been the work of the generation at the very end of the fourth century B.C., when the historical Pythagoras (of the sixth century) was a figure so remote as to be scarcely discernible (even supposing the authors of the aretalogies had wished to discern him, which they did not), and the lives of Pythagoras which we have complete are products of the second and third centuries A.D. In this respect—as in many others—the aretalogical treatment of his life resembles that of the life of Moses, which, of our four, began next after the Pythagorean legend : it is already found in Jewish works written in Egypt in the second century B.C., and the complete examples are preserved in works of the first century A.D.

By contrast with the lives of Pythagoras and Moses, the four canonical Gospels were written within less than a century of Jesus' death. Therefore they are especially interesting as showing how the aretalogical pattern could be imposed on the life of a man while his contemporaries were still living. It is not unlikely that this imposition was facilitated by the fact that Jesus had been aware of the pattern and had deliberately followed it. He lived in a world in which the figure of the sage already existed, and he therefore was able to act the part. Apollonius of Tyana, the fourth of our figures, undoubtedly did so, and aretalogical accounts of his life were also produced by his contemporaries, although, unfortunately, we have only a rewriting of them (and of other material) from the early years of the third century A.D., about a hundred and twenty-five years after Apollonius' death in the late nineties.

Apollonius, however, is the only one of our figures of whose aretalogy we have only one preserved example. For Pythagoras, Moses, and Jesus we have several works each. These works parallel each other to such an extent that few would wish to read them all. For purposes of example and comparison, therefore, it has seemed best to select one work dealing with each man. For Pythagoras, there is a fairly short life by Porphyry that has not hitherto been easily available in English translation. This it has seemed worthwhile to translate entire. By contrast, the life of Moses by Philo and that of Apollonius of Tyana by Philostratus are long works that, for the purpose of convenient comparison, it has seemed best to summarize. For Jesus, too, a summary of the long Gospel according to Luke has been preferred to a full reprint of the shorter Mark, partly because aretalogical traits are more prominent in Luke than in Mark, partly because it was thought a new and summarizing translation might help readers notice the content of stories to which they had long been accustomed.

The object of these summaries is to present fully, but as briefly as possible (while retaining narrative style) the aretalogical content of the works summarized. Speculations by the authors, literary developments of dialogue and description, and so on, have all been eliminated, but reports of the sages' actions and teachings have been retained. Abbreviation of course necessitates choice between the essential and the secondary, but this choice has been made in the spirit of the aretalogist, not the historical critic. That is to say, nothing has been cut out because it was "unhistorical." The object of these retellings is not to present the "historical"

Pythagoras or Moses or Jesus or Apollonius, but to sketch the aretalogies of which they were made the heroes.

Of these there was never any single authoritative form. The four Gospels, for instance, are not four developments of a single, original text. There was only the general tradition composed of innumerable stories and sayings that every preacher shaped and developed according to his own needs and tastes and those of his circle. Even the tradition about Moses was never coextensive with the text of the Pentateuch. Rather that text is an accumulated deposit of several documents which embodied parts of a much more extensive oral tradition. This tradition continued to live, change, and develop apart from the written text, and was eventually so much reworked that a part of it assumed something like the form in which Philo presented it. Therefore we must not think that by comparison of the several accounts of a single man we can recover the original tradition with which all his aretalogists began. That original tradition never had a single or fixed form and never existed as a whole in the mind of anyone. Behind the variants known to us lie other variations, and so on back ultimately to the various followers of the heroes, each of whom told different stories about the man he followed—and told them, probably, in different forms at different times. Our task, therefore, is not to present as a whole the original tradition that never existed as a whole, but to present as briefly as possible one form that the tradition about each man did assume.

Even the casual reader will notice immediately the similarity of these forms. To those who reflect on the evidence presented in the preceding chapters it will be amply clear that much of this similarity is due to the influence of the aretalogical tradition described therein. However, one trait of particular importance for the understanding of these following works may be noted here : none of them is properly a "life" of its hero. Each begins with legends of his birth and youth (to represent him as a *Wunderkind*) then turns to his work. Of this work the record included a collection of unrelated stories and sayings. These the authors tried to adapt to the requirements of Greco-Roman literary form by imposing on them a chronological and geographical framework. But the authors were not successful. Each one had left over a lot of miscellaneous material not attached to his frame, and he had to dispose of it as best he could. Porphyry and Luke inserted it in great chunks, Philo collected it in a second book as a postscript to his "historical" outline, Philostratus scattered it throughout his work in bits and pieces here and there (a method also followed in part by Luke). All of them, finally, concluded with a developed account of the hero's death and/or ascension to heaven. The predominantly religious rather than biographical interest and the dependence at least in part upon oral and anecdotal ("haggadic") tradition are clear in all instances. Equally clear are the differences between the works, reflecting the basic differences of historical fact and social background in the traditions which confronted the authors. That from material so clearly diverse the four authors should have produced works so clearly similar shows the strength of the common Greco-Roman culture, and especially of the common aretalogical tradition, which produced the similarity.

XII. *THE LIFE OF PYTHAGORAS*

BY PORPHYRY

INTRODUCTORY

PORPHYRY, whose life of Pythagoras is translated in the following pages, was a Syrian or Tyrian, originally called Malchus. Born in 232/3 A.D., he studied at Athens and then went to Rome, where at about the age thirty he became a devoted disciple of the Neoplatonic philosopher Plotinus, whose works he edited shortly before his own death about 305. His life of Pythagoras is an excerpt from a history of philosophy he wrote as a young man, before his attachment to Plotinus. Like other such works of about the same time, it quotes a great many "authorities" without much effort to reconcile or evaluate their different opinions. The quoted authorities are the following:

Antiphon, of uncertain date and background.

Antonius Diogenes, of unknown origin, wrote about 100 A.D.

Apollonius of Tyana, died about 97, the hero of the fourth of the lives presented in the volume.

Aristoxenus of Tarentum, a musical theorist and philosopher, born about 360 B.C. He came to Athens, was a pupil of a Pythagorean philosopher and also of Aristotle, and lived till about the end of the century.

Dicaearchus of Messina in Sicily, a pupil of Aristotle. He wrote from about 320–280 B.C. on philosophy, politics, history, biography, and geography.

Diogenes = Antonius Diogenes, above.

Dionysophanes, unknown.

Eudoxus, a famous mathematician, astronomer, and geographer, from Cnidus in southwestern Asia Minor. He lived about 408–355 B.C.

Hippobotus, of the late third century A.D., collected material on the history of philosophy.

Lycus, of uncertain identity.

Moderatus of Gades (modern Cadiz), an important interpreter of Pythagorean philosophy who worked in the second half of the first century A.D.

Neanthes of Cyzicus (a city on the sea of Marmora), a credulous historian and biographer, who worked in the early third century B.C.

Nicomachus of Gerasa in TransJordan, an eminent mathematician and Neopythagorean philosopher who worked from about 100–150 A.D.

Timaeus, a famous Sicilian historian who lived about 356–260 B.C.

The opinions cited from these authorities show the various developments that the Pythagorean legend underwent.

From the time of Neanthes and even earlier we have attempts to connect Pythagoras by race with the eastern peoples to whom Greeks with a taste for occultism were already attributing knowledge of ancient mysteries. (The Etruscans, in Greek legend, had come from Asia Minor.) Apollonius, as part of his Hellenizing reaction, made Pythagoras the son of the pre-eminently Greek god, Apollo. Yet another miraculous account of Pythagoras' origin probably lies behind the story reported in §10 from Antonius Diogenes. Here the miraculous child found feeding on manna was probably Pythagoras. The legend has been reconciled with the common account (that Pythagoras was the son of Mnesarchus) by renaming the miraculous child and having Mnesarchus adopt him and give him to Pythagoras.

There are various attempts to tie together the history of Greek philosophy by making Pythagoras a pupil of Pherecydes (author of a mythological cosmology) or of the great Milesian philosopher Anaximander, and the teacher, through a supposed son, of the even greater Democritus. At least the last two of these are almost certainly worthless —had there been any such relation, it would have been better attested. On the other hand, Hermodamus of Samos, who is also mentioned as the teacher of Pythagoras, is known in this connection only, and therefore probably was Pythagoras' teacher.

The attempt to connect Pythagoras' teachings if not his person with the supposed ancient oriental wisdom is so widespread that Porphyry can present it as the common opinion (which he is happy to do). Connection with the mysterious East was a standard trait of the holy man; thus Matthew brings the Magi to acknowledge the superiority of Jesus, and thereafter sends the Holy Child to Egypt (details the other Evangelists had not heard of). The opposite side of the coin is shown in the Greek claim that Pythagoras was the teacher of Zalmoxis (the chief deity of the Getae, a barbarous people in Thrace), while Greek occultism is represented by the story that Pythagoras visited Crete and was there initiated into the tradition of the Dactyls (legendary craftsmen and magicians supposed to have lived on Mt. Ida).

The lack of any coherant tradition as to Pythagoras' work in Italy is obvious from the central section of the *Life*. Here, as in the other works resting on aretalogical traditions, we are dealing with a collection of disjointed anecdotes presented by different authors in ways clearly contradictory. Compare, for instance, the statement in §22, "He utterly destroyed factionalism . . . for many generations . . . ," with the account in 56 of the great factional riots "everywhere" that preceded his death. Now Porphyry had perhaps the best philosophical training of any of our authors. That he could include such flagrant contradictions in his work when he found them in his sources should diminish our surprise at the contradictions in the works of less learned authors, e.g., the Evangelists.

Porphyry's general arrangement of his material on Pythagoras' work is another interesting parallel to the Gospels. He begins with an account of the great sensation made by his hero on arrival, and his gathering a body of followers (18–20; cf. Luke 4:14–5:11, Mark 1:14–39, John 2:1–11); then comes a preliminary account of his legal and moral teaching (21-22; cf. Luke 5:12-6:49, Mark 1:40-4:34), and then a collection of miracle stories (23–31; cf. Luke 7 and 8:22–9:17, Mark 5, 6, and 7:24–8:26). After this comes an account of his daily regimen and diet (32–35), an example of Greco-Roman biographical interests alien to the aretalogical tradition. Then comes the fuller account of his teaching, with careful distinction between what he taught in public and what he taught secretly to the inner circle of his disciples (37–53; cf. Luke 9:18–21:38, Mark 8:27–13:37, where the same distinction is emphasized; see also Mark 4). It is particularly noteworthy that the tradition about teachings seems to have been generally separate from that about miracles, and both of these from that about the main course and events of the hero's life. This existence of at least three different kinds and bodies of tradition, kept distinct even though they all concern the same man and may be handed down by the same men, is also conspicuous in the Gospels and is of basic importance for critical discussion. Finally, like the Gospels, the story closes with an account of the hero's death and the survival of his teaching through his followers.

Note: the numbers in the margins
refer to the divisions of
the Greek text.

IT IS AGREED BY MOST that Pythagoras was the son of 1
Mnesarchus, but there has been disagreement concerning
Mnesarchus' race. Some say he was a Samian, but Neanthes in
the fifth book of his work on Pythagoreanism says he was a Syrian

from Tyre in Syria. When Samos was in the grip of a grain short-age, Mnesarchus sailed to the island as a trader with a cargo of grain, sold it, and was honored with citizenship. Since Pythagoras from childhood on was gifted for every study, Mnesarchus took him to Tyre, and having introduced him to the Chaldaeans there, made him study with them for a considerable time. When Pythagoras came back thence to Ionia, he first was a student of Pherecydes of Syros, next, in Samos, of Hermodamas the son of

2 Creophylius, who was already an old man. Neanthes also says there are others who state that Pythagoras' father was one of the Etruscans who settled Lemnos; thence he came on business to Samos, remained there, and became a citizen. When Mnesarchus sailed to Italy, Pythagoras sailed with him while yet a youth. He saw the country was extremely fertile, and then later returned to it. Finally, Neanthes records two brothers of Pythagoras, Eunostos and Tyrrenos, both elder than he.

Apollonius, in his book *On Pythagoras,* also gives the name of Pythagoras' mother, Pythaïs, a descendant of Ancaeus, the founder of Samos. Apollonius says, too, that some declare Pythagoras was by procreation the child of Apollo and Pythaïs, and only nominally the child of Mnesarchus. As a matter of fact, one of the Samian poets does say, "Pythagoras, the friend of Zeus, whom Pythaïs, most beautiful of the Samians, bore to Apollo." Finally, that he was a pupil not only of Pherecydes and Hermo-damas but of Anaximander too, is also stated by Apollonius.

3 Duris of Samos, in the second book of his *Samian Chronicles,* declares that Pythagoras had a son, Arimnestus, who was the teacher of Democritus. Arimnestus, when he came back from exile, dedicated in the temple of Hera a bronze pillar nearly two cubits [three feet] in diameter, on which the following epigram was inscribed, "Arimnestus, the dear son of Pythagoras, dedicated me, he who discovered in words many proportions." Simos, the writer on the theory of harmony, destroying this, appropriated Arimnestus' musical canon and published it as his own. There-fore, although the proportions originally listed were seven, by reason of the one, which Simos took away, the others recorded in the votive offering also disappeared.

Yet others record a son of Pythagoras named Telauges and a 4
daughter, Myia, and some say, also Arignota, born of Theano,
of Cretan race, the daughter of Pythonax, and they report that
Pythagorean writings by these have been preserved. Timaeus,
moreover, writes that the daughter of Pythagoras, while still a
girl, was the leader of the chorus of girls in Croton [the south
Italian town where Pythagoras settled], and after her marriage,
the leader of the women. He says that the people of Croton made
Pythagoras' house a temple of Demeter, and called his street
Museum Street.

Lycus, in the fourth book of his histories, reports that some 5
authorities differ even concerning Pythagoras' native land. He
says, "If you do not know the land and the city of which this man
happened to be a citizen, do not be disturbed, for some say he
came from Samos, some from Phleius [in the Peloponnesus], and
some from Metapontum [in southern Italy]."

Further, as concerns his teaching, most writers say he learned 6
the sciences called mathematical from the Egyptians, Chaldaeans,
and Phoenicians (for from ancient times the Egyptians have
studied geometry, the Phoenicians number theory and arithmetic,
and the Chaldaeans astronomy and astrology). However, they
say that in matters dealing with the services of the gods and the
other concerns of life, he was a student of the Magi and took his
doctrines from them. Now his doctrines are almost commonly 7
known, since they are to be found in various treatises, but the
rest of his practices are less known. However, Eudoxus, in the
seventh book of his *Tour of the Earth,* says he practiced so great
purity, especially in avoidance of slaughter and slaughterers, that
he not only ate no animal food but also never went near cooks
and hunters.

Antiphon, in his book *On the Life of Those Who Excelled in
Virtue,* describes the endurance Pythagoras showed in Egypt,
saying that because he approved the way of life of the Egyptian
priests and was anxious to participate in this, he besought the
tyrant Polycrates [of Samos] to write his friend and former host
Amasis king of Egypt, and ask that he [Pythagoras] might be
permitted to share in the training of these aforesaid priests. Com-

ing to Amasis, he received letters to the priests and, when he had spent some time with those at Heliopolis, was sent on by them to Memphis, as if to their seniors, though in fact this was merely a pretense of the Heliopolitans, and from Memphis, as a result of the same pretense, he went to the priests of Diospolis [ancient

8 Thebes, in upper Egypt]. They were not able, from fear of the king, to allege any causes [for refusing to initiate him]. However, they thought to turn him away from his attempt by the greatness of the hardship it would entail. Therefore they ordered him to submit to harsh rules that were quite alien to the Greek way of life. But when he willingly accomplished these things, they so admired him that he was authorized to sacrifice to the gods and to be present when they were taken care of, something not known to have happened in the case of any other alien.

9   When he came back to Ionia (Antiphon goes on to say) he built in his native city the semicircular lecture hall which is still called that of Pythagoras and in which the Samians meet to deliberate on their public affairs. Outside of the city he adapted a cave to the requirements of his philosophy and in this spent most of the day and the night, together with a few friends.

Artistoxenus says that when Pythagoras was about forty years old, he saw the tyranny of Polycrates was so severe that a man of free spirit would do better not to endure its rule and despotism. Accordingly he made his departure for Italy.

10   Since Diogeres, too, in his book *The Things Incredible beyond Thule,* gave an accurate account of matters concerning Pythagoras, I have decided not to pass over his statements. He says Mnesarchus was an Etruscan by race, of those who inhabited Lemnos, Imbros, and Scyrus, and traveling thence, visited many cities and many lands. Once upon a time he came on a baby boy lying under a great and beautiful white poplar tree. When he drew near, he saw the child gazing upward into the sky, looking at the sun without blinking, while in its mouth was a short and narrow reed like a flute. He saw with astonishment, too, that the child was nourished by dew dripping down from the poplar. Therefore he took the child with him, supposing it must be of some divine origin. When the child grew to be a man, in Samos,

he was taken up by Androcles, a native of the island, who turned the care of his household over to him. Meanwhile, however, Mnesarchus, being well to do, brought up the child, whom he called Astraeus, with his own three children, Eunostus, Tyrrenus, and Pythagoras, whom Androcles also adopted as his son when he was yet very young. While he was a boy, he sent him to study with 11 a lyre player and a gymnast and a painter; when he became a youth he sent him to Anaximander in Miletus, to learn geometry and astronomy.

Moreover, Diogenes declares, Pythagoras went to the Egyptians and to the Arabs and Chaldaeans and Hebrews, from whom he also learned accurately the diagnosis of dreams. And he was the first one to practice divination by incense.[1] In Egypt, too, he was with the priests and mastered the knowledge and the language of the Egyptians, including their three different alphabets, episto- 12 lographic and hieroglyphic and symbolic, of which some are communicative in the common fashion, by imitation, others allegorically, by certain enigmas. And he learned something more [than is commonly known] concerning the gods. In Arabia too he spent some time with the king, and in Babylon he was with the other Chaldaeans and also was introduced to Zaratos [= Zarathustra], by whom he was both purified of the pollutions of his former life and instructed as to those things from which the pious should keep themselves pure. Further, he heard the teaching [of Zaratos and the other Chaldaeans] about nature and about the sources of all things. For it was from his travel among these peoples that Pythagoras acquired the greater part of his wisdom.

Mnesarchus gave Astraeus to Pythagoras, who, on receiving 13 him, from his features and from consideration of the ways his body moved and rested, diagnosed his character and educated him accordingly. For Pythagoras was the first to master this science about men, learning what each man was like by nature. And he never made any friend or acquaintance without first judging from the man's features what sort of person he was.

---

[1] "This is what the text says. It should probably be emended to read: among whom he both learned . . . and first practiced."

14   Besides Astraeus he had another lad, too, whom he got from Thrace and whose name was Zalmoxis, because when he was born, a bearskin was wrapped about him (for the Thracians call a pelt *zalmon*). Pythagoras loved him and instructed him in astronomical theory and the things concerning sacrifices and the other services of the gods. Some say he was also called Thales. The
15 barbarians worship him as Hercules. However, Dionysophanes says he was a slave of Pythagoras, but when Pythagoras was driven into exile by his opponents, Zalmoxis fell into the hands of robbers and was tattooed, and wore a bandage over his forehead because of the tattooing. And some say the name Zalmoxis means "an alien."

When Pherecydes was sick in Delos, Pythagoras took care of him and buried him when he died. Thereafter he returned to Samos, because of his desire to be with Hermodamas the son of Creophylus. Spending some time there, he supervised the training of Eurymenes, the Samian athlete who, although of small body, by the wisdom of Pythagoras defeated many bigger men and was a victor at the Olympic games. For while the other athletes still ate cheese and figs, according to the ancient fashion, Eurymenes, following the advice of Pythagoras, was the first one to eat a prescribed amount of meat daily and so gained strength in his body. However, when Pythagoras progressed in wisdom, he advised men to participate in athletic contests but not to win, since one should undergo the hardships but avoid the jealousies that arise from winning. Moreover, it also happens, that those who win and are pelted with leaves are not free from pollution.

16   After this, when the tyranny of Polycrates took control of the Samians, Pythagoras decided that it was not fitting for a man who loved wisdom to live under such a government, and therefore was minded to depart for Italy. Sailing thither he landed to visit Delphi and wrote on the tomb of Apollo an elegy in which he explained that Apollo was the son of Silenus, was killed by Pytho, and was buried in the so-called "Tripod," which received this name because three maidens, the daughters of Triopas, bewailed
17 Apollo there. Coming to Crete, he visited the initiates of Morgos, one of the Idaean Dactyls, by whom he was also purified with a

meteorite, a ritual in which he lay prone beside the sea at dawn, and at night, wreathed with the wool of a black ram, lay beside a river. Going down with black wool into the so-called "Idaean cave," he spent the prescribed thrice nine days there and made offerings to Zeus and saw the couch that is spread for him annually, and inscribed on his tomb an epigram beginning : "Here, having died, lies Zan, whom they call Zeus." Above this he wrote : "Pythagoras to Zeus."

When he landed in Italy and arrived in Croton, Dicaerchus 18 says a great sensation was created by the coming of a man widely traveled and extraordinary and blessed by fortune with many natural advantages, for his appearance was noble and full of great beauty, and his voice and his manner and all other things about him were elegant. The city of Croton was so captivated that after he preached to the college of elders, saying many and noble things, he again, at the request of the civic officials, delivered to the young men exhortations suitable to their age, and after this to the boys, who came together in a single assembly from the schools, and then to the women, since even a meeting of women was arranged for him.

At these events a great reputation grew up around him, and 19 he derived many disciples from this city, not only men but also women (of one of whom the name, Theano, has become famous), and also many, both kings and rulers, from the neighboring barbarian territory. What he said to those who studied with him no one can state with certainty, for they kept unusually silent about this. However, it became well known to everyone that he declared first that the soul is immortal, and second, transmigrant into other kinds of animals, and further, that all events recur at certain periods and nothing is absolutely new, and that all animate creatures should be thought of like race. For it is commonly reported that Pythagoras was the first to bring these doctrines into Greece.

Thus he turned every man to himself, so that, as Nicomachus 20 says, by one single lecture that he gave when he arrived in Italy he captured by his words more than two thousand men. They did not return home, but together with children and wives, establishing a great school of fellow hearers, built a city in that country

everyone calls Magna Graecia in Italy. They received from him
laws and commandments as if they were divine covenants, and
would do nothing whatever in transgression of these. They both
communized their possessions and counted Pythagoras among the
gods. Therefore, choosing one detail of their secret teachings—a
subtle concept, however, and related to many solutions of physical
problems, the sum of the first four numbers—by means of this they
invoked Pythagoras, like some god, in their oaths, all of them
uttering, after all things which they asseverated, "Verily, by him
who gave the sum of the first four numbers to our generation,
that which contains the source and root of eternal nature."

21   The cities which, on his arrival in Italy and Sicily, he found
enslaved to one another—some of them for many years, others
recently—he set free, filling them with free-spirited thought
through his disciples in each. Such were Croton and Sybaris and
Catana and Regium and Himera and Agrigentum and Tauromenium and certain others, to which he also gave laws through
Charondas of Catana and Zaleucus of Locri (and by these laws
they became and long remained worthy of the envy of their neighbors). Simicus, the tyrant of Centoripae, hearing him, abdicated
his rulership and gave some of his money to his sister, the rest of
22   the citizens. To Pythagoras there came, as Aristoxenus says,
Lucanians and Messapians and Peucetians [three south Italian
peoples] and Romans. He utterly destroyed factionalism, not only
among those who knew him, but also among their descendants
for many generations, and generally from all the cities in Italy
and Sicily, destroying not only factionalism within the city but
also that between cities. For he constantly repeated to all, whether
many or few, this saying: "One must drive out by every device,
and with fire and sword and all means whatever cut off from the
body disease, from the soul ignorance, from the belly luxury, from
the city factionalism, from the household dissidence, and from all
at once disproportion."

23   Moreover, if the ancient and reputable authors who wrote
accounts of his life are to be credited, his admonitions extended
even to irrational animals. For catching the Daunian bear, that
is said to have wounded many of those who lived in its country,

he stroked it for a long time and fed it with barley cake and acorns, and having sworn it never again to touch living creatures, let it go. Thereupon it went off into the mountains and thickets, and was never again seen attacking any animal at all. Again, 24 when he saw an ox in Tarentum eating green beans in a pasture that contained many sorts of food, he went up to the oxherd and advised him to tell the ox to abstain from beans. The oxherd answered him with ridicule and said that, himself, he didn't speak ox language. So Pythagoras went near and whispered in the ear of the ox. It not only left the beanfield at that moment but never again touched beans. It lived to an extreme old age in Tarentum, staying near the temple of Hera, and was called the sacred ox and ate such food as the passers-by offered it. Yet again, at 25 Olympia, when he chanced to speak to his acquaintances concerning auguries from the flights of birds and omens and signs from the sky, saying that these too are messages of a sort from the gods to those among men who are truly dear to them, it is reported that he drew to earth an eagle that was flying over, stroked it, and again, let it go.

Once he came upon fishermen drawing in their nets from the deep with a great catch, and he foretold to them how many fish they were pulling, specifying the number. When the men undertook to do whatever he might order, should this number turn out to be correct, he commanded them to let the fish go again, alive, after they had counted them accurately. What was yet more marvelous, although the fish stayed out of water for all the long time it took to count them, none of them died while he was present.

He called back to the memories of many whom he met the 26 former lives their souls had lived at some long-ago time before being bound in this body. And by indisputable signs he proved himself to have been Euphorbus, the son of Panthoüs. And of the Homeric poems, the verses he particularly recited and sang most melodiously to the lyre were the following:

"His (Euphorbus') long hair, like that of the Graces, was drenched with blood, and his locks, which were bound with gold and silver. As when a man nourishes a verdant olive sapling in a lonely garden, where plentiful water bubbles up, a beautiful thing and flourishing, but the blasts of many winds shake it, and when at last it bursts open with white bloom, the wind coming suddenly, with a great storm, roots it up from its hole and spreads it on the ground, thus when the Atreïd, Menelaus, killed the son of Panthoüs, Euphorbus of the good spear, he took his armour as spoil" [Iliad 17.51–60].

27   We pass over as too generally known the things told about the shield of this Phrygian, Euphorbus, that in Mycenae is dedicated with other Trojan spoils to the Argive Hera.

It is reported that once when Pythagoras with many of his companions was crossing the river Caucasus, he spoke to it and the river, loud and clear, in the hearing of all, uttered, "Greetings, Pythagoras." Almost all authorities assert that on one and the same day he was present and talked together with his companions both in Metapontum of Italy and in Tauromenium of Sicily, although the distance between these two cities is one of a great many stadia, both by land and by sea, and not to be traversed in

28   many days. It is commonly told that when Abaris, of the Hyperboreans [a legendary people of the far north], guessed him to be the Hyperborean Apollo, of whom Abaris was a priest, Pythagoras showed him that his thigh was of gold, thus confirming that the guess was right. Equally common is the story that when a ship was putting in to land and his friends were praying that they might have the cargo, Pythagoras said, "So you'll get a corpse." And the ship sailed into port with a corpse on board.

Ten thousand other things yet more marvelous and more divine are told about the man, and told uniformly in stories that agree with each other. To put it bluntly, about no one else have greater

29   and more extraordinary things been believed. For he is reported to have uttered proclamations which earthquakes would not transgress, spells which rapidly drove off plagues and checked violent winds and hailstorms and calmed the waters of rivers and seas, so that his companions could easily cross them. It is said, moreover, that these were handed down to Empedocles and Epimenides and Abaris, who thus in many places performed similar miracles, as their poems clearly evidence. Besides, Empedocles was known as "the averter of winds," and Epimenides

as "the purifier," and Aba:is as "air-walking" because, riding on
the arrow given him by the Hyperborean Apollo, he crossed rivers
and seas and impassible places, somehow walking on the air,
which some suppose Pythagoras to have done on that occasion
when he spoke with his followers in both Metapontum and
Tauromenium in the same day.

Pythagoras also charmed away both psychic and somatic suf-   30
ferings and passions, by rhythms and tunes and incantations he
adapted to the needs of his followers. But he himself listened to
the harmony of all things, understanding the universal harmony
of the spheres and of the stars that move according to them—a
harmony we do not hear because of the pettiness of our nature.
Empedocles bears witness to these things, saying of him : "There
was one among them, a man who knew countless things, who had
truly attained the greatest wealth of intelligence, and was most
sovereign over all sorts of wise works, for whenever he desired
with all his mind, he easily beheld every detail of all things, even
in ten or in twenty ages of men." The words "countless" and "he   31
beheld every detail of all things" and "wealth of intelligence"
and the like are particularly indicative of Pythagoras' extraordinary constitution, which was more accurate than that of other men
in seeing and hearing and thinking.

Pythagoras maintained that the nine Muses were the utterances of the seven planets and of the sphere of the fixed stars,
and besides this, of the sphere which we cannot discern but which
they call the "counterearth." That which is at once the mixture
and harmony and, as it were, bond of all things, of which, since
it is eternal and unbegotten, each thing is a part and effluence, he
called Mnemosyne [Memory, the mother of the Muses].

Diogenes, describing his daily course of life, says that he urged   32
everyone to avoid the love of honors and praise, which particularly
occasions envy, and to shun public discussions. He himself, beginning at dawn, studied in his house, attuning his soul to a lyre
and singing certain ancient paeans of those composed by Thales.
Further, he sang those parts of Homer and Hesiod that he had
found pacified the soul. He also danced certain dances that he
thought made for bodily agility and health. He did not go walk-

ing with many followers, in a manner likely to occasion envy,
but went with one or two in temples or groves, choosing the most
33 tranquil and most beautiful landscapes. He was unusually devoted
to his friends and was the first to declare, "What friends own, they
own in common," and "A friend is a second self." When they
were well, he always spent his time with them; when sick in body,
he cured them; when ill in soul, he comforted them, as we have
said, some with incantations and magic spells, others with music.
For he had songs that were remedial even for bodily illnesses and
that raised the sick from their beds when he sang them. And he
had others that produced forgetfulness of sorrow and mollified
anger and destroyed untoward desires.

34   Of his diet, the breakfast was honeycomb or honey, the dinner
bread of millet or barley and vegetables, whether boiled or raw.
He would eat only rarely of the flesh of sacrificial victims, and
this not from every part of the body. Generally, when he was
about to descend into adyta of the gods and remain there for some
time, he used foods that would keep away hunger and thirst. That
which would keep away hunger he composed of poppy seed and
sesame and the skin of a squill washed carefully until cleansed
of the juice around it, and flower stalks of asphodel, and leaves of
mallow and barley groats and barley corns and chick peas, of all
which he chopped up equal quantities and soaked the choppings
with honey from Hymettus. That which would keep away thirst
he made of cucumber seeds and juicy raisins, from which he took
out the seeds, and coriander flowers and seed of mallow (again)
and purslane and cheese gratings and the finest wheat meal and
35 cream, all of which he mixed with honey from the islands. He
said Hercules had learned these recipes from Demeter when he
was sent into waterless Libya. As a result of this diet Pythagoras
kept his body always in the same condition, as if in a scale. He
was not sometimes healthy and sometimes sick, nor again sometimes getting fatter and increasing in girth, sometimes losing
weight and thinning down. His soul, too, always revealed through
his appearance the same disposition, for he was neither much
relaxed by pleasure nor withdrawn because of pain, nor did he

ever seem to be in the grip of joy or grief; indeed, no one ever saw him either laughing or weeping.

In sacrificing to the gods he practiced simplicity, propitiating 36 them with barley groats and a cake and frankincense and myrtles, and least of all with animal offerings, except occasionally with cocks and with the tenderest pigs. He once sacrificed an ox, however (but according to the more accurate authorities, it was an ox made of dough), when he found the square of the hypotenuse of a rightangle triangle equal to the sum of the squares of the other sides.

The things he discussed with those who came to him he taught either explicitly or by a parable, for he used two forms of teaching. And of those who came, some were called learners, others 37 hearers. The learners were those who mastered the more detailed account of the science, worked out accurately; the hearers were those who heard only the summarized instructions from his works, without any more accurate explanation. He taught men to speak 38 well of the race of gods and supernatural beings and heroes and to think well of them, to be grateful to parents and benefactors, to obey the laws, to make worship of the gods not something done by-the-way but to set out from home for this specific purpose, and to sacrifice things in odd numbers to those of underworld, for he declared that of the opposing powers in the world the better was the monad and light and on the right and equal and enduring and straight, the worse was the duad and darkness and on the left and unequal and curved and transient. He also taught things 39 like the following : one should neither destroy nor damage any cultivated plant that bears good fruit nor any animal that is not harmful to mankind; one should faithfully keep a deposit, not only of money but also of words, for him who left it; one should recognize three classes of important matters that should be pursued and undertaken : first the honorable and noble, next those beneficial for life, third and finally the pleasant. He did not tolerate the popular sort of pleasure that casts a spell over men, but only that which is secure and most reverend and free of accusation. For there are two sorts of pleasures. That which through luxury pleases the stomach and the sexual capacities he compared to the man-destroying songs of the Sirens, but that found in things noble and righteous and necessary for life, which is both immediately pleasant and remains unchanged into the future, he 40 said was like a harmony of the Muses. He advised that two times of the day should be given special attention, the one when a man turns to sleep, and the other when he arises from sleep. For in the first of these one should review the things he has done, and in the second the things about to happen, and each man should receive correction from himself for what has happened and should take thought for the future. Accordingly, before sleep everyone should sing to himself the following verses : "I will not admit sleep to the soft eyes before thrice reviewing each of the day's actions. In what way have I transgressed? What have I accomplished? What have I not done that I should have?" And before arising, the following : "On first awaking from sweet sleep it is well to scrutinize what-41 ever actions you will perform in the day." Such were the things he counseled; and especially, to tell the truth. For only this can make men like God. Indeed, as he learned from the Magi, even of God, whom they call Horomazda, the body is like light and the soul like truth. He taught other, similar things, too, which he said he had heard from Aristokleia[2] in Delphi.

He also said some things in a secret way by the use of symbols; these Aristotle has reported more fully. For example, that he called the sea a tear, the Big and Little Bear the hands of [the goddess] Rhea, the Pleiades the lyre of the Muses, the planets the hounds of Persephone. He said the noise coming from struck bronze was the 42 voice of one of the demons shut up in the bronze. Besides these he used another sort of symbols, like the following : he commanded his disciples not to step over a scale, that is, not to be avaricious; not to poke the fire with a knife, that is, not to move with edged words a man swelling with anger; not to pluck a wreath, that is, not to harm the laws, for these are the wreaths of the cities. Again, other such symbols are : not to eat the heart, that is, not to grieve oneself with griefs; not to sit on a bushel basket, that is, not to live idly; not to turn back when going on a journey, that is, not

[2] Presumably a Pythia, i.e., one of the women who were inspired by the god and uttered the words with which he replied to the questions asked him.

to cling to this life when dying; not to walk the highways, by which he forbade his disciples to follow the opinions of the majority—they should pursue instead those of the few and learned; not to allow swallows in the house, that is, not to live under the same roof with talkative men and insatiable tongue-waggers; to help load men carrying a burden, but not to help unload them, by which he taught that they should cooperate with no one in laxity but only in virtue; not to wear images of the gods in rings, that is, not to make the praise of the gods nor the teaching about them something open and easily available, nor to bring it out in public; to pour libations to the gods from the ear-sides of the cups, by this he indicates that one should honor the gods and hymn them with music, for this goes through the ears; not to eat things it is not right to eat—beginning, increase, source, end—nor things from which comes the first inception of all things; his meaning was to abstain from the loins and testes and genitals 43 and brains and feet and heads of sacrificial victims, for he called the loins a foundation, since animals are erected on these as on foundation, the testes and genitals beginning, for without the work of these no animal comes into being, and he called the brain increase, since it is the cause of growth in all animals, and the feet source, and the head end, since it has the greatest administrative powers over the body. Similarly, he taught his disciples to abstain from beans as if from human flesh. They say he forbade all sorts 44 of beans because when the first source and beginning of things was thrown into confusion and many things were brought to-gether and sown together and rotted together in the earth, begin-ning and distinction presently arose together, animals coming into being and plants growing up at the same time. At this time, from the same putrefaction, men arose and the bean sprouted. Of this he brought clear proofs. For if anyone bite through a bean and crush it with his teeth and then put it for a little while in the warmth of the sun's rays, go away and return shortly after, he will find it smelling like a murdered man. And if one take a little of a bean plant, when it has sprouted and is blooming and the flower is beginning to turn dark, and put it in a pottery vessel, put on a lid, bury it in the earth and wait ninety days after the burial, then digging it up, take it and remove the cover, he will find that instead of the bean either the head of a child or the vagina of a woman has developed.

45   Pythagoras also advised the avoidance of other foods, such as sea-wombs and red mullet and sea anemones and almost all other sea foods whatever. And he traced himself back to men who had formerly lived, saying he was first Euphorbus, second Aithalides [a son of the god Hermes, he was said to have been one of the Argonauts], third Hermotimus,[3] fourth Pyrrus [a fisherman of Delos], and now Pythagoras, by which means he showed that the soul is immortal and in those who have been purified it attains to memory of its ancient life.

46   He practiced a philosophy of which the object was to deliver and set free of such fetters and bonds [as incarnation] the mind that had been separated from the cosmic mind for incarnation in us. Apart from this mind no one can learn anything sound or true whatever, nor can he even perceive anything by means of the senses. For the mind by its own nature sees all and hears all, but other things are blind and dumb. To one who has been purified, therefore, the mind should bring something beneficial. It does so by conceiving various arts, first leading itself gently toward the vision of the eternal and bodiless beings that are kin to itself and always exist with the same relationships and in the same way. It leads itself on from lower things little by little lest, terrified by the sudden and total change, it should turn back and give up on account of its nourishment being so bad for so long a time.

47   Accordingly, it uses mathematics and the sciences dealing with the borderland between bodies and the bodiless to train in advance the eyes of the soul, turning them little by little toward the truly existent and away from bodily things that never remain, however briefly, with the same relationships and in the same way in the same place. Thus with technical training it leads itself to the desire of intellectual nourishment, and thus introducing the

[3] A man of the early seventh century, who lived in the city of Clazomenae, on the coast of Asia Minor. His mind had the power of leaving his body for long periods and travelling about in distant places. Once, while his mind was absent, his body was murdered.

vision of things truly existent, renders blessed those men who follow its teaching. Practice in mathematics was therefore taken into the Pythagorean program for this purpose.

According to a number of authorities, and especially Modera- 48 tus of Gades, who had made a very intelligent collection in ten books of the doctrines of the Pythagorean school, the study of numbers was pursued for the following reason. Since the Pythagoreans were unable to express clearly in speech the first forms and first principles, because these are difficult to comprehend and explain, they turned to numbers for the sake of clear teaching, imitating the geometers and the grammarians. For example, the latter, wishing to express the elements of speech and their powers, turned to the written letters, saying—as far as primary teaching was concerned—that these were the elements, although later they teach that the letters are not elements but that through them an idea is given of the true elements. Similarly, 49 the geometers, since they are not able to present by speech the bodiless forms, turn to the drawings of the shapes, saying, "This is the triangle," although they mean that *the* triangle is not the visible thing but what is similar to that, and thus, through the visible drawing, they present the concept of the triangle. Accordingly, in the case of the first reasons and forms the Pythagoreans did the same thing : since they were not able to express in words the bodiless forms and the first principles, they turned to the explanation by means of numbers. And thus they called "one" the reason for unity, and that for identity, and that for equality, and the cause of the union and sympathy of all things and of the preservation of that which remains the same. For truly the unity that exists between individuals is of this sort, being united to the individuals and yet existing as a unit by reason of its participation in the first cause. Similarly, they called "duad" the dual 50 reason for diversity and inequality and everything that is divided and in change and now one way, now another; for the nature of two is of this sort, even in individual objects. The existence of these reasons, moreover, is not a matter asserted by the Pythagoreans but denied by the other philosophers. On the contrary, the others too can be seen to have left undisputed the existence of certain powers that unify and maintain all things, and in their teachings too there are certain reasons for equality and inequality and difference.

For the sake of clear teaching, then, the Pythagoreans call these reasons by the names of "the one" and "the duad," for it makes no difference to them to say "biformed" or "of unequal form" 51 or "of diverse form." And similarly, in the case of the other numbers the same rule holds, for each one is set in correspondence to certain powers. For again there is something in the nature of things that has a beginning and middle and end. In correspondence to this sort of form and this sort of nature they declared the number "three" its symbol. Therefore they declare that everything that has a middle term is triform, and they thus denominate everything that is complete. And if something is complete, they say it has availed itself of and been arranged according to this principle, for which—because they cannot otherwise name it—they use the name of the number three. In this way, by means of this external form, they lead us, as they desired, to the conception of this principle. And the same rule applies to the other numbers.

These, then, are the cosmic reasons in correspondence with 52 which the aforesaid numbers were set. Both these and the numbers following them are comprised under one single idea and power. This they called "decad," inasmuch as it is a receptacle [in Greek, *dekada*]. Therefore they say ten is a complete number, or rather the most complete of all, having within itself every difference of number and every form of reason and proportion [i.e., $10 = 1 + 2 + 3 + 4$; $10 = (1 \times 4) + (2 \times 3)$; etc.]. For if the nature of all things is defined according to reasons and proportions expressed by numbers, and if everything that comes into being and increases and comes to completion conducts itself according to reasons expressed in numbers, and if the decad contains every reason and every proportion and every form expressed by numbers, how can it not be called complete number?

53　　The number theory of the Pythagoreans, then, was of this sort. And as a result of this it came about that this philosophy, which had been first of all, became extinct primarily because of its enigmatic expression, further, both because its written works

were written in Doric Greek, a somewhat obscure dialect, and
because even the teachings which it stated were suspect as
spurious or misunderstood, since those who gave them to the
public were not themselves Pythagoreans. In addition to these
causes, Plato and Aristotle [and their followers] Speusippus and
Aristoxenus and Xenocrates, as the Pythagoreans say, took as
their own the fruitful elements, with minor adaptation, while
the superficial and trivial and those suited for refutation and
ridicule of the school were later put forward by envious fault-
finders for anyone to collect and write down as characteristics of
the sect. These things, however, happened later.

For a long time both Pythagoras himself and the disciples with 54
him were so much admired in Italy that the cities even committed
their government to persons coming from him. At long last they
became the objects of envy, and a plot arose against them, more
or less as follows : Cylo, a man of Croton, stood above all
his fellow citizens in respect of family and ancestral glory and
excess of income, but otherwise he was ill-tempered, violent, and
tyrannical, and used the protection afforded by his friends and
the power afforded by his wealth to strengthen his hand for in-
justices. This man judged himself worthy of all other things that
he thought good, and he considered himself most worthy to share
in Pythagoras' philosophy. He comes to Pythagoras, praising himself as one who wished to be with him. Pythagoras at once dis-
cerned the man's character from his features and saw what sort
he was from the bodily signs that he [Pythagoras] was careful to
look for in persons who came to him. Accordingly, he told him to
go away and mind his own business.

This grieved Cylo not a little : He thought himself treated con-
temptuously, and he was a man generally ill-natured and unable
to contain his anger. Accordingly, assembling his friends, he 55
spoke against Pythagoras and prepared a plot against him and his
associates. As a result of this some say that when Pythagoras' companions were gathered in the house of Milo, the athlete, the
plotters set fire to the house on every side and there burned and
stoned them all. (According to this story Pythagoras was out of
the country at the time, for he had gone to Delos to Pherecydes

of Syros, who had been his teacher; Pherecydes had been afflicted with lice—an affliction reported to have killed him—and Pythagoras went to nurse him, and buried him.) Only two of his disciples escaped from the fire, Archippus and Lysis, so Neanthes says. Of these Lysis went to live in Greece and settled in Thebes and was associated with [the great Theban general] Epaminondas, of whom he also became the teacher.

56   However, Dicaearchus and the more accurate authorities say Pythagoras was present at the time of the plot (for Pherecydes had died before Pythagoras' departure from Samos). Forty of his companions were caught together sitting in someone's house, but most were killed in the town wherever they happened to be, here and there about the city. Pythagoras, since his friends siezed him, at first fled to the harbor of Caulonia, thence again to Locri [neighboring towns along the sole and toe of Italy]. When the Locrians learned of his coming, they sent some of the elders to the borders of their land. These, meeting him, said, "We, O Pythagoras, hear that you are a wise man and a capable one. But we have no fault to find with our own laws. We shall therefore try to continue with those we have, and you go somewhere else, taking from us whatever you need by way of necessities." So when he was turned away in the fashion thus stated from the city of Locri, he sailed to Tarentum, and again, after having had experiences there like the ones in Croton, he came to Metapontum. For everywhere there were great riots, which even now the inhabitants of these places remember and tell about, calling them the riots in the time of the Pythagoreans, for all of the faction that followed him were called Pythagoreans.

57   Pythagoras himself is said to have died in the neighborhood of Metapontum,[4] after having taken refuge in the temple of the Muses and gone for forty days in want of the necessities of life. But others say that when the fire was consuming the house in which he and his companions were gathered, the latter, putting themselves into the fire, made a way of escape for their teacher, bridging the fire with their own bodies. But when he had escaped

[4] Or: "in the riot that took place in Metapontum." The Greek is ambiguous.

from the fire, Pythagoras, despairing because his followers were gone, himself withdrew from life.

When this catastrophe seized upon the men, the knowledge likewise came to an end with them, since it had been kept as a secret in their breasts until that time, only the enigmatic symbols being mentioned when outsiders were present, and since there was no written work by Pythagoras. But those who escaped, Lysis and Archippus and such as happened to be out of the country, preserved a few sparks of the philosophy, but obscure and difficult to grasp. For having been isolated and despairing at what had 58 happened, they were scattered hither and thither, avoiding association with men. However, fearing lest the name of philosophy should wholly perish from men and lest they should be hated by the gods themselves for this reason, they collected the writings of the elders and such things as they remembered, and they composed summary memoranda which they left behind, each where he happened to die, commanding sons or daughters or wives to give these to no one outside the family. And their descendants in succession kept this injunction for a long time, giving the same commandment to their offspring.

These descendants were not negligent in avoiding friendships 59 with persons outside their own circle, but most carefully guarded against and shunned them, while on the other hand for many generations they preserved undiminished their friendship for each other. Of this we may judge, Nicomachus says, from the things that Aristoxenus, in his book on the life of Pythagoras, says he himself heard from Dionysius II, the tyrant of Syracuse [367-357 B.C.], who, having lost his throne, taught letters in Corinth. He writes as follows : these men avoid lamentations and tears and all such things as far as is possible. And the same rule applies for flattery and supplication and entreaty and all suchlike. But some people said that if they were caught, they would not keep faith with each other. Dionysius, therefore, on one occasion, wishing to test them, made the following experiment : Phintias[5] was arrested and brought before the tyrant. Dionysius accused him of

[5] Phintias and Damon are unknown apart from this oft-told story and the further legends that accrued to their names.

conspiring against him and said this had been proved, and he was sentenced to die. Phintias thereupon, since this was the ruling of the tyrant, asked that the rest of the day be granted him so that he might set in order his own affairs and those of Damon, for Damon was his companion and partner, and since he (Phintias) was the elder, he had taken many of the matters of management upon himself. Therefore he asked to be let go, offering Damon as a surety. When Dionysius agreed, Damon was sent for, and hearing what had happened, he consented to be security and remain until Phintias should return. Dionysius was astonished at these events, and those who from the first had instigated the test mocked Damon, saying that he would be left in the lurch. But when the sun was setting, Phintias came to be put to death, whereupon they all were astonished. But Dionysius embraced and kissed the men and asked that he himself be admitted as a third in their friendship. They, however, would by no means agree to this, though he much besought them. These things, then, Aristoxenus reports that he heard from Dionysius himself. But Hippobotus and Neanthes tell [the same story] about Myllius and Timycha.[6]

---

[6] Myllius and his wife Timycha were another Pythagorean pair, of uncertain date and history.

XIII. A SUMMARY OF

ON THE LIFE OF MOSES

BY PHILO

INTRODUCTORY

PHILO, the author of the following treatise *On the Life of Moses,* was a Jew of Alexandria. He was born about 15 B.C. (the date commonly given, 30 B.C., has recently been proved to be too early) and lived until about A.D. 45. His family was a very wealthy and distinguished one; it was allied with the royal Herodian house, of which a number of members ruled in Palestine as representatives of Roman interests. Philo himself headed a delegation sent by the Jewish community of Alexandria to Emperor Gaius in 39–40. Other members of his family became pagans, one of them rising to be Roman governor of Egypt, but Philo was a devout Jew and spent a great deal of his life expounding and defending his religion.

His effort was to show that the books of Moses, properly understood, taught the true philosophy and that the peculiar practices of Judaism were to be understood and practiced as allegorical expressions of philosophic truths and as useful exercises for the development of the philosophic mind. His notion of "the true philosophy," however, was derived less from a study of the books of Moses than from his excellent classical education. That presented him with a wealth of philosophical opinions from which he selected those he could best adapt to the biblical text; he patched them together into a sort of system and read this system, by allegorical exegesis, into the Mosaic books (which, of course, had no such meanings to begin with). Allegorization was a particularly useful device because it permitted him, when worst came to worst, to declare that the sacred text simply could not mean what it said and that some hidden, philosophical meaning must therefore be found in it. The result was a compromise faithful neither to the plain sense of the Bible nor to the clear spirit of Greek philosophy.

This compromise is clearly seen in *On the Life of Moses,* where Philo adapts the biblical story of Moses to the aretalogical pattern. Moses, therefore, becomes a "Chaldean" by birth (the term could mean simply "Babylonian," but had come to mean "astrologer," "magician," almost "oriental sage"). He was taught in childhood not only the ancient wisdom of the Egyptians but also Greek philosophy and Chaldean·astrology. He distinguished himself by his practice of Stoic asceticism and his constant study of philosophy. He was suspected, as philosophers often were, of plotting a revolution, and for this reason he had to flee Egypt. All this is quite unknown to the Bible, while on the other hand characteristic biblical traits are discreetly omitted: the Bible says Moses fled Egypt because he had committed a murder and was afraid it would become known. It declares that God spoke with him directly from the bush; Philo inserts a mediating angel. The Bible says that when Moses was on the way back to Egypt, the Lord tried to kill him (Exod. 4:24); Philo says nothing of this interesting adventure. Philo's Moses "despised" sexual intercourse "almost from the time when he first began to prophesy" (II.69); the Moses of the Bible married a negress, presumably as a second or later wife and probably at or after the height of his prophetic career (Num. 12).

Philo's whitewashing of divine revelation did not stop with his remodeling of Moses as an ascetic philosopher. He also made Aaron and his sons pre-eminent for "piety and holiness" (II.142) and therefore suppressed the Bible's reports that it was Aaron who made the golden calf (Exod. 32) and that two of Aaron's four sons were burnt up by fire from God, in the course of their ordination, because of their wickedness (Lev. 10). Details of this sort could easily be multiplied, but there is no need to illustrate the obvious. In general, Philo's work is of particular interest for this collection because the main source he used—the biblical account —is known. This makes it possible for the interested reader to compare Philo's work with his source and so to determine precisely the changes Philo made by addition and subtraction. Comparison of these changes with the content of the aretalogical tradition (as revealed by comparison of the other works) will then show rather accurately the extent to which that tradition influenced Philo's life of Moses.

This influence was exerted primarily through Philo himself. Primarily, but not exclusively. The stories written down in the Bible had never, surely, exhausted the fund of Israelite legends about the great leader, and as the books of the Bible gained acceptance and became sacred, the wider body of legend from which the books had originally been drawn lived on beside them as commentary. Because this commentary was oral and disjointed, a multitude of anecdotes and explanations—what the rabbinic tradition was to call *haggadah*—it was easily adapted to suit the interests of new environments. In the Jewish community in Egypt it had begun to assimilate to the aretalogical tradition at least a century before Philo's time. Earlier stages of the assimilation are to be seen in the preserved fragments of the Alexandrian Jewish historians of the second and first centuries B.C., where, for instance, Moses is identified with the Greco-Egyptian god Hermes-Thoth and is declared to have been the teacher of Orpheus (Artapanus in Eusebius, *Praeparatio evangelica* 9.27). Philo's work is to be understood, therefore, as influenced by and in part a reaction against the extremes of this anecdotal, Hellenizing *haggadah*. What appealed to Philo in the aretalogical tradition was its combination of the traits of philosopher, prophet, and wonder-worker. This enabled him to represent the prophet and wonder-worker of the Bible as a philosopher, someone socially acceptable to the Hellenized Jewish aristocracy of Alexandria. For this purpose, therefore, Philo used the haggadic-aretalogical tradition; beyond this he was reluctant to go. He knew, for instance, the aretalogical stories of Moses' transfiguration and ascension (II.288, 291), but he transformed the first into a philosophical allegory, and he passed over both it and the second with the briefest possible mention. Miracles were not to be denied, of course, but enough was enough.

I

MOSES BY RACE WAS A CHALDAEAN, but was born and brought up 5 in Egypt. Because of a long famine that had afflicted Babylon and the lands around it, his ancestors had come with their whole households to Egypt in search of food. His father and mother were 7 of the best of their contemporaries, and although members of the same tribe, were related even more by like-mindedness than by race. He himself was the seventh in descent from the first settler, who was the founder of the whole Jewish people.

As a result of the following circumstances, he was given the 8 education of a king. The Jewish immigrants were multiplying rapidly, and the king of the land, fearing lest they become too strong for control, ordered that the male children born to them should be put to death. Now when Moses was born, he was more 9 handsome than an ordinary child, so his parents, as far as was possible, set aside the decrees of the tyrant. It is said that he was nursed at home for three whole months without his existence becoming known. Then, however, fearing lest it be discovered 10

and bring ruin on them, his parents reluctantly decided to
12 abandon him and left him on the bank of the Nile. They went
off, grieving, but his sister, a girl still unmarried, waited at a little
13 distance to see what would happen. Now the king of the land had
an only daughter, whom he dearly loved. She had long been
married but had never conceived a child, though she particularly
14 wanted a boy, who could inherit his grandfather's throne. Although she was always downcast and sighing, on this particular
day she bade farewell to her cares, and whereas her custom was to
stay at home and never cross the threshold, she went down with
15 her handmaidens to the river, where the child lay. She saw him,
ordered him brought to her, found him handsome and healthy,
and pitied his tears. Knowing that he was a child of the Hebrews
and fearing the commandment of the king, she was in a quandary
as to how she could raise him, for she thought it would not be
16 safe to take him to the palace. While she was still at a loss, the
baby's sister, who guessed what was in her mind, ran up and asked
if she wanted him nursed by a woman of the Hebrews who had
17 lately been with child. When the princess said she did, the girl
brought her own and the baby's mother, as if a stranger, who
gladly promised to nurse him for pay. Thus the foresight of God
provided that the first food of the boy should come from his own
mother. Then the princess gave him a name, Moses, because he
was taken from the water (the Egyptians call water *möu*).
18   The boy grew rapidly and was weaned earlier than customary.
His mother then took him to the princess. He seemed to be a handsome child and of good stock, and better grown than usual at his
19 age. The princess, seeing him, liked him even better than before
and passed him off as her son. In order that he might be thought
legitimately born, not adopted, she first pretended to go through
a pregnancy. (God facilitates whatever he wills, even things
otherwise most difficult of accomplishment.)
20   Thus having been granted a royal upbringing, the child did
not, as if wholly childish, rejoice in jokes and laughter and games,
although those who had care of him let him do as he liked and
showed no severity. But he was naturally modest and serious and
gave his attention to those things that would benefit his soul.

Various teachers from various regions promptly presented them- 21
selves, those from Egypt coming of their own accord, those from
Greece hired for high salaries. But little Moses soon surpassed
their powers, anticipating their teachings by his natural gifts, so
that one would think he was remembering, not learning; indeed,
he himself even thought out in advance solutions of problems
theretofore believed insoluble. Nonetheless, the learned Egyptians 23
taught him arithmetic, geometry, rhythm, harmony, metrics, and
all music, both instrumental and theoretical. Moreover, they also
taught him the philosophy expressed in symbols, which is indicated in the hieroglyphics and in the reverence for those animals
to which they pay divine honors. Greeks taught him the other
subjects of a liberal education, and scholars from the neighboring
countries taught him Assyrian writing and Chaldaean astrology.
Astrology he acquired also from the Egyptians, who have particu- 24
larly studied this branch of mathematics. Thus learning accurately
the teachings of both schools and in what they agreed and disagreed, he sought the truth without becoming involved in their
quarrels as a partisan of either side.

When he began to pass the limits of childhood, he increased 25
his prudence, not letting his youthful desires go unbridled, as
some do (though he had the innumerable opportunities that
palaces afford), but reining them in by temperance and self-
restraint. Thus he kept strict control of his passions and impulses, 26
as of horses that must be tamed and submitted to the direction of
reason, their charioteer. Consequently his fellow students and all 27
other men were astonished by him and speculated as to what sort
of mind inhabited his body and was carried about in him like a
god in an image. Was it human or divine, or a mixture of the
two? At all events, it was nothing like that in most men but
towered above them and was lifted up toward what was greater.
For he gave nothing to his stomach beyond the necessary tribute 28
set by nature, and he did not even think of sexual pleasures except
insofar as they were involved in the begetting of lawful children.
Since he desired to live for the soul alone, not for the body, he 29
particularly practiced the reduction of his needs to a minimum.
No one else was so scornful of the life of luxury. Thus he demon-

strated the teachings of philosophy in his daily practice, saying what he thought and acting in accordance with what he said, so that his life and his speech agreed in musical harmony.

32   Moreover, although he was believed the grandson of the king and everyone hoped he would be the successor to his grandfather, so that he was regularly called "the young king," nonetheless he particularly devoted himself to the tradition of his physical ancestors, thinking the good fortune of his adoptive parents, although momentarily more brilliant, nevertheless alien to him, but the lot of his natural parents, although temporarily more obscure,
33   nevertheless his own. As an incorruptible judge he repaid those who begot him with love, those who adopted him with gratitude.

This gratitude would no doubt always have continued, had
34   not the king of the country been guilty of a great injustice : he reduced to slavery the Jews who had come to his country as free
38   suppliants, and he put them to hard labor—making bricks and gathering straw and building houses and digging canals and the
40   like. Moses was grieved and angered by this but could neither punish the wrongdoers nor help those who were being wronged. Whatever he could do, he did, urging the overseers to be moderate and not to enforce the full severity of the law, the workers to bear their present troubles nobly, behave like men and not weary in
43   soul as in body, since everything in the world is changeable. His task was made considerably more difficult by the savagery of
44   some of the overseers. One of the most violent of these was a man who would never give way and was made even harsher by entreaties, beating those who did not do their work without grumbling or delay, humiliating them to the point of death and subjecting them to all sorts of bad treatment. Him Moses killed, judging this to be a righteous act. And indeed it was righteous that one who lived for the destruction of men should be destroyed.

45   Hearing of these things, the king was angered, thinking it a most serious matter, not that someone died or killed, justly or unjustly, but that his grandson did not agree with him nor have
46   the same enemies and friends as he, but the contrary. This opinion was encouraged by those courtiers who thought the young man would punish them for their part in his grandfather's policies.

They persuaded the king that Moses was plotting a revolution, 47
and Moses withdrew to Arabia where he could live in safety, praying God to deliver the unfortunate, pay back the unjust, and,
with double kindness, grant him to see both these eventualities.

While awaiting the fulfillment of these prayers, Moses was 48
exercised in virtue by the trainer, reason, that dwelt within him
and prepared him for the best theoretical and the best practical
life. He was always studying the doctrines of philosophy and
quickly grasping them and committing them to memory, never
to be forgotten, and at once bringing his actions into accord with
them, for he desired truth rather than seeming, because his one
goal was nature's right reason, which is the sole source and
fountainhead of virtues.

Moved by his concern for righteousness and thinking righteous- 50
ness sufficient power for any purpose, he did not hesitate to come
into conflict with powerful persons in the land where he was an
exile. Thus when he saw shepherds taking advantage of the 52
weakness of seven shepherd girls (who were daughters of a priest
of that country) and driving away the girls' flocks in order to 53
bring their own to the water that the girls had drawn, he ran up
and, standing near by, said, "Will you not cease doing wrong,
thinking the loneliness of the place an advantage? Are you not
ashamed of nourishing your shoulders and arms for idleness?
You are long hair and meat, not men. The girls act like young
men, and work willingly; the young men are already taking it
easy, like girls. Won't you go away? Won't you give way to those 55
who came before you and to whom the water belongs? You should
rightly have drawn for them, so that there would have been plenty
of water, yet you try to take away what they have made ready.
But by heaven, the eye of righteousness that sees even what
happens in the loneliest places, you shall not take it away. For 56
heaven has ordained me as an unexpected helper, and I am an
ally to those who are being wronged. I have a strong hand which
the rapacious may not see, but you shall feel it striking from the
invisible if you do not change your practices." While he delivered 57
himself of these sentiments, he was inspired and transformed into
a prophet. The shepherds were frightened, thinking he was de-

livering divine oracles, and accordingly drove their flocks away from the drinking troughs and led back those of the girls.

58 When the girls reported these events to their father, he blamed them for not bringing back the stranger and sent them after him.

59 They found him not far off and persuaded him to come home with them. Their father was so well impressed, first by his appearance and afterward by his disposition, that he gave him the prettiest of his daughters to wife.

60 After the marriage, Moses took over the sheep. (Shepherding
63 is the best preparation for kingship, as hunting is for war.) He was best of the shepherds of his time and a capable provider of whatever was useful for the benefit of the flocks. Because he never shirked his duty but did with spontaneous and industrious desire what was necessary for his charge, he increased the herds with
64 pure and guileless honesty, so that he was soon envied by the other shepherds, who saw nothing similar in their own flocks, which were deemed lucky if they got no worse, whereas for Moses' this was thought a misfortune because of their customary improvement.

65 As he was leading his flock into a well-watered and grassy place, he came near a certain glen where he saw a most astounding spectacle. There was a thorny bush, of the most fragile sort, which suddenly, although no fire came near it, was kindled and wholly enveloped from root to tip in a mass of flame that seemed to well up from some fountain. Yet the bush was not burned and remained undamaged as if it were some imperishable substance,
66 not itself food for fire but using the fire as its food. In the midst of the flame was a most beautiful form, like none of all things visible, an image of most divine appearance blazing forth a light more brilliant than that of the fire, a form that might be thought the likeness of Him Who Is, but shall here be called a messenger,[1] because with a silence clearer than voice, it all but announced
67 through the miraculous vision the things that were to be. For the bush was a symbol of those who were being wronged, the fire, of those who wronged them, and the messenger, of the providence

[1] The Greek word for "messenger" is that which we transliterate as "angel."

of God, which would quietly, against all expectations, make the most fearful things harmless.

Having showed this marvel to Moses, God also began to urge 71 him by oracles to hurry to care for the people, since he was soon to be a contributory cause of their freedom and leader of their departure. God promised to help him in all things, saying that 72 He knew the people's sufferings and had heard their prayers. He 73 told Moses that the former king had died, and the new ruler would not take action against him. Therefore he should return to Egypt without fear and tell the elders of the people that by an oracle from God the people were called to go three days' journey beyond the frontiers of the country and sacrifice in their ancestral fashion.

Moses foresaw that his fellow Jews and everybody else would 74 disbelieve this message. Therefore he said, "If they ask me, 'What is the name of the one who sent you?' and I cannot say, shall I not seem a deceiver?" "First of all," God answered, "say to them 75 that I am He Who Is, in order that, learning the difference between the existent and the nonexistent, they may learn besides that no name whatever can be properly applied to me, to whom existence alone is attributable. But if, being too weak by nature 76 [to make do with philosophy], they still seek some appellative, reveal to them not only this, that I am God, but also that I am the god of the three men named for their virtues, god of Abraham and god of Isaac and god of Jacob, of whom the first is the paradigm of learned, the second of natural, and the third of ascetic wisdom. And if they yet disbelieve, they will come over when you show them three signs that no man before ever saw or heard of."

The first sign was that when he threw his stick to the ground, 77 it at once wriggled and became a huge snake. When Moses started to run from it, God both ordered him and gave him courage to take hold of its tail. It immediately stopped wriggling, 78 straightened itself out and was turned back into the same stick as before. The second sign was that when he put one of his hands 79 into the bosom of his garment and brought it out a little later, it had turned whiter than snow; when he put it back and brought

81 it out again, it turned back to its own color. The third sign he
could not be shown in advance, but he was told what it would be :
when he poured water from the Nile onto the earth, it would become blood, both in its color and in all its properties.

83   Nevertheless, Moses asked to be excused from the mission, since
his voice was feeble and he spoke slowly and was not eloquent,
especially by comparison with God. Moreover, being cautious by
nature, he judged that great affairs were not for him and besought
84 God to choose someone else. God, however, assured him that He
could make him eloquent, and added that if he still needed an
interpreter, he could use his brother.

85   On hearing these promises—since further opposition might not
have been safe—Moses set out with wife and children for Egypt.
On the road he met his brother and persuaded him to go along.

86 When they arrived, they first assembled the elders of the people
and told them in secret the oracles of God and his promises to
87 set them free and lead them to a better land. Next, they dared
speak to the king about sending the people out of the country
to sacrifice according to their ancestral customs, which differ
88 from those of other men. The king not merely refused permission but ordered the overseers of the works to treat the people
89 yet more harshly so that they would not have time for such non-
90 sense. The people therefore suffered worse hardships than before
and blamed Moses' followers as blasphemous deceivers. Accordingly, Moses began to show forth his miracles.

91   When all the nobles of Egypt were assembled in the palace
before the king, Moses' brother, taking the staff and waving it
conspicuously, threw it to the floor. It immediately became a
snake. Those who had been standing around at once marveled
92 and started to run. But the magicians who were present said,
"Why are you terrified? We are not unpracticed in such matters,
but use arts that can do similar things." Then each one of them
threw down the staff he had, and there was a tangle of snakes,
93 and they coiled around the first one. But it, towering above them,
spread its hood and opened its mouth and sucked them all in like
a draught of fishes, and then changed back into a staff.

94, 95   In spite of this clear demonstration of the will of God, the

Egyptians did not change their treatment of the Jews, so they 96, 97
were punished by a series of ten plagues, three sent by Moses'
brother from the thicker elements of earth and water, which are
the source of bodies, three sent by Moses from air and fire, which
are the source of souls, one sent by both together, and three by
God himself.

The first were those from the water, because the Egyptians 98
particularly honor water and think it the primary principle of all
things. Moses' brother brought down the staff on the river, which 99
was immediately changed into blood, from Ethiopia to the sea,
as was all other water in the country. When the Egyptians dug
new wells, blood shot up from these as from cut veins. All the 100
fish died, and everything was filled with the stink of rotting
bodies. Crowds of men, dead of thirst, lay in heaps on the cross-
roads. The plague lasted seven days, until the Egyptians besought 101
Moses' followers, and these God, to pity those who were dying.
He, being merciful by nature, changed the blood back to water.
The Egyptians then went back to their former injustice. Therefore 102–3
Moses' brother was again commanded to stretch out the staff
on the canals and lakes and marshes. When he did so, a multitude
of frogs emerged and filled not only the markets and all the open
places but also all houses and temples. The Egyptians could 104
neither stay inside nor go out. Therefore the king promised the 105
Hebrews that he would permit their exodus, they pacified God
with prayers, and the frogs either went back to the river or died.
As soon as the Egyptians recovered strength, however, they went 106
back to their former malpractice. Accordingly, God now told 107
Moses' brother to strike the ground with the staff. At this a stream
of gnats poured forth and spread like a cloud over all Egypt. These 108
not only bit the skin of the Egyptians but got into their ears and
noses and eyes, so that they were forced to acknowledge, "This 112
is the finger of God."

These plagues from earth and water were followed by those 113
brought by Moses from air and heaven. First the air—although 118
Egypt normally has no winter—brought streams of rain, heavy
hail, violent winds, cloudbursts, and continuous lightnings and
thunderings, that frightened the inhabitants both by their novelty 119

(which made them seem, as they were, evidence of divine wrath)
and by the damage they did, for trees, crops, and animals were
120 destroyed alike by the cold, the hail, and the lightnings. When
this plague abated and the king and his party again became insolent, Moses, on God's command, stretched the staff into the air,
and a violent south wind fell on the country, a dry wind that it-
121 self caused no little damage and discomfort but that also brought
an incalculable multitude of locusts, filling all the air and eating
whatever the lightning and the hail had left, so that no growing
122 thing was to be seen in all the land. Then at length the officials,
realizing their misfortunes, urged the king to let the Jews go, and
he consented. Moses prayed again, and a wind arose from the
123 sea and scattered the locusts. When the king thereupon regretted
his promise, a worse plague followed. From brilliant day the land
124 suddenly was plunged into darkness, a darkness even fire could
not light, that deafened men and left them unable to use any
125 of their senses, until Moses, taking pity, prayed to God, and light
was restored.

126   A seventh plague was brought by Moses and his brother to-
127 gether : at God's command they took ashes from a furnace in their
hands. Moses scattered a little in the air. Then a dust settled on
128 men and animals, causing ulcers all over their skins, until each
became one huge ulcer from head to foot, a condition that abated
129 only when Moses prayed for them. This plague was administered
by Moses and his brother because it involved both material from
the earth [the ashes] and the air.

130-1   The three remaining plagues were brought by God himself with-
133 out human agency. The first was flies, the second murrain, the
134 third the death of the first born children, beginning with the
135 eldest son of the king himself. For in the middle of the night, although healthy and strong of body, all of them were suddenly
killed without apparent cause. It is said that no household
136 escaped this disaster. In the morning, when they saw their dearest
unexpectedly dead, the whole land, from one end to the other,
137 was filled with lamentation. When they learned, however, that
138 their calamity was common, fearing for those who still lived, they
ran to the palace, crying out against the king as the cause of all

the catastrophies that had befallen them and demanding that 139
the Hebrews should be sent out of the country immediately.

The Hebrews, for their part, being driven out, called to mind 140
their own nobility and undertook an act of daring worthy of free
men, for they carried away much spoil, not from love of money 141
but as pay for the time of their servitude and as retaliation, albeit
inadequate, for their enslavement. It should be noted, too, that 143
of all the plagues that afflicted the Egyptians none harmed the
Hebrews in any way. They were, throughout, the spectators of the 146
sufferings of others and were taught by the spectacle the most
excellent and useful of lessons—piety.

Of those who went out, the men of military age numbered over 147
six hundred thousand, the multitude of old men, children, and
women could not easily be counted, and a bastard crowd of persons of mixed descent, rabble and servants, went with them—
persons born of Egyptian women to Hebrew men, converts, and
the like.

The appointed leader ୯୮ all of these was Moses, who received 148
the kingship on account of his virtue and nobility of conduct and
benevolence, and above all because God gave it him as a reward.
Since, out of nobility of soul, he had voluntarily given up the 149
kingship he might have had as adopted grandson of the Pharaoh,
therefore God rewarded him with the kingship of a more numerous and better people, that was destined from among all others
to be priests, always praying for the race of men.

On being made king Moses did not attempt to advance his 150
two sons so as to make them his co-rulers and future successors.
As a good judge he conquered his natural affection toward his
children by means of his incorruptible reason. For the one goal 151
he set himself was to benefit those whom he ruled and to do everything in deed and word for their good. He alone of all rulers of all 152
ages neither stored up gold and silver nor levied tributes nor
acquired buildings or flocks or servants, though he could have
had plenty of all these. But thinking the concern for material 153
wealth a result of spiritual poverty, he despised such wealth as
blind, while he honored that of nature which sees, and was
zealous for it as perhaps no other man has ever been. In clothing

and food and the other elements of physical life he affected nothing for the sake of majesty but practiced the economy and contentedness of a private citizen. In those things of which a

154 ruler should be avaricious his display was truly royal—self control, endurance, continence, shrewdness, understanding, learning, labor, patience, contempt of pleasure, righteousness, exhortation to excellence, lawful blame and punishment of wrongdoers, lawful praise and honor of those who did well.

155 Because of his contempt for human wealth God rewarded him with the greatest and most perfect wealth, which is that of the whole earth and sea and all other elements. For God saw fit to declare him His partner in His realm and yielded to him the whole

156 world as a possession appropriate to His heir. Accordingly, each of the elements obeyed him as a master, changing whatever property it had and giving way to his commandments. There is nothing marvelous in this, for if, as the saying goes, "What friends have, they have in common," and the prophet is called the friend of God, it follows that he shares control of creation, insofar as

157 this is useful. For God, having all things, needs nothing, but the good man has nothing, properly speaking, not even himself, yet he partakes, so far as he is able, of the treasures of God, and this appropriately, for he is a citizen of the world and therefore rightly is not enrolled in any of the earth's cities, but receives as

158 his portion not a piece of land but the whole world. And did Moses not enjoy even greater partnership with the Father and Maker of all things, since he was thought worthy of the same title as the Father? For he was called God and King of the whole people. And he is said to have gone into the darkness where God was, that is, into the formless and invisible and bodiless archetypal essence of existing things, since, using mortal nature, he comprehended the invisible. And he set forth himself and his life like a well-painted picture, a supremely beautiful and godlike

160 work, as a model that those who wished might imitate. Thus he

162 became the example for all the people, as the ruler must be. And as he was to be lawgiver, he himself, by divine providence, first became the reasonable and living Law.

163 Since he now had received the rulership from willing subjects,

God awarding and approving it, he directed their emigration toward Phoenicia and Palestine, then called Canaan, of which the
boundaries were three days' journey distant from Egypt. How- 164
ever, he did not lead them the short way, partly because he feared
that if they encountered opposition they might be frightened and
go back to Egypt, partly because he wished to test their obedience
in difficult country. Therefore, turning aside from the straight 165
road, he found a diagonal path he thought led down to the Red
Sea, and began to follow it. It is said that a cloud in the shape of 166
a great column preceded the multitude and by day gave off a
light like the sun, by night like flame, that they should not go
astray in their journey but should follow an inerrant leader. It
may be that one of the officers of the great King, an invisible
angel that bodily eyes may not behold, having wrapped himself
in the cloud, was their guide.

When the king of Egypt saw that the people had lost the road, 167
as he thought, and were making their way through wild and trackless desert, he was delighted and pursued them with the pick of
his army, thinking either to enslave them again or to kill them all.
He caught up with them when they were encamped by the sea- 169
shore. The unexpected arrival of the Egyptian army terrified the 170
Hebrews, and they blamed Moses for having led them out of
Egypt: he should have realized that servitude was better than 171
death. Moses, remembering the oracles, with his mind invisibly
entreated God while with his voice he encouraged the people, 173
reminding them that God and man do not fight in the same way,
God can find a way out of any difficulties, and so on. Soon he 174-5
became possessed, inspired by the spirit that customarily visited
him, and prophesied that the pursuing army should never be seen
again; within that very night it would disappear in the depths,
and no trace of it would remain.

While he was saying these things, the sun set, and a violent 176
south wind rushed down, driving the sea, which was ebbing already, before it. No star was visible; thick, black cloud covered
all the heaven, terrifying the pursuers. Moses, on God's order, 177
struck the sea with the staff. The sea was divided. Of the two
parts, the one rose up to a great height and became solid like a

wall, the other was held back in its course as if by invisible reins. Between them, where the break occurred, the bottom of the sea became a dry, broad road. Seeing this, Moses marveled and rejoiced, encouraged his followers, and urged them to get under

178 way as soon as possible. When they were about to pass through, the cloud that had hitherto preceded them moved around to their

179 rear as a guard. The Hebrews thus crossed the sea at early dawn; the Egyptians pursuing them were swallowed up by the two parts

180 of the sea, which rolled in on them from both sides. The astonished Hebrews celebrated their bloodless victory by setting on the seashore two choirs, one of men, the other of women, to sing hymns of thanksgiving to God. Moses led the men, his sister the women.

181 After their departure from the sea, they were for a while free of the fear of enemies, but when for three days they found no water, they were again despondent, because of thirst, and again

182 began to find fault. Matters were made worse by disappointment when they came upon some springs that turned out to be bitter.

184 Moses therefore prayed God for speedy relief. God at once sent forth his merciful power, opened the sleepless eye of his suppliant's soul, and showed him a tree that he commanded him to put

186 into the springs. When this was done, the springs ran sweet water.

187 The people slaked their thirst, filled their water jars, and set forth again as if from a banquet, drunk not with wine but with that sober intoxication of which their ruler's piety had given them the first taste.

191 Soon after this, however, they were famished by want of food and particularly depressed because, besides their immediate need,

192 they saw no hope of finding further provisions in their long

193-4 journey through an utterly sterile desert. They complained bitterly that Moses had led them from the plenty of Egypt to die

196 of hunger in the wilderness. Moses was grieved not so much by their accusations of him as by their fickleness. Having experienced so many unexpected events, they should have learned to trust not

197 appearances but him. However, when he took into consideration

198 their need and the natural instability of any crowd, he forgave them, and God sent them relief partly because of His clemency

and love for men, partly to honor the leader whom He had
ordained. Therefore, on the next day at dawn He sent a strange 200
dew of tiny white grains that lay about the tents in heaps. When 201
the people asked what it was, Moses was possessed by inspiration
and declared in an oracle, "The deep-earthed plain is given to
mortals. They plough it with furrows and sow and perform the
other actions of farming to secure the seasonable produce for
abundance of the necessities of life. But to God is subject not one
portion of the universe but the whole cosmos and its parts, serving
him as slaves for any service he may will. Now, therefore, he has 202
seen fit that the air should bring food instead of water, since earth
has often brought water [as well as food]. For what is the river
in Egypt, annually flooding to water the fields, save rain pouring
up from beneath?" Moreover, to make the miracle yet greater, it 203
was renewed every morning, and the grain would not keep over 204
night. But the holy hebdomad was particularly honored, for since 205
no work may be done on the seventh day, God rained down a
double portion on the day before and commanded that two
days' supply be gathered, and what was kept over night to the
Sabbath did not spoil. This regimen continued throughout all 206
their forty years in the wilderness, and thus they were given proof 207
that the Sabbath was the birthday of the world.

The food thus provided was presently augmented by quail, 209
which flew in great flocks over the camp and were easily caught.
Thus the danger of starvation was removed, but presently they 210
again found themselves short of water. When they were beginning to despair, Moses took that holy staff by which he had done
the miracles in Egypt and, moved by divine inspiration, struck the
steep rock, which thereupon spouted forth water sufficient not 211
only to relieve their immediate thirst but also to provide plentiful
drink to so many myriads for a longer time, for they filled all their
water vessels, as they formerly had at the springs of which the
waters were sweetened. (If anyone disbelieve these stories, he 212
neither knows God nor has ever sought him, for if he had, he
would know immediately that these marvels are the child's play
of God by comparison with things truly great like the creation
of the world, the order of the stars and planets, and so on, which 213

are neglected merely because we are used to them, while even tiny things, if unaccustomed, amaze us.)

214 At length, after crossing much trackless land, they sighted the borders of the inhabited country for which they were bound. The 215 inhabitants were Phoenicians, and the king called up the youth 216 of the cities and attempted to defend the land by force. Moses, knowing from lookouts that the hostile army was not far off, selected the young men and chose as general one of his officers named Jesus. Then he himself hastened to his greater ally. For having cleansed himself with the customary purifications, he ran to a nearby hill and besought God to shield and give victory to 217 the Hebrews. When they were about to engage in battle, a most portentous thing happened to his hands, for they became alternately very light and very heavy. When they were light and rose up, the Hebrews prevailed; when they sank down, their opponents. Thus God indicated that earth was the proper inheritance of the opponents and the most holy ether of the Hebrews, and as heaven rules earth, thus the holy people will overcome their 218 opponents. For a while, then, the hands fluctuated, and for so long the battle, too, was dubious. But suddenly they became weightless, flew up on high like winged creatures, and remained aloft until the Hebrews had undisputed victory and their enemies were slaughtered, young and old alike, suffering justly what they 219 had tried to do unjustly. Thereupon Moses founded an altar that he called "Refuge of God," on which, with prayers of thanksgiving, he offered the sacrifices due for the victory.

220 After this battle he decided that he should investigate the land 221 in which the people was to settle. He therefore chose twelve men, one leader of each tribe, so that no part of the people might feel 224 dissatisfied. He ordered these men to discover the strength and number of the inhabitants of the land, the locations and fortifications of the cities, and the quality of the soil—whether or not 228 it was worth fighting for. They found it very fertile and well 229 watered, but they also found the cities strategically located and strongly fortified and the inhabitants gigantic, if not giants. 231 With these reports and with a cluster of grapes so large that it 232 had to be carried on a beam between two men, they returned. But

after their return they disagreed as to what should be done. Two 234
wished to go on and attempt to conquer the country, ten thought
the attempt hopeless. The ten prevailed, but God's anger at their 235
counsel was soon demonstrated. They and their supporters were 236
killed off by a plague, and the people were compelled to wander 237
in the wilderness for thirty-eight years more as expiation of their 238
impiety in doubting the power of God and hesitating to carry out
his will.

When they again approached the frontiers of the land, they 239
found living near them a people to whom they were related, the 240
descendants of a brother of their ancestor. The brothers, however, 242
had quarreled, and the descendants of the other had kept alive
the old feud. Moses could have conquered them at once but, be- 243
cause of their relationship, did not think this right and requested
merely the right of passage through their land, promising to pay
for whatever his people used on the way. Even to this, however,
their relatives would not agree but threatened them with war if
they crossed their borders. At this insult the people were ready to 244
fight, but Moses dissuaded them, arguing that although the insult 245
deserved punishment, they were not the ones who should inflict
it. He then led them around by another way and so avoided a 246
conflict. Thus he displayed two of the greatest virtues, prudence 249
and benevolence, for to take care to avoid damage shows intelligence and to refrain from taking revenge on relatives shows an
unusual love of mankind.

When they had passed these cities, the king of the adjacent 250
country, Hananes by name, learned from his lookouts that their
army was not far off. He attacked them, won an initial victory, took
some captives, and pressed on to attack the main body. Here, how- 251
ever, the people not only encouraged each other for the fight but 252
also vowed to sacrifice to God, as first fruits, the cities of the king
and their citizens. God granted their prayers, inspired them with
courage, and caused them to capture the opposing army. They ac- 253
cordingly paid their vows, taking nothing of the spoil for themselves but sacrificing the cities, the men, and all their treasures 254
as the first fruits of their coming conquests.

Rejoicing in these ever-recurring yet unexpected blessings, 257

Moses led the people on, putting the young men as guards in the front and the rear, the old men, women, and children in the
258 middle. A few days later, entering the country of the Amorites, he sent ambassadors to the king, whose name was Seön, asking permission to cross and promising to pay for whatever the people used. Seön not only refused permission but came out with his
261 army to do battle. He was completely defeated, his forces were
262 annihilated, and his cities became at once empty of their former inhabitants and full of better men.

263 　This war terrified all the peoples of Asia, but particularly those near by. One of the neighboring kings, Balakes by name, ruler of a great and populous region of the east, despaired of victory in combat and sent to Mesopotamia for a famous diviner to come
274 and put a curse on the Hebrews. This plan, however, was foiled by God, who took possession of the diviner against his will at the crucial moments and uttered through his mouth blessings instead
292, 295 of curses. The king, of course, was furious. The diviner, to pacify him, explained to him that the Hebrews could not be defeated
296 unless they could be led to disobey God and advised him, therefore, to order the women of his country to prostitute themselves
298 to the Hebrews but, before yielding, to demand as the price of their compliance that their lovers participate with them in
300, 301 idolatrous worship. This plan was wonderfully successful until the son of the high priest, Phineas, was moved to an act of violence
302 worthy of a good and true man. Seeing a Hebrew openly and shamelessly going in to consort with a harlot, he ran in after him, surprised the man and the woman in bed, killed them both, and in addition, ripped up the woman's genitals because they had
303 served for unlawful seed. Seeing this, on Moses' orders, some of those who were zealous for the pattern of continence and godliness imitated Phineas and killed all their relatives and friends who had been initiated into idolatrous rites, showing mercy to none. Thus the people was purged of impurity; the killers were considered pure and their attacks deserving of the truest praise.
304 It is said that twenty-four thousand were killed in one day. Moses therefore sought to give a worthy prize to the son of the high priest, but God forestalled him, granting by oracles to Phineas the

greatest good, peace, which no man can give, and besides this, perpetual possession of the priesthood as a portion never to be taken away from himself and his descendants.

Since all the evildoers among the people had thus perished, this seemed the right time for an attack on Balakes. Moses decided not to use the whole army but selected twelve thousand of the best young men—a thousand from each tribe—and chose Phineas as general for the war. After favorable sacrifices he sent out the soldiers, encouraging them with the reminder that this war was not to seize political control or the property of others but was to defend piety and holiness, of which their friends and fellow tribesmen had been deprived by the enemy. It would be unreasonable, having killed their own relatives for transgressing the law, to spare enemies whose actions had been worse and who, by forcing [!] the Hebrews to sin, had been the causes of all their misfortunes. Thus encouraged, the soldiers went forth and won a complete victory, after which they destroyed the enemy's cities so thoroughly that no one could have told they had ever been inhabited. Having taken an incalculable number of prisoners, both men and women, they killed them, but spared the little boys and the girls who were still virgins. Finally, they brought back to the camp an enormous booty. Moses praised their exploits and especially the fact that they had not appropriated the booty for themselves but presented it as common property in order that those who had remained in the tents might share in it. He also commanded them to stay outside the camp for some days and ordered the high priest to purify from slaughter those who had been involved in the fighting. Shortly thereafter he divided the booty, giving half to those who had gone on the campaign— these were relatively few—and half to those who had stayed in the camp. One fiftieth of the share of the latter and one five-hundredth of the former he sanctified, giving the five-hundredth to the high priest, the fiftieth to the temple officers, who are called Levites. Moreover, the officers of the campaign brought what gold they had found in the booty as a thank offering, and Moses, admiring their piety, laid this up in the consecrated tent as a memorial.

305 306 307 308 309 311 312 313 315 316 317

319   All these wars were fought while they had not yet crossed the
320 Jordan. The land thus conquered was good cattle country.
      Therefore, of the twelve tribes, two who had much cattle now ap-
      proached Moses and asked him to assign them portions in this
321 land. Moses thought they were planning to withdraw from the
322 army while the land of Canaan itself was yet to be conquered. He
      therefore angrily rebuked them, calling their proposal unjust and
327 cowardly, and assuring them that the portions would not be
      assigned until the whole of the promised land had been conquered
328 and its previous inhabitants exterminated. They bore his rebuke
      humbly, for they knew he was not made arrogant by the
      authority of his office but was careful for all and honored justice
      and equality, and when he expressed his hatred of evil, he did so
      not for the sake of blaming, but for correction of those who could
329 be improved. Therefore they explained to him that they had no
330 intention of withdrawing, but wished merely to leave their wives,
      children, and cattle in fortified cities in the land they now held,
      while they themselves went on with the army until the completion
331 of the conquest. This pacified Moses, and he gave them permission
332 to do as they proposed.
334   Thus Moses' deeds as king have been recounted.

II

4 Since it is a king's task to order what should be done and forbid
5 what should not, the king is in effect a living law. Further, the
      king and lawgiver must exercise the highest priesthood in order
      that by perfect sacrifices and with perfect knowledge of how God
      should be worshiped he may ask of the deity aversion of evils and
6 participation in what is good. And since in spite of all his gifts
      the king, lawgiver and high priest, is a mortal to whom many
      things both human and divine are unknown, he must also have
      the gift of prophecy in order that by the providence of God he
      may discover what he cannot grasp by reasoning. All these gifts
      Moses possessed, being at once king, lawgiver, high priest, and
      prophet.

His work as a lawgiver exemplified all four of the virtues a law-   8, 9
giver should have : love of men, love of justice, love of what is
good, and hatred of evil. These qualities are clear in the sacred   11
books he wrote under the guidance of God and handed down (to
those worthy to use them) as images of the archetypal forms
carried in the soul. That he was the best of all lawgivers of all   12
countries and that his laws are the best and are truly divine and
lack nothing they should contain, is proved by the fact that all   13
other laws have been altered, but Moses' alone remain unchanged
from the day they were written to the present and will remain so to
the end of time. Moreover, they have been honored and accepted   17
not only by the Jews but by almost all other peoples. What   21
country does not respect the sacred seventh day as a day of rest,
or the great annual feast? That the laws were translated into   23, 27
Greek under the auspices of Ptolemy Philadelphus is further   30
evidence of the respect shown them by non-Jews.

But this external evidence for the excellence of the laws is sur-   45
passed by the content of the laws themselves. They are divided   46
into historical and strictly legal sections. The historical, in turn,   47
is composed of an account of creation and a properly historical
part, the latter dealing with punishments of the wicked and reward of the righteous. The legislator began with the historical   48
section and put the legal commandments and prohibitions in
second place, in order to show that there was one father and
creator of all things and that consequently to obey the laws was
to live in harmony with nature. Similarly, he cast the laws rather   51
in the form of exhortations than of orders and surrounded them
with proems and epilogues, so as to persuade rather than compel.

The harmony of the laws with nature is shown by the stories of   52
the flood and the destruction of Sodom and its neighboring cities
by fire from heaven. These demonstrate that for the worst sinners
are reserved extraordinary punishments by the most drastic elements of nature—fire and water. At the same time, they show   57
the extraordinary salvation of individual righteous men from
general catastrophies.

Moses was not only king and lawgiver but also, as declared   66
above, high priest and prophet. As high priest he was dis-

tinguished especially by his piety, the most necessary quality of a priest. For this he was gifted by nature and cultivated by the practice of philosophy, improving himself by the contemplation of most excellent teachings until he brought forth the perfect

67 fruit of virtue in both words and deeds. He both loved God and was loved by God as few others; he honored Him and was honored by Him. The honor befitting a sage is to serve that which truly exists, and priesthood is concerned with the service of God. Of this reward, than which there is no greater good, Moses was thought worthy and was taught by oracles everything that concerned the divine service.

68 First of all, he had to purify his body as well as his soul, ridding it of every passion and of all things pertaining to mortal nature

69 —food and drink and sexual intercourse. This latter he had despised almost from the time when he first began to prophesy and to be inspired, since he thought he should keep himself always ready for oracles. Food and drink he did without for forty days in succession, since he had better nourishment from visions with which he was inspired from heaven and which, through his soul, improved first his mind and then his body, increasing the

70 strength and good condition of both. By divine command he went up into the highest and holiest mountain of the region, a mountain inaccessible and trackless, in which he is said to have remained for the time specified, eating no food. He came down so much better in appearance than he went up that those who saw him were astonished and could no longer look at him because of the blaze of sunlike brilliance he radiated.

71 While he stayed on the mountain, he was instructed in all the mysteries concerning the priesthood, and first of all in those

73 concerning the temple and the things in it. Since the people were still wandering in the desert, it was suitable that they should have a portable temple in order that in their journeys they might offer

74 sacrifices and the like. Accordingly, a tent was to be made, a most holy work, of which the structure was described to Moses on the mountain by divine utterances. He beheld with his soul bodiless

76 forms of the physical objects to be made. These were then copied

77 in the appropriate materials. The resultant tent, with its sur-

rounding courtyard, the ark in the holy of holies containing the 95
laws, the cherubim on the ark, the altar of incense, candlestick 101, 104
and table of shewbread in the holy place, the altar for sacrifices 106
in the courtyard before the tent, the garments of the high priest, 109
and the basin for ablutions at the entrance to the courtyard were 136
all of them, therefore, symbolic either of the powers of God or the
elements and structure of the cosmos or the nature and duties
of men, or all of these at once—multiple symbolism being 134
facilitated by the facts that the cosmos is the Son of God and
that the duty of man is to carry the pattern of the cosmos within
himself and so model himself upon it as to be transformed into a
microcosm.

When Moses had described the forms to be made and the tent 141
was being prepared, he had next to choose the persons best suited
to be priests and to teach them how the sacrifices should be
offered. On the basis of merit he chose his brother to be high priest 142
and ordained the latter's sons as priests. His choice was determined
not by consideration of family but by the piety and holiness he
saw in the men. This is proved by the fact that he did not appoint
either of his own sons. Those whom he chose he ordained first 143
by washing and clothing them—the high priest in the symbolic
garments, his sons in linen clothes designed for decency—then 144, 146
by anointing the high priest, together with the tent and its equip-
ment, and finally by offering appropriate sacrifices, a calf for 147
forgiveness of sins (since sinning is congenital with every creature
born) and two rams, one as a thank offering and one for 148-9
the purification and sanctification of those being ordained. Of the 150
blood of this latter he poured some around the altar, with some
he anointed the ends of the right ears, right thumbs, and right
big toes of the initiates. Then he sprinkled the initiates with a 152
mixture of the blood from the altar and the anointing oil. All of
these actions had, of course, symbolic meaning, in general sym-
bolizing the virtues the priests should exemplify.

After other sacrifices had been offered—some by the priests for 153
themselves, some by the elders for the whole people—Moses
entered the tent, taking his brother with him. This was the eighth
and final day of the initiation. Inside, he taught his brother how

the high priest should accomplish the ceremonies to be performed
154 there. Then both, coming out and lifting their hands before their
heads, offered the appropriate prayers for the people. While they
were praying, a mass of flame leapt out from the adytum to the
altar and consumed all that was on it, an evident proof the cere-
155 monies had not been performed without divine supervision. For
156 it was appropriate that the fire of the altar should be not
the ordinary substance of fire, which is put to menial and destruc-
158 tive uses, but a pure, ethereal fire rained down from heaven.

159   Because of the number of the people and their piety great numbers of sacrifices were offered daily, and this necessitated a great
160 number of temple attendants. For this purpose Moses chose one
of the twelve tribes, on the basis of merit, and gave it the ordina-
161 tion as a prize and reward of a deed well-pleasing to God. The
deed was as follows : Moses had gone to the nearby mountain and
spent several days alone with God. While he was gone, those of
unsteady nature turned to impiety and, forgetting the worship
162 of the Existent, became devotees of Egyptian images. They
shaped a golden bull, which they thought a likeness of the most
sacred animal of Egypt, and offered sacrifices of a sort that should
not be offered and instituted dances that should not be danced
and sang hymns no different from threnodies and, having filled
163 themselves with unmixed wine, spent the night in orgies. When
the constant shoutings of the multitudes in the camp resounded
so far that their echoes came even to the mountaintop, Moses
was at a loss what to do. Because he loved both God and men,
he could not bear to leave his conversation with God nor could
164 he overlook the evil doings of the mob, for he knew from the sound
that the disturbance had sprung from drunkenness and was cul-
165 minating in wantonness. God, however, cut short his hesitation
by ordering him to go back to the people and telling him what
166 they had done. Nevertheless, as a mediator and advocate he did
not go at once but first besought God to pardon the sins of the
people. Next, having placated the Deity, he went back at once
rejoicing and depressed—rejoicing that God had accepted his
entreaty, depressed by the transgression of the multitude.

167   When he arrived in the midst of the camp, he saw that some

were still unaffected by the spiritual epidemic and retained their hatred of evil. Wishing to distinguish these and any who might repent from those hopelessly infected, he proclaimed, "If any is 168 on the side of the Lord, let him come to me." At this one of all 170 the twelve tribes, that of Levi, rushed to him immediately. Moses, seeing them coming like racers from a mark, said, "If 171 you hasten to us not only with your bodies but also with your minds, let this be proved at once. Let each one, taking his sword, kill those, worthy of a thousand deaths, who have left the true God and have made false ones, using the title of the Incorruptible and Uncreated for corruptible and created substances. Kill relatives and friends alike, considering that the friendship and kinship of good men consists only in holiness."

They were more than ready for this exhortation, since they had 172 been alienated from the others ever since they saw the transgression beginning. Therefore they killed some three thousand of those who a little before had been their dearest. This put the fear 173 of God into the mob, and Moses, approving their noble action, thought of a prize worthy of the deed. For it was fitting that those who had undertaken a voluntary war for the sake of God's honor and had quickly triumphed should be thought worthy of his service and should receive consecration.

There are two orders of consecrated persons : one group—the 174 priests—is entrusted with prayers and sacrifices and similar holy rites and have access to the inner parts of the temple, while the other has nothing to do with these things but has supervision and guard, day and night, over the temple and things in it. This latter group some call the temple attendants. Since it was much more numerous than the priests, its members began to attack the priests and thought to take over their privileges. Lest this innovation 175 should seem their private project, they persuaded the eldest of the twelve tribes to share their opinion, and this tribe was followed by many individuals of the rasher sort. Moses recognized 176 that this great opposition was growing up against him. Although he had acted according to oracular directions in choosing his brother as high priest, nevertheless there were charges that he had forged the oracles and had made the choice because of his kingship

177 and his liking for his brother. Naturally he was grieved by these charges, and since he did not think it easy to persuade the prejudiced, he besought God to give them clear proofs that he had

178 falsified nothing in regard to the choice. God commanded him to take twelve rods and write on eleven the names of the leaders of the elven other tribes, on the twelfth the name of his brother, the high priest, and then to bring them in to the adytum of the

179 temple. He did as directed. Next day in the presence of all the people he went in and brought out the rods. The others were no different than before, but that one on which his brother's name was written had sprouted all over with new shoots and was laden

181 with an abundance of nuts. The nut is the symbol of perfect virtue.

187   Finally we come to Moses' role as prophet. Here it must be stated at once that all things written in the holy books are oracles

188 given through him. But of these things some are spoken by God

191 himself through Moses as an interpreter. These are too great for human praise, and an interpreter is not the same as a prophet; consequently these will not be considered. Others, however, are presented as divine replies to questions by Moses or as inspired utterances of Moses himself, and these are relevant here.

192   An example of prophecy given through question and answer

196 is afforded by the case of the half Jew, half Egyptian who was so insane as to curse God. Moses had no doubt that he should be

197 killed and would himself have killed him had he not feared this might be too light a punishment. But no man could conceive any

201 punishment adequate for so great an offense. Therefore Moses put the man in prison and asked God what should be done with him,

203 and God ordered him stoned. This was the occasion of a new law, that otherwise might not have been thought worth writing: "Whoever curses god, let him be adjudged guilty of sin, and who

204 ever names the name of the Lord, let him die." Since this sets a heavier penalty for naming than for cursing, the word "god" in the first half must refer to the pseudonymous "gods" of the Gentiles: even these are not to be cursed, in order that the word "god" should not be used casually.

209   Another case of the same sort was that of the man caught

gathering sticks on the Sabbath. Those who apprehended him 214
brought him to Moses, who was sitting teaching philosophy, as is 215
customary on the Sabbath, instructing the people as to what
should and should not be done. Here again Moses knew the man 217
deserved death but was at a loss to make the punishment fit the
crime. Therefore he shut him in prison and inquired of God what
should be done with him. God ordered this one stoned likewise. 218

Two other cases may be cited in which legal questions were 221
similarly settled by inquiry and divine response. One was that 222
of men who, by reason of a recent death in the family, were un- 225
clean at the time of Passover and therefore could not perform the 226
paschal sacrifice. They appealed to Moses. Moses on the one hand 227-8
recognized the justice of their plea and sympathized with their
misfortune, on the other he felt himself constrained by the laws
fixing the date and conditions of the ceremony. He therefore put
the case to God, who replied that persons prevented by no fault 230
of their own from sacrificing at the appointed time might perform
the sacrifice in the same fashion a month later. Another case 234
was that of the daughters of a man who died without sons. Since
the law then limited inheritance of real property to male heirs,
they appealed to Moses, not in pursuit of wealth but desiring
to preserve the name and reputation of their father. Moses ad- 236
mired their piety but found himself bound by the principle that
real property should be awarded to men as compensation for
military service, and women should therefore have no claim to it.
Consequently he referred this case also to God, who ruled that 237, 242
if a man had no sons, his daughters should inherit, not, however,
by right but by legalized charity.

Another type of prophecy were those pronouncements uttered 246
by the prophet speaking by inspiration [but in his own name].
His first experience of being possessed by the Deity occurred at
the Red Sea, when the people were in despair between the sea 249
and the Egyptian army. At this moment Moses, no longer in himself, was carried away by God and uttered the following oracle :
"On the one hand, fright is necessary; the cause of terror is near, 250
and the danger is great. In front is the gaping sea; there is no
landing place from which to embark for flight, there are no ships.

Behind, the enemy troops are near, they advance in unresting pursuit. Whither can one turn, whither can one swim? Everything from every side has suddenly attacked us—earth, sea, men,
251 the elements of nature. But take courage; do not be disheartened; stand with unwavering minds; await the invincible help of God. Self-sent, it is already present; unseen, it takes the lead in the battle. You have often already experienced it invisibly protecting you. I see it preparing for combat, noosing the necks of the opponents. It drags them down into the sea; like lead they sink into the depths. You perceive them yet alive, but I envision them as
253 dead, and you too shall today see them corpses." So he said, prophesying things beyond all hope, and the people presently discovered by experience the truth of the pronouncement.
258 This was the beginning of Moses' prophesying while possessed by God. Later he also prophesied concerning the food that heaven
259 rained down daily, saying while inspired, "Those who have experienced God's benefactions in deeds greater than could be hoped for should believe him. Let the food not be stored up nor
260 kept. Let no one leave any part of it over to the next day." This prophecy too was confirmed not only by the spoiling of that food
262 some doubters kept over night but also by God's continued re-
264 newal of the gift each morning. When Moses learned that on the sixth day the supply was doubled and that kept over to the seventh did not spoil, he did not so much guess as, divinely in-
265 spired, prophesy the doctrine of the Sabbath. Such conjectures are closely related to prophecy, for the mind would not have hit the mark so directly had not the spirit guiding it to the truth been
268 divine. Further, in the same connection, Moses prophesied that the air would give no food on the Sabbath, and this prophecy too was verified by the facts.
270 Another prophecy, although it might seem to be rather an exhortation, was that uttered when the people turned to worship
271 the golden calf. Moses was horrified, not only that the people should suddenly become so blind but also that an idol should
272 have the power to quench so great a light. He no longer remained the same man; his appearance and his mind were changed, and, divinely inspired, he said, "Who is there who has not been carried

away by the error nor attributed validity to the invalid? Let every
such man come to me." And when one tribe, filled with hatred 273
for the godless, came to him, seeing their anger he was yet more
possessed by God than before, and said : "Each one of you, taking
a sword, run through all the camp and kill right and left, not only
persons with whom you have no connection, but the closest of your
friends and relatives. And think the task most holy, as done for
the truth and the honor of God, which it is the lightest of labors
to champion and defend." Accordingly, when they had killed 274
three thousand, they not merely did not defend their action but
enrolled it among the noblest of heroic deeds and were thought
worthy of consecration as temple attendants as the most proper
reward.

A further and more miraculous oracle was given in connection 275
with the dispute over the priesthood described above. The charge 278
that he had forged divine decrees and given the priesthood to his
brother out of family feeling so outraged Moses that, although
meekest and mildest of men, he not only prayed God to reject the 279
sacrifice of his opponents but also, kindled by righteous wrath, 280
became possessed by God, was transformed into a prophet, and
prophesied as follows : "Unbelief is a bitter thing only to the un-
believers. Them no word but only works will teach. Since from
learning they did not know that I was not lying, they will know
it from suffering. This will be judged from the end of their lives.
For if they die a natural death, I have forged the oracles, but if 281
some new and extraordinary death, my love of truth will be
evidenced. I see chasms of the opening earth spreading wide and
long, populous families going to destruction, houses dragged
under and swallowed down with the men still in them, live men
going down into Hades." When he finished speaking, the earth 282
was split by an earthquake, and the tents of the wicked, with those
in them, were swallowed whole. A little later the leaders of the 283
opposition, 250 men, were suddenly destroyed by thunderbolts
so that nothing was left of them for burial. Thus God testified to 284
the truthfulness of the prophet.

Later, when he was to be sent hence to heaven and, leaving 288
mortal life, was to be immortalized at the call of the Father, who

resolved him from the duality of soul and body into a monadic nature, transforming him wholly into a sun-bright mind, then possessed by God, he no longer seemed to prophesy in general to the whole people at once but foretold to each tribe in particular the things that were to be and should come to pass hereafter. Of these some have already happened, others are still expected, for the accomplishment of those past is evidence of those to come.

290   These things are marvelous, but most marvelous is the con-
291 clusion of the holy books, which, as in an animal, is the head of the whole body of legislation. For when he was already about to be taken up and, like a runner on the mark, to fly up the road into heaven, the divine spirit inspired him and he prophesied while still alive the story of his own death, telling how he was buried when no one was present—evidently not by mortal hands but by immortal powers—how he was not laid in the tomb of the patriarchs but in a special grave that no man knew, and how all the people mourned him, weeping, for a whole month, grieving with common and particular grief because of his indescribable benevolence and care for each one and for all.

XIV. A SUMMARY OF THE GOSPEL
ACCORDING TO LUKE

INTRODUCTORY

ALMOST ALL WE KNOW about Jesus comes from the four Gospels accepted and handed down by that party that eventually became dominant within the Christian movement. These four were by no means all the gospels written during the first and second centuries. We know the names of many others, and there must have been many more of which even the names have been lost. Their loss was largely accidental. Most of them were presumably written on papyrus, and a sheet of papyrus fibers (though it might survive for millennia if left undisturbed in dry sand) was a fragile thing and would go to pieces if it had much handling. Therefore, only those gospels survived that were accepted and copied and recopied by particular parties. When these parties were stamped out by persecution (whether by the pagans or later by that Christian party which reached an agreement with the Roman government) the gospels they had preserved generally perished with them, whereas the four Gospels accepted and kept in circulation by the triumphant party survived.

Of these four, the third is commonly attributed to "Luke." The attribution is no doubt intended to make the reader think the author was that Luke mentioned by Paul in his letters to the Colossians (4:14) and to Philemon (vs. 24) and either by Paul or some imitator of Paul in II Timothy (4:11). The reason for this attribution is that the third Gospel was certainly written by the same man who wrote the Acts of the Apostles, and the second half of the Acts deals chiefly with the career of Paul. To authenticate this, an attribution to one of Paul's companions was most desirable. However, there is little likelihood that the attribution is correct. The author seems to have used in Acts a source written as if by a companion of Paul—it tells how "we" traveled from one place to another—but he used it only here and there, and when he was not using it, he showed himself ignorant of Paul's theology and wrote an account of Paul's early career which contradicts that given by Paul himself in Galatians.

If we suppose, then, that the author of Acts wrote at least ten or twenty years after the companion of Paul, whose work he used as a source, we shall date Luke and Acts in the eighties at the earliest. But they might be twenty or even thirty years later. There is no evidence for their existence prior to A.D. 130, and Papias, a Christian writer of about that time, gave an account of the origins of Matthew and Mark but seems to have said nothing of Luke, which suggests that he either did not know or else did not accept it. By that time, however, it was almost certainly in existence, for soon thereafter it began to be used by other christian writers (Marcion, Valentinus, Justin).

"Luke," whoever he was, addressed his gospel to a friend called Theophilus and prefaced it with a brief statement of purpose (1:1—3): "Since many have undertaken to draw up accounts of the fulfillments [of prophecy] in our times, as those who from the beginning were witnesses and agents of the teaching have reported [it] to us, I also, having followed up all [the reports] accurately, have seen fit to write you an orderly [account], my dear Theophilus, so that you may know the reliability of those statements about which you have been taught."

Of the many accounts to which Luke refers here, one was certainly the Gospel according to Mark, which Luke used as a source off and on through his chapters 3 or 4 to 9 and 18 to 24. Of his other sources at least one was also used by Matthew (unless Luke used Matthew itself, which seems unlikely). Others are known to us only from Luke's use of them and therefore cannot be identified with any confidence.

But one thing is certain: all of his source material came from Christian communities that had preserved, shaped, developed, and sometimes invented it to suit their own interests. As an account of those interests it is a primary and reliable source, as an account of the life of Jesus it is a secondary source and unreliable. Worst of all, the fact that a story could have served a community interest does not prove that it was invented to do so. Therefore, even material that is patently motivated cannot be dismissed for that reason alone as clearly false. Nor can we suppose that we know all the motives early Christians had for inventing gospel material. Therefore, even material which seems to us unmotivated cannot be accepted for that reason alone as certainly true.

Consequently, the comparison of Luke with the aretalogical tradition, which the following summary is intended to facilitate, should not be pressed for immediate conclusions as to the actual events of the life of Jesus. In particular, it would be mistaken to suppose that aretalogical material necessarily represents early Christian invention rather than historical fact. As was said above in the chapter on "Lives," it is not unlikely that Jesus may have deliberately acted like a conventional (or conventionally unconventional) "sage." There is no doubt that the Greek ideal of the philosopher exercised a great influence in shaping the "wise man" (the *hakam*) of rabbinic Judaism, and this influence was exercised and this figure shaped in Palestine during the century within which Jesus' lifetime fell. Jesus seems to have been in closer touch with the Hellenizing elements of the Palestinian population than were the Pharisees; it would be 'surprising if he were less open to Hellenistic influences. At all events, before any judgment can be passed on the historicity of the aretalogical traits in the Gospels, those traits must be identified, and the character of the tradition from which they derive must be recognized. It will be seen from the material in Luke that this tradition is closely akin to that which lies behind the other aretalogical works and also to that which lies behind much rabbinic material. It is a Hellenized haggada, composed for the most part of disjointed stories and sayings, the material of different types handed down separately in different written (and probably different mnemonic) collections, that have been combined and confused only in the more recent stages of the development of the present literary text.

JESUS WAS DESCENDED on the side of his adoptive father from 3:23 King David, whose genealogy the Bible traced to Adam, who was the son of God. On his mother's side he was of priestly family, 1:5, 36 and one of his mother's relatives was the wife of a high priest, named Zacharias.

When Zacharias was serving in the Temple at Jerusalem, he 1:8 saw an angel of the Lord standing to the right of the altar of incense. He was terrified at the sight, but the angel told him not 1:12 to fear, his wife would bear him a son whose name he should call John and who would be a great minister of the Great King, would not drink wine or strong drink, would be filled with the Holy Spirit while yet unborn, and would turn many of the children of Israel back to the Lord their God, going before him with the spirit and the power that the prophet Elijah once had, to prepare a people for the Lord.

Zacharias hesitated to believe this announcement, for both he 1:18 and his wife were well on in years. The angel therefore punished him by striking him dumb and told him his dumbness would last until the prophecy was fulfilled. Shortly thereafter, when Zacharias had completed his period of service in the Temple and returned to his house, his wife Elizabeth conceived a child.

About six months later the angel Gabriel was sent from God 1:26 into Nazareth, a city in Galilee, to a virgin named Mary, who was

engaged to a man named Joseph. Coming to her he said, "Rejoice, favored one, the Lord is with you." She was deeply troubled
at this saying and wondered what sort of greeting this might be.
The angel thereupon told her not to fear, she had found favor
with God and would bear a son and call him Jesus. He would be
great and would be called the son of the Highest; God would
give him the throne of his ancestor David, and he would reign
over the people of Israel for ever and ever. But Mary said to the
angel, "How will this be, since I have not known a man?" The
angel answered her, "The Holy Spirit will come upon you, and
the Power of the Highest will overshadow you; therefore, the holy
child engendered will be called Son of God." He added that
Elizabeth too had conceived and was now in her sixth month.
Mary said, "I am the maidservant of the Lord; may this happen
to me as you have said." And the angel left her.

1:39   Thereupon Mary went at once to Judea to see Elizabeth. When
Elizabeth heard Mary's voice, the baby in her womb leaped and
she herself was filled with the Holy Spirit and cried out, "You
are the most blessed of women, and blessed is the child you will
bear. How have I deserved that the mother of my Lord should
come to me?" She then prophesied that the things Mary had
been told by the Lord would be fulfilled. Mary replied with a
hymn of thanksgiving to God, celebrating the great things he had
already done for her, and his promised deliverance of Israel. She
stayed with Elizabeth about three months and then returned to
her own house.

1:57   When Elizabeth's time came, she gave birth to a son. At his
circumcision her neighbors and kinsfolk were going to call him
Zacharias, after his father, but his mother said, "No, he shall be
called John." Thereupon they made signs to his father, asking
him what he wanted the boy called, and he took a pencil and
wrote, "His name is John." At that moment his power of speech
returned and he blessed God, saying God had fulfilled the
promises made through the prophets and had sent one of the
family of David to save Israel. He said, too, that his own child
would be called the prophet of the Highest because he would go

before the Lord to prepare for his coming and to give his people knowledge of salvation by remitting their sins.

About this time Emperor Augustus ordered that a census be 2:1 taken of all the empire. So everyone went to his own city to be entered on the rolls, and Joseph went up from Nazareth to Bethlehem, the city of David, in Judea, because he was a descendant of David. With him went his fiancée, Mary, who was pregnant. While they were there, the time came for her to give birth, and she bore her son, her first child, and wrapped him up and laid him in a manger because there was no room for them in the inn.

Now there were shepherds out in the country there, living out 2:8 of doors to keep watch during the nights over their sheep. And the angel of the Lord came to them, and the glory of the Lord shone around them, and they were terribly frightened. But the angel said to them : "Do not be afraid. I bring you good news of something that will be a great joy to the whole people. Today a deliverer, who is the Messiah promised by the Lord, has been born for you in the city of David. And let this be a sign to you : you will find a baby wrapped up and lying in a manger." And suddenly, with the angel there were many of the heavenly army, praising God and prophesying peace to his chosen people. So when the angels went away from them into the sky, the shepherds said to each other, "Let us go over to Bethlehem and see what has happened, and what the Lord has made known to us." And they hurried over and found Mary and Joseph and the baby lying in the manger. Seeing him they told about the prophecy, and everyone marveled.

When the eighth day came and he was circumcised, he was 2:21 called Jesus, the name given by the angel before he was conceived. Next, when the time set by the Mosaic Law for his mother's purification was completed, they brought him up to Jerusalem to present him to the Lord, according to the Law, and to offer the legally prescribed sacrifice. Now there was in Jerusalem a righteous man named Simeon, who awaited the consolation of Israel, and the Holy Spirit used to come upon him and had revealed to him that he should not see death until he saw the Messiah promised by the Lord. So, inspired by the Spirit, he came into the Temple, and when the child Jesus was brought in, he took him into his arms and blessed God that the promise made him had been fulfilled and his eyes had seen the means of deliverance God had prepared as a light for the Gentiles and a glory for His people, Israel. While Jesus' parents marveled at the things said about him, Simeon blessed them and uttered further mysterious prophecies. Moreover, a prophetess named Anna, a very old woman who never left the Temple but worshiped there night and day, fasting and praying—she too came up at this time and gave thanks to God and spoke about the child to all those who waited for the deliverance of Israel.

2:39   When they had done everything prescribed by the Law of the Lord, they returned to Galilee to their city, Nazareth. The child grew and became strong and was filled with wisdom, and the grace of God rested on him. When he was twelve, his parents took him with them to Jerusalem to the feast of Passover. When they started home, he stayed behind without their knowledge. They went a day's journey, then looked for him among their relatives and acquaintances in the company with which they were traveling, and then went back to Jerusalem, searching for him. After three days they found him in the Temple sitting among the teachers, hearing them and asking questions. Seeing him, they were amazed, and his mother said to him, "Child, why have you treated us in this way? See, your father and I have been frantic, hunting for you." But he said to them, "Why did you have to hunt for me? Didn't you know that I should be at my Father's?" However, they did not understand what he said to them, so he went down with them to Nazareth and was subject to them.

3:1   In the fifteenth year of Emperor Tiberius (c. 29 A.D.), when Pontius Pilate was governor of Judea and Herod Antipas ruler of Galilee, the word of God came to John, the son of Zacharias, in the desert, and he came into the Jordan valley proclaiming that there was a baptism for the repentant that would remit sins. Thus he fulfilled the prophecy of Isaiah, that when someone cried out in the wilderness, urging men to prepare the way of the Lord, all obstacles would be removed and all men would see the deliverer sent by God. When crowds came out to be baptized, John told them that they must not merely claim to be penitent but must make their works correspond to their words, for the day was near when all evildoers would be destroyed. He therefore urged them to practice justice and to share with the poor whatever belongings they had. When everyone began to speculate as to whether or not he was the Messiah, he said, "I baptize you with water, but there is coming one stronger than I, who will baptize you with the Holy Spirit and fire. He brings a winnowing shovel to clean his threshing floor, and will gather the wheat into his granary but burn the chaff with unquenchable fire." Thus John spread the good news. But since he denounced the many wicked things done by Herod Antipas, Herod did one more by shutting him in prison.

When all the people were being baptized, Jesus was baptized 3:21 too. And at the time of his baptism, when he prayed, the heavens were opened and the Holy Spirit came down on him in bodily form as a dove, and there came a voice from heaven : "You are my beloved Son, with you I am satisfied."

Jesus was about thirty when he began. He returned from the 3:23; 4:1 Jordan full of the Holy Spirit and was driven about the wilderness by the Spirit for forty days, being tempted by the devil. He ate nothing in those days, and when they were over, he was hungry. So the devil said to him, "If you are the Son of God, tell this stone to become bread." But Jesus answered him, "It is written, 'Man shall not live by bread alone.' " Then leading him up to a high place, the devil showed him all the kingdoms of the world in a moment of time and said, "I will give you all these if you will worship me." But Jesus answered him, "It is written, 'You shall worship the Lord your God and Him only.' " So he led him into Jerusalem and stood him on the cornice of the temple and said to him, "If you are the Son of God, throw yourself down, for it is written, 'He will order his angels to take care of you' and, 'they will carry you on their hands, lest you should strike your foot on a stone.' " But Jesus answered him, "It has been said, 'You shall not tempt the Lord your God.' " Having exhausted all his temptations, the devil left him until next time.

So Jesus, having the power of the Spirit, returned into Galilee, 4:14

and rumor about him spread through all the country round, while he himself was teaching in their synagogues and all men were praising him. When he came to Nazareth, where he had been brought up, he went into the synagogue on the Sabbath according to his custom, and stood up to read the lesson. He was given the book of the prophet Isaiah and, opening it, found : "The Spirit of the Lord is upon me because he has anointed me to bring good news to the poor. He has sent me to proclaim release to prisoners and recovery of sight to the blind, to set free the oppressed, to proclaim the year chosen by the Lord." Having rolled up the book and given it back to the attendant, he sat down, and all eyes in the synagogue were fixed on him. He began to preach on the theme : "Today this prophecy is fulfilled." They marveled at his eloquence and said, "Is not this the son of Joseph?" He said to them : "You will certainly tell me the proverb, 'Doctor, cure yourself.' Do here, too, in your home town, such things as we have heard happened in Capernaum. I tell you truly, no prophet is acceptable in his home town. There were many widows in Israel in the days of prophet Elijah, but the prophet was sent to one only, and she was a Sidonian, and there were many lepers in the days of the prophet Elisha, but none was cured except a Syrian." This so angered them that they took him up to the brow of the hill on which their city was built, to throw him down. But he passed through the crowd and went away.

4:31   He went down into Capernaum, a city of Galilee, and was teaching them on the Sabbaths. They were astonished at the authority with which he taught. On one occasion a man possessed by a demon was in the synagogue and shouted, "Go on, what have you got to do with us, Jesus of Nazareth? Have you come to destroy us? I know who you are, the holy one of God." But Jesus rebuked it, saying "Be silent and come out of him." And the demon, throwing him down, came out of him without hurting him at all. Everyone was astonished and talked of Jesus' authority, and his fame spread accordingly.

4:38   From the synagogue he went to the house of Simon. Simon's mother-in-law was sick with a high fever, so they asked him to help her, and he went to her and rebuked the fever, and it left her; she got up at once and waited on them. Towards sunset all those who had sick brought them to him, and he laid his hands on each one of them and cured them. Moreover, demons went out of many, screaming and saying, "You are the Son of God." But he rebuked them and did not permit them to speak, because they knew he was the Messiah. At daybreak he went out to a lonely spot, but the crowds followed him and tried to prevent him from going away. He said to them, however, "I must proclaim the good news of the Kingdom of God in the other cities, too; for this I was sent."

Once when the people were crowding around him to hear the 5:1 word of God and he was standing by the lake of Galilee, he saw two ships on the lake, for the fishermen had left them and were washing their nets. Going into one of the ships, he asked its owner, a man named Simon, to put out a little distance from the land. Sitting down, he taught the people from the ship. When he finished speaking, he told Simon and his companions to go out further into the lake and cast their nets. Though they had been fishing all night and had caught nothing, they did as he ordered and immediately caught more fish than the boats could carry. Simon, therefore, fell at Jesus' feet and said, "Go away from me, Lord, I am a sinner." For he and his partners, James and John, the sons of Zebedee, were terrified. But Jesus said to him, "Do not fear. From now on you will be catching men." So, when they brought the ships back to land, they left everything and followed Jesus.

Another time when he was in one of the cities, a man full of 5:12 leprosy, seeing him, fell down and entreated him, "Lord, if you will, you can cleanse me." Jesus stretched out his hand and touched him, saying, "I will; be cleansed." And immediately the leprosy left him. Jesus ordered him to tell no one but to go and show himself to the priest and make the offerings for his cleansing, as Moses ordered for proof to them. Such miracles spread the talk about Jesus yet further, and great crowds came to hear and be cured, but he withdrew into lonely places and devoted himself to prayer.

One day when he was teaching in the presence of Pharisees 5:17

and legal experts who had come from every village of Galilee and Judea and Jerusalem, men came carrying a paralytic on a stretcher. When they could not bring him in because of the crowd, they went up on the roof and let him down, stretcher and all, in front of Jesus. Seeing their faith, Jesus said, "Man, your sins are forgiven you." Thereupon the scribes and Pharisees said to themselves, "Who is this who utters blasphemies? Who can forgive sins except God alone?" Jesus, knowing their thoughts, said, "Which is easier, to say, 'Your sins are forgiven you,' or to say, 'Get up and walk'? That you may know that the Son of Man has authority on earth to forgive sins"—he said to the paralytic— "I tell you, get up and take up your stretcher and go home." And the man did so at once, praising God, and they were filled with fear.

5:27   After this Jesus went out and saw a tax collector[1] named Levy sitting in his office, and said to him, "Follow me." And leaving everything, he followed him. Later Levy gave a big reception for him in his house, and a great crowd of tax collectors and such like dined with Jesus. The Pharisees and scribes reproached his disciples with this, but Jesus answered, "Those who are well do not need a doctor, but those who are sick. I came to call, not the righteous, but sinners to repentance." To the further objection that the disciples of John and of the Pharisees fasted and prayed, while his ate and drank, Jesus said, "You cannot make the members of a bridal party fast while the bridegroom is with them. There will come a time when the bridegroom shall be taken from them, and then they shall fast." He also told them parables : "Nobody cuts a patch from a new garment and puts it on an old one, and nobody puts new wine in old wineskins, and nobody drinking old wine wants new."

6:1   Once, on a Sabbath, he was going through grain fields, and his disciples were picking and eating the ears of grain, husking them by rubbing them in their hands. The Pharisees said, "Why do you do what is not permitted on the Sabbath?" Jesus answered

---

[1] Tax collectors were triply unpopular with pious Jews: as suspect of extortion and other practices prohibited by the Law, as agents of the Roman government, and as tax collectors.

that David had done worse when he was hungry, he had eaten the holy bread from the table of the Lord, which was prohibited to all save priests. Further, he said to them, "The Son of Man is lord of the Sabbath."

On another Sabbath he went into a synagogue, and a man was 6:6 there whose right arm was withered. The scribes and Pharisees watched him to see if he healed on the Sabbath, to find material for an accusation of him. Knowing their thoughts, he said to the man, "Get up and stand here in the center." He did so, and Jesus said to them, "Let me ask you if it is permissible on the Sabbath to do good or to do evil, to save life or to destroy it?" And looking round the circle of them, he said to the man, "Stretch out your arm." He did so, and his arm was restored. They were furious and discussed among themselves what they could do to Jesus.

At about this time he went out into the hills to pray and spent 6:12 the night in prayer to God. When it became day, he called his disciples and selected twelve, whom he named apostles, a group headed by Simon, whom he also called Peter, and including Simon's brother Andrew, James and John, and also Judas Iscariot, who became the traitor. Coming down with these he stood in a plain with a great crowd of his disciples and a multitude of the people from all Judea and Jerusalem and the coast of Tyre and Sidon, who came to hear him and be healed. Looking 6:20 at his disciples, he said, "Blessed are you who are poor, for yours is the Kingdom of God. Blessed are you who hunger now, for you shall be filled. Blessed are you who weep now, for you shall laugh. Blessed are you when all men shall hate you because of the Son of Man, for your reward is great in heaven." He balanced these blessings with woes on the rich, the well fed, the people who laugh and are in good repute. But he warned his followers that they must love their enemies, do good to them, bless them, pray for them, and offer no resistance to any who would mistreat or rob them. They should give to any who asked of them, and, in one word, act as they wished men would act to them. "For it is no special virtue," he said, "to love your friends or help those who help you, or the like. Even sinners do that. But if you love your enemies and do good without any hope of reward, then your reward will be great and you will be sons of the Highest, for He too is good to the evil. Be merciful, as He is. Do not judge, and you will not be judged. Give, and you will receive. The blind cannot lead the blind, nor can a man with a plank in his eye remove a speck from someone else's. As trees are known to be good or bad by their fruits, so are men by their words. But words are no avail without works." His teaching, he insisted, must be not only heard but also followed. To hear it but not follow it was to build a house without foundation, that would fall in the time of trouble. After his sermon, he returned to Capernaum.

7:2   A certain centurion had a slave whom he valued greatly and who was on the point of death. He sent elders of the Jews for Jesus, asking him to come and save the man. They entreated earnestly on the centurion's behalf, assuring Jesus that he was a friend of the Jews and had himself built their synagogue. So Jesus went with them. But while he was still far off, the centurion sent friends, urging him not to bother coming but merely to say the word and order the slave healed. Jesus marveled at this and said he had not found such faith among Jews. And when those who were sent returned, they found the slave well.

7:11   Next day he went with his disciples and a great crowd to a city called Nain. As he came near the city gate, he met the funeral of a widow's only son. Seeing the mother, he pitied her and said to her, "Do not weep." And going up, he touched the bier and said, "Young man, I tell you, get up." The dead man sat up and began to talk. Fear seized everyone, and they praised God.

7:18   John's disciples told him about all these things, so he sent two of them to the Lord to ask him, "Are you the one who is to come, or do we look for another?" After their question Jesus healed many and said to them, "Go tell John what you have seen and heard. The blind see, the lame walk, lepers are cleansed, the deaf hear, the dead are raised, the poor hear good news, and blessed is he who finds no offense in me." When the messengers of John went off, he told the crowds that John was at once a prophet and greater than a prophet: he was the forerunner of the Lord, spoken of by the prophet Malachi. None born of women was greater than he, but the least in the Kingdom of God was greater. Those who had listened to John and had gone to him for baptism—the common people and the publicans—had acknowledged the righteousness of God, and those who had not —the Pharisees and the lawyers—had denied it. But they were the ones who also denied Jesus' authority. They were like contrary children, nothing would suit them. John came neither eating bread nor drinking wine, and they said, "He's crazy!" The Son of Man came eating and drinking, and they said, "See, a glutton and a drunkard, a friend of tax collectors and sinners." But God's wisdom is justified by all its children.

One of the Pharisees asked him to dinner, and he accepted. 7:36 While he was at table, a woman who was a sinner came into the Pharisee's house, bringing a flask of myrrh, and stood behind Jesus, weeping. She washed his feet with her tears, dried them with the hair of her head, kissed them and anointed them with myrrh. Seeing all this the Pharisee said to himself, "If this man were a prophet, he would know what sort of woman this is who touches him." Jesus said to him, "A certain creditor had two debtors, one owed him twenty-five dollars and the other two hundred and fifty. He forgave both their debts; which one will love him more?" The Pharisee said, "I suppose the one to whom he forgave more." Jesus said, "You are right. Now consider this woman. I came into your house. You gave me no water for my feet, but she washed my feet with her tears and dried them with the hair of her head. You gave me no kiss, but since she came in, she has not ceased kissing my feet. You did not anoint my head with oil but she has anointed my feet with myrrh. Therefore I tell you her many sins are forgiven her because she loved much, but he to whom little is forgiven loves little." And he said to the woman, "Your sins are forgiven; your faith has saved you; go in peace."

Thereafter he went from city to city and village to village, pro- 8:1 claiming the good news about the Kingdom of God. With him went the twelve and many women who had been cured of evil spirits and diseases and who from their property helped to meet the expenses of the company.

When a great crowd was present, he taught through parables : 8:4

"A sower went out to sow, and some of the seed fell by the roadside and was trampled, and the birds ate it. Some fell on stony ground and died for lack of soil. Some fell among thorns and was choked, but some fell in good ground and bore a hundredfold. Whoever has ears to hear, let him hear." When his disciples asked him the meaning of this parable, he said: "To you it has been given to know the mysteries of the Kingdom of God; to the rest they are told in parables so that, seeing, they may not see, and hearing, may not understand." The seed, he went on to say, is the word of God, and the different grounds are persons who receive it differently. None receive it properly save those who put it into practice. Only for them is the seed sown, not for the others. For a lamp is not lit to be put under a basket, and in general nothing is hidden except to be revealed. Therefore be careful how you hear, for anyone who has received the word to good purpose shall receive more, but from one who has not, even that which he seems to have shall be taken away.

8:19   His mother and brothers came but were not able to get to him because of the crowd. When it was told to him, "Your mother and brothers are standing outside and want to see you," he said: "My mother and brothers are these who hear the word of God and do it."

8:22   One day when he and his disciples were sailing across the lake, he fell asleep in the boat. A sudden storm arose, and when they were in danger of sinking, they woke him. He rebuked the wind and waves, and they ceased. Then he said to his disciples, "Where is your faith?" And they feared and were amazed.

8:26   When they came to land, they met a demoniac who fell at his feet and cried out, "What have you got to do with me, Jesus, Son of the Highest God? I entreat you, do not torture me." But Jesus made the spirits in him tell their name, and then at their request he permitted them to go into a herd of pigs feeding on the hill. When they did so, the herd rushed off a cliff into the lake and were drowned. Their keepers fled and told of what had happened. Crowds came to see and found the demoniac in his right mind, sitting at Jesus' feet. They were terrified and besought Jesus to leave their country, so he went off in the boat. The man from whom the demons had gone out begged to go with him, but Jesus told him to go home and report what God had done for him.

When Jesus landed again, he was met by a man whose only 8:40 daughter had died and who besought him to come to her. As he was going, a woman who had suffered for twelve years from a hemorrhage came up from behind and touched the edge of his garment, and at once her hemorrhage ceased. Jesus said, "Who touched me?" Everyone denied it, and Peter pointed out that the crowd was pressing all around him. But Jesus said, "Someone touched me, for I know power has gone out of me." The woman, seeing her action had not gone unnoticed, came and fell at his feet and declared in front of everyone why she had touched him and said that she had been healed immediately. He said to her, "Daughter, your faith has cured you. Go in peace." Then he went on to the house where the dead girl was. There he would not permit anyone to go in with him except Peter, James and John, and the girl's parents. To the others he said, "Do not weep, she has not died but is sleeping." They laughed at him, knowing she was dead, but he took hold of her hand and cried, "Child, get up!" And she got up at once. He ordered them to give her something to eat and told her parents to tell no one what had happened.

Calling the twelve together he gave them power and authority 9:1 to cure all persons afflicted by demons and diseases, and sent them out to proclaim the Kingdom of God and to heal. He ordered them to take nothing for the road, not food nor money nor even a begging bag, and not to go from house to house, but when they came to a city, to stay in the first house that received them, and if they were not received at all, to knock the dust off their shoes when they went out of the city. Accordingly, they went from village to village, spreading the good news and healing.

Herod Antipas heard what was happening and did not know 9:7 what to make of it, because some said that John, whom Herod had beheaded, was risen from the dead, others that Elijah had appeared, and so on. Therefore Herod wanted to see Jesus. So when the apostles returned, Jesus, taking them, went off to the territories of a city called Bethsaida [outside the realm of Herod]. The crowds, knowing this, followed him, and he spoke to them

about the Kingdom of God and healed those in need of it. When
the day wore on, the twelve asked him to send the crowd away
to find food, but Jesus said, "You give them food." They said
they had only four loaves and two fish and asked him if he wanted
them to go off and buy food for all the crowd—about five thousand. He told them to make the people lie down by fifties, then,
taking the loaves and fish, he looked up to heaven, blessed them,
broke them, and gave to the disciples to give to the crowd. They
all ate and were filled, and there were twelve basketfuls
left over.

9:15   Once when he was alone with the disciples, he asked them,
"Who do the people say I am?" They answered, "John the
Baptist, but others say, Elijah, and others, that one of the
old prophets has arisen." "But who do you say I am?" Peter answered, "The Messiah of God." He ordered them to tell this to
nobody, saying, "The Son of Man must suffer many things and
be rejected by the elders and high priests and scribes and be killed
and be raised on the third day." But he said to everyone, "If anyone wants to come after me, let him deny himself and take up his
cross daily and follow me. For whoever wishes to save his life
shall lose it, but whoever loses his life for my sake shall save it.
For whoever is ashamed of me, the Son of Man will be ashamed of
him when he comes in his glory, and the Father's and the holy
angels'. And I tell you truly, there are some of those standing
here who will not die until they see the Kingdom of God."

9:28   About eight days after this he took Peter, John, and James and
went up on the mountain to pray. While he was praying, the
appearance of his face changed, and his clothing became glitter-
ing white, and two men appeared and talked with him. These
were Moses and Elijah, who appeared in glory and foretold the
destiny he was to fulfill in Jerusalem. Peter and those with him
were heavy with sleep, but, awaking, they saw his glory and the
two men standing with him. Just as the latter were departing,
Peter spoke, and a cloud covered them. They were frightened as
they went into the cloud. Then a voice came from the cloud, saying, "This is my Son, the chosen one, hear him." And when the
voice had spoken, Jesus was found alone. They kept silent about

the matter and told no one at that time anything of what they had seen.

Next day when they were coming down from the mountain, a 9:3 crowd met them, and in it was a man who besought Jesus to cure his son, who was a demoniac. He said he had asked Jesus' disciples to cast out the demon, but they had not been able. Jesus said, "O unbelieving and perverse generation, how long shall I be with you and bear you? Bring your son here." And he healed the boy, and they all were astonished.

When everyone was marveling at his miracles, he said to the 9:43 disciples, "Remember what they are saying, for the Son of Man will be handed over to men." But they did not understand this saying and were afraid to ask him about it.

A dispute arose among them as to which of them was greatest. 9:46 Jesus, knowing their thoughts, showed them a child and said, "Whoever receives this child in my name receives me, and whoever receives me receives Him who sent me, for he who is least of you all, he is great." John replied, "Master, we saw a man casting out demons in your name, and we forbade him because he does not travel with us." Jesus said, "Do not forbid him, for whoever is not against you is on your side."

When the time came for him to be taken up, he was determined 9:51 to go to Jerusalem and sent messengers before him. In one village of the Samaritans[2] the people would not receive him, because he was apparently going to Jerusalem. Seeing this, James and John said, "Lord, do you want us to order fire to come down from heaven and consume them?" But he turned around and rebuked them, and they went to another village.

When one man said to him, "I will follow wherever you go," 9:57 Jesus answered, "The foxes have holes, and the birds nests, but the Son of Man has no place to lay his head." When he said to another, "Follow me," the other said, "Let me first go bury my

[2] The Samaritans were a people living chiefly in central Palestine. They accepted the Mosaic Law but held that the worship for which the Law provided should be performed at Mount Gerizim, in their territory, rather than at Jerusalem. Between them and the Jews there was at this time considerable hostility. Some of Jesus' enemies accused him of being a Samaritan; cf. John 8: 48.

father." But Jesus answered, "Let the dead bury the dead. You go proclaim the Kingdom of God." Yet another said, "I shall follow you, Lord, but first let me put my house in order." Jesus said to him, "Nobody who puts his hand on the plough and looks back is fit for the Kingdom of God."

10:1   After these events Jesus appointed 72 others and sent them, two by two, into every place he was to visit and said to them : "The harvest is great, the workers few, so pray the Lord of the harvest to send workers." He went on to give them essentially the same directions he had given the twelve when he sent them out, adding that it would be more tolerable in the day of judgment for Sodom than for any city in which they were not received. If Tyre and Sidon had seen the miracles done in the cities of Galilee, he exclaimed, they would long ago have repented and sat in sackcloth and ashes; therefore it would be more tolerable for them on the day of judgment than for the cities of Galilee. "I send you out," he said, "like sheep among wolves. He who hears you hears me, and he who rejects you rejects me." They returned with joy, reporting that even the demons were subject to them in his name. He said, "I saw Satan falling from heaven like lightning. See, I have given you authority to tread down snakes and scorpions and every power of the enemy, and nothing shall wrong you. But do not be glad of this; be glad that your names are written in heaven." At this time he was inspired by the Spirit to rejoice and say, "I thank you, Father, Lord of heaven and earth, that you have hidden these things from the wise and understanding and revealed them to the childlike. All things have been given me by my Father, and none knows who is the Son except the Father nor who is the Father except the Son and one to whom the Son may choose to reveal Him." And turning to his disciples he said privately, "Blessed are the eyes that see what you see, for I tell you that many prophets and kings wished to see what you see and did not."

10:25   A lawyer asked him, "What shall I do to inherit eternal life?" Jesus said, "What is written in the Law?" He answered, "You shall love the Lord your God with all your heart and soul and strength and mind, and your neighbor as yourself." Jesus said,

"You have answered rightly. Do thus and you shall live." But he said, "And who is my neighbor?" Jesus answered, "A man once fell into the hands of thieves and was left half dead on the roadside. A priest came along, saw him, and went by on the other side of the road. So did a Levite. Then a Samaritan came along and pitied him and helped him. Which of the three was his neighbor?" "The one who pitied him." "You go and do likewise."

In one village he was received by a woman named Martha. 10:38 Her sister, Mary, sat at his feet and listened to his teaching, leaving Martha to do the work. Martha asked Jesus to tell Mary to help, but Jesus said Mary had chosen the better part, which should not be taken from her.

His disciples once said to him, "Lord, teach us to pray, as John 11:1 taught his disciples." He said to them, "When you pray, say: Father, may your name be hallowed, may your Kingdom come, give us each day our daily bread, and forgive us our sins—for we, too, forgive everyone who owes us anything—and do not bring us into temptation." And he said to them, "If you go late at night to a friend's to borrow something and your friend will not get up out of mere friendship to give it to you, you can get him up if you keep pounding the door. So I tell you, ask and it will be given you, seek and you will find, knock and it will be opened. No father among you will give his son a snake instead of a fish or a scorpion instead of an egg. If you who are men know enough to give good gifts to your children, you can be sure the Father from heaven will give the Spirit to those who ask him."

Some said of him that he cast out demons by Beezeboul, the 11:14 ruler of the demons. But, he said, "Any kingdom divided against itself will fall; if Satan is divided against himself, how will his kingdom stand? And if I cast out demons by Beezeboul, by whom do your followers cast them out? But if I cast them out by the finger of God, then the Kingdom of God has come upon you." These arguments he supported by others to the same point and by an explanation of why persons from whom he had cast out demons were sometimes seized again (the demon regretted leaving his pleasant house). While he was saying these things, a woman shouted from the crowd, "Blessed is the womb that bore

you and the breasts you sucked." "Rather," he said, "blessed are
those who hear the word of God and keep it." He went on to re-
proach the men of his generation for asking a sign. They should
have seen their sign in the Son of Man, as the men of Nineveh
did in the prophet Jonah, at whose preaching they repented.
They should have come to hear him, as the Queen of the South
came to hear the wisdom of Solomon. For he was greater than
Jonah and greater than Solomon. Therefore, in the judgment,
the examples of the pious heathen (the men of Nineveh and the
Queen of the South) would condemn them.

11:37   While he was speaking, a Pharisee asked him to dine, and he
went in to dinner. The Pharisee marveled that he had not washed
before the meal, but the Lord said to him, "You Pharisees clean
the outside of the cup and platter, but the inside of you is full of
greed and wickedness." And he went on to denounce them for
attending to petty regulations while neglecting to do justice and
love God. At this one of the lawyers complained that he was
attacking them too, so Jesus went on to make the attack explicit,
saying the lawyers loaded men down with heavy burdens that
they themselves would not stir with one of their fingers. They had
taken away the key of wisdom and would neither go in themselves
nor permit others to enter. Their fathers had killed the prophets,
and they built the tombs for them. Therefore the murders of all
righteous men since the beginning of the world would be punished
on this generation.

11:53   When he left, the scribes and Pharisees began to attack him
bitterly and tried to find things he said that could be used against
him. For his part, he warned his disciples against the hypocrisy
of the Pharisees, saying that nothing was hidden which would not
be revealed, and that one should not fear those who could only kill
the body, but rather Him who, after killing the body, could cast
the soul into Hell. Nothing escapes His eye. It notes the cheapest
sparrow, it has numbered all the hair of the head. Therefore, he
will not overlook those who have acknowledged the Son of Man
before men and will be acknowledged by the Son before the
angels. Nor will he overlook those who have denied Jesus and
who will be denied. For while anyone who speaks against the Son

of Man will be forgiven, anyone who blasphemes against the
Holy Spirit will not be forgiven.

When a man from the crowd asked that his brother should be   12:13
ordered to divide an inheritance with him, Jesus answered, "Man,
who made me a judge over you?" And he went on to warn against
avarice, telling of the rich man who spent his day planning how
to store his riches and died that night. "Therefore," he said, "take
no thought for what you shall eat or what you shall wear. Life is
more than food, and the body than clothing. Consider the ravens,
they neither sow nor reap, but God feeds them, and you are more
important than they. Consider the lilies, they neither spin nor
weave, yet I tell you, not even Solomon in all his glory was attired
as one of these. If God so clothe the grass in the field, which
today is and tomorrow is thrown in the stove, how much more
will he clothe you. O men of little faith!" Since God would take
care of them, he went on, they need fear nothing, but should sell
their belongings, give to the poor, and so lay up their treasures
in heaven, where they would be safe. For where their treasure was,
their hearts would be. Thus they would be always ready, like servants waiting for their lord, who might come at any moment,
or like the owner of a house, on the lookout for a thief. For the Son
of Man would come when they did not expect him.

Peter said, "Lord, do you tell this parable for us or for every-   12:41
one?" Jesus replied that it was told for the servant whom the lord
would put in charge of his house. If the lord found him performing his office faithfully, he would be rewarded; if not, punished;
and the more responsible the servant, the severer the punishment,
for much would be demanded of him to whom much was given.

"I have come to set fire to the earth," he cried out. "And how I   12:49
wish it were already kindled! I have to be baptized, and how I am
hampered till that is done! Do you think I came to give peace
on earth? No, I tell you, but division. From now on there will be
five in one house divided, three against two and two against three,
father against son and son against father, mother against daughter and daughter against mother." Saying these things he
reproached the crowd for their inability to discern the signs of the
times. They could foretell the weather but could not see the signs

of God's coming judgment; for if they could, they would hasten to satisfy his demands. Some who were present told him of the Galileans whose blood Pilate had mingled with their sacrifices. He said those men had not been extraordinary sinners; neither had the men recently killed in Jerusalem by the collapse of a tower. Unless the rest repented, they would all similarly perish. The world was like a fig tree that bore no fruit; God was giving it a last chance; unless fruit appeared soon, he would cut it down.

3:10   One Sabbath when he was teaching in a synagogue he saw a woman who was bent over and for eighteen years had not been able to stand up straight. He said to her, "Woman, you are freed from your infirmity." And he put his hands on her, and she straightened up at once and praised God. The head of the synagogue, however, rebuked him for healing on a Sabbath. But Jesus said, "You hypocrites! Doesn't every one of you on the Sabbath loose his ox or his donkey from the manger and take it out to water? And this woman—a daughter of Abraham whom Satan had bound for eighteen years—was it not fitting that she should be loosed on the sabbath day?" Thus he shamed all his opponents, and all the crowd rejoiced in the glorious things he did.

13:22   So he went from city to city and village to village, teaching and making his way to Jerusalem. Once someone asked him, "Lord, are the saved few?" He replied, "Try to get in through the narrow door, for many, I assure you, will try to get in and will not be able. And once the door is closed, you will stand outside and knock in vain. There will be weeping and gnashing of teeth when you see Abraham and Isaac and Jacob and all the prophets in the Kingdom of God, and yourselves cast out. And men will come from east and west and north and south to the banquet in the Kingdom of God, and those who are last will be first, and the first last."

13:31   At this time some of the Pharisees came to him saying, "Leave and go elsewhere, for Herod wants to kill you." But he said to them, "Go tell that fox I shall cast out demons and perform cures today and tomorrow, and on the third day I shall be perfected. But I must go on today and tomorrow and the next day, for it cannot be that a prophet should perish outside Jerusalem.

Jerusalem, Jerusalem, city that kills the prophets and stones those sent to her! How often have I wanted to gather your children as a hen gathers her chicks under her wings, and you were not willing! See, your Temple is abandoned by God. For I tell you, you will not see me until the time comes when you say, 'Blessed is he who comes in the name of the Lord.' "

Once when he went on the Sabbath to eat at the house of a   14:1
ruler of the Pharisees and they were watching him, there was a man sick of dropsy present, and Jesus said to the lawyers and the Pharisees, "Is it lawful to heal on the Sabbath, or not?" But they said nothing, so he healed the man and sent him away, and said to them, "If your son or ox fall into a pit, which of you will not pull him up at once on the Sabbath?" They could not reply to this. He then noticed how the guests picked the best seats and advised them, when invited to a party, to choose the worst ones. (If they chose the best, their host might have to humiliate them by asking them to give way to some more valued guest, but if they chose the worst, he would honor them by asking them to take a better.) Further, he told his host that he should not invite friends or relatives or rich neighbors to his parties, since they might invite him back and pay off the debt, but he should invite the poor, the lame, and the blind, and since they could not repay him, he would be rewarded in the resurrection of the just. Hearing this, one of the other guests said, "He'll be a lucky man who eats in the Kingdom of God." Jesus replied by telling of a man who gave a great dinner and invited many, but all the invited guests refused, so he sent his slaves out into the streets to bring in the poor and the lame and the blind, and these got the dinner.

Great crowds traveled with him, but he said to them, "If a man   14:2
comes to me and does not hate his father and mother and wife and children and brothers and sisters, and himself too, he cannot be my disciple. Whoever does not take up his cross and come after me cannot be my disciple. Just as a man must count the cost before he starts to build, or a king calculate his forces before he goes to war, so one who would be a disciple must renounce all his belongings. For disciples are like salt : if they go bad, they are utterly useless. Whoever has ears, let him be sure to hear."

15:1   The Pharisees and scribes continued to grumble that he ate
with sinners, but he answered their objections with a number of
parables : "What man, having a hundred sheep and losing one of
them, does not leave the ninety-nine and go after the lost one and
rejoice when he finds it? Thus, I tell you, there is more joy in
heaven over one sinner who repents than over ninety-nine
righteous, who do not need repentance. Or what woman having
ten drachmas and losing one of them does not hunt for it everywhere and rejoice when she finds it? Thus the angels of God rejoice
when a sinner repents. There was a man who had two sons, and he
divided his property between them. The younger went off and
squandered his share in loose living. Then, when he was at the
verge of starvation, he went home. His father saw him coming
and ran and fell on his neck and kissed him, but he said, 'Father,
I have sinned against Heaven and against you. I am no longer
worthy to be called your son.' His father, however, ordered the
slaves to dress him in fine garments and make a feast to celebrate
his return. While they were feasting, the elder son came home
from work. He heard the singing, called one of the slaves, and
asked what was going on. When he learned, he was angry and
would not go into the house, so his father came out and pleaded
with him. But he retorted, 'Just see how many years I've slaved
for you and never broken a rule of yours, and you've never given
me anything. But when this son of yours who ate up your property
with whores came back, you gave him a party.' But his father said,
'My child, you are always with me, and everything I have is yours.
We ought to rejoice, because your brother was dead and has come
back to life, was lost and is found.' "

16:1   He also said to his disciples : "A rich man had a steward whom
he intended to discharge. When the steward learned of this, he
called in the debtors of his employer and gave them their old
promissory notes in return for new ones in which the amounts
of the debts were substantially reduced. Thus he made friends
who would take him into their homes after his discharge. And his
master praised him for acting prudently, for the children of this
world in their time are more prudent than the children of light.
And I tell you, make yourselves friends with the wealth of this

unrighteous world, so that when it fails, you may be received into eternal dwellings. No servant can serve two masters; he is sure to hate one and love the other. You cannot serve God and money."

The Pharisees, who loved money, heard all this and mocked 10:14 him, so he said to them : "To men you make yourselves seem just, but God knows your hearts, for what is exalted among men is an abomination in the sight of God. There was a rich man who was clothed in purple and fine linen and lived splendidly, and at his gate lay a beggar named Lazarus, covered with sores. The beggar died and was carried by angels to the bosom of Abraham; the rich man died too and was buried. And when he was being tortured in Hell, he saw Abraham far off with Lazarus in his bosom, and he begged him to send Lazarus to give him even a drop of water, but Abraham told him that was impossible. Then he begged Abraham to send Lazarus to warn his brothers, so that they too would not come into such torture. But Abraham said, 'They have Moses and the prophets, they should listen to them.' 'No, father Abraham,' he said, 'but if someone goes to them from the dead, they will repent.' But Abraham said to him, 'If they will not listen to Moses and the prophets, neither would they be persuaded if one should rise from the dead.' "

In this connection he warned his disciples of the terrible pun- 17:1 ishments awaiting sinners and therefore urged them to correct each other if any should sin, and to forgive each other if any should repent. When they besought him to increase their faith, he told them that if they had the least bit of faith, they could do miracles, and he reminded them that, being slaves of God, they should not think they deserved any special favor merely for doing all they were told. That was their duty.

In one village that he entered on his way to Jerusalem ten 17:11 lepers met him and begged him to have mercy on them. He said to them, "Go show yourselves to the priests." As they went, they were cleansed. One of them, seeing this, came back, praising God, and fell at Jesus' feet, thanking him. This man was a Samaritan. Jesus said, "Where are the nine? Was there none to praise God save this alien?"

17:20   Asked by the Pharisees when the Kingdom of God would come, he answered them : "The coming of the Kingdom of God is not observable. People will not say, 'See, here !' or 'There !' For the Kingdom of God is within you." And he said to his disciples : "The time will come when you shall desire to see one of the days of the Son of Man and shall not see it. People will say to you, 'See, there; see, here.' Do not follow them. For the Son of Man in his day will blaze like lightning from one end of the sky to the other. But first he must suffer many things and be rejected by this generation. As it was in the days of Noah, so it will be in the days of the Son of Man : they ate, they drank, they married and were married, until the day when Noah went into the ark, and the flood came and destroyed all of them. When that day comes, do not pause to take anything with you. He who tries to save his life will lose it. In that night there will be two men in one bed; one will be taken and the other left." They said to him, "Where, Lord?" He said, "Where the body is, there will the vultures gather."

18:1   He also told them a parable, that they should always pray and not lose heart : "There once was a judge who feared neither God nor man, but a widow got her rights from him by pestering him relentlessly. So if God's elect keep at Him, He will vindicate them. But when the Son of Man comes, will he find faith on the earth?"

18:9   He told another parable against some who thought themselves righteous : "Two men went up into the Temple to pray, one a Pharisee and the other a tax collector. The Pharisee prayed, 'O God, I thank you that I am not like the rest of men, avaricious, unjust, adulterers, or even like this tax collector. I fast twice a week, I give tithes of everything I get.' But the tax collector, standing far off, did not even dare to lift his eyes to heaven, but beat his breast, saying, 'O God, be merciful to me, a sinner.' I tell you, he rather than the other went home justified. For whoever exalts himself shall be humbled, and whoever humbles himself shall be exalted."

18:15   People brought little children for him to touch, and the disciples rebuked them, but Jesus called them to him, saying, "Let little children come to me, for of such is the Kingdom of God. I tell you truly, whoever does not receive the Kingdom of God as a child will never enter it."

A ruler asked him, "Good master, what shall I do to inherit 18:18 eternal life?" Jesus said to him, "Why do you call me good? None is good save God alone. You know the commandments; keep those." He said, "I do." Jesus said, "You lack one thing. Sell all you have and give to the poor, and you shall have treasure in heaven; and come, follow me." Hearing this he was grieved, for he was very rich. Jesus said, "How hard it is for people with money to enter the Kingdom of God! It is easier for a camel to go through the eye of a needle than for a rich man to enter the Kingdom of God." His hearers said, "So who can be saved?" He answered, "Things impossible to men are possible to God." Peter said, "We, leaving everything, have followed you." He answered, "I tell you truly there is no one who has left anything for the Kingdom of God who shall not, in this present age, receive many times as much and, in the age to come, eternal life."

Taking the twelve aside he again told them that they were 18:31 about to go up to Jerusalem and that the things written by the prophets about the Son of Man would be fulfilled: he would be handed over to the Gentiles, abused and put to death, and would rise on the third day. But they understood none of these things.

When he came near Jericho, a blind beggar sitting by the road 18:35 cried out, "Jesus, son of David, have mercy on me." Those in the fore of Jesus' party tried to silence him, but he kept repeating his cry, so Jesus cured him, and all the people praised God.

As he was going through Jericho, a man named Zacchaeus— 19:1 a chief tax collector, and rich—was so anxious to see him that he climbed a tree by the route. Jesus, coming to the tree, looked up and said, "Zacchaeus, hurry down, for I must stay in your house today." He hurried down and received him gladly. Everyone grumbled at Jesus' going to stay with a sinner, but Zacchaeus was moved to give half his goods to the poor and to promise to repay fourfold anything he had got by false assessment. Whereupon Jesus told the company, "Salvation has come to this house today, since even this man is a son of Abraham, for the Son of Man came to seek and save what was lost."

19:11   To these things he added a parable, because he was near Jerusalem, and they thought the Kingdom would appear forthwith. So he said : "A noble man went to a far country to receive royal authority and return. He called his slaves and gave them fifty dollars each and told them to do business with this capital until his return. The men of his city hated him and sent an embassy after him, saying, 'We do not want this fellow to rule over us.' When he came back, having received the authority, he called his slaves and rewarded them according to the profits they had made. When one of them merely returned him the original sum, he gave him no reward and gave the money to the one who had made most profit (for to him who has shall be given, and from him who has not, even what he has shall be taken away). And finally, he had his enemies brought and killed before him."

19:28   So saying, he went on towards Jerusalem. When they neared the suburbs on the Mount of Olives, he sent his disciples into a village to find a colt, which they brought him. They threw their cloaks over it, and Jesus rode on it, while others spread their cloaks on the way, and all the company praised God, shouting, "Blessed is the King who comes in the name of the Lord." Some of the Pharisees told Jesus to silence them, but he said, "If these keep silence, the stones will shout." When he saw the city, he wept over it, and prophesied that it would be destroyed because it had not known the things necessary for its peace nor the time when it would be visited.

19:45   Going into the Temple he began to drive out the traders, telling them, "It is written, 'My house will be a house of prayer.' But you have made it a den of thieves." And he taught daily in the Temple. But the high priests, scribes, and leaders of the people sought to kill him, though they could not think of what to do, because all the people hung on his words. One day they asked him by what authority he acted as he did. He countered by asking them whether John's baptism was from heaven or from men—a question they could not answer because they had not accepted John, but all the people were convinced that he had been a prophet, and would stone them if they denied it. Accordingly, they said they did not know, and Jesus replied that if they would not answer his question, he would not answer theirs.

Then he told the people a parable : "A man rented a vineyard 20:9 to farmers who refused to pay the rent. When he sent slaves to get it, they beat them up. So he sent his son, and him they murdered. What will he do? He will come and destroy those farmers and give the vineyard to others. This is the meaning of the prophecy. 'The stone the builders rejected has become the cornerstone.' "

At this the scribes and high priests wanted to lay hands on him, but they feared the people, so they sent some who pretended to be just [i.e., anti-Roman] and who asked him whether or not it was permissible to pay tribute to the emperor. He saw through them, however, and said, "Show me a coin. Whose is the image and the inscription?" "The emperor's". "Very well, then, give him what is his and God what is God's."

Some of the Sadducees, who deny the resurrection, said to him, 20:27 "There were seven brothers, and one married and died childless. Whereupon, according to Mosaic law, his next brother was obligated to marry the widow. That brother too died childless, and so on through all seven. And finally the woman died. In the resurrection, whose wife will she be?" "Those found worthy of resurrection," said Jesus, "neither marry nor are married, for they cannot die thenceforth, for they are equal to angels and are children of God, being children of the resurrection. But Moses too intimated that the dead are raised, where he says, 'The God of Abraham and the God of Isaac and the God of Jacob.' For God is not of the dead but of the living." At this some of the scribes praised him, for they dared to ask him nothing further. He then said to them, "How do they say the Messiah is the son of David, for David himself in the Psalms calls him Lord?" Further, in the hearing of all the people he warned his disciples against the scribes, their love of prestige, hypocrisy, and exploitation of the poor. And when many were making gifts to the Temple, he praised above all the mite given by a poor widow, saying that the others had given from their excess but she from her poverty.

When some were praising the magnificence of the Temple, he 21:5 said the time would come when not one stone should be left on another. Asked when this would be and what sign would show it was about to happen, he said, "Beware lest you be misled. For many will come in my name, saying 'I am,' and 'The time is near.' Do not follow them. When you hear of wars and disturbances, do not be frightened. These things must happen first, but the end will not come immediately." Then he told them that there would be earthquakes, famines, plagues, terrifying signs in the sky, and first of all they themselves would be persecuted, but he would give them wisdom and speech that none of their opponents could withstand. Betrayed by wives and brothers and relatives and friends, some of them would be put to death. They would be hated by everyone, but not one hair of their heads would be lost, and they would gain their lives by their endurance. Further, he said that when they saw Jerusalem surrounded by armies, they should flee to the mountains, for the city would be destroyed and many Jews sold into slavery or killed. There would be further signs in the heavens, and men on earth would be terrified, and then they would see the Son of Man coming in a cloud with power and great glory. The Kingdom of God would follow on these signs are surely as summer follows on the budding of the trees. "I tell you truly," he said, "this generation will not pass away until all this has happened. Heaven and earth will pass away, but my words will not pass away." Therefore, he warned them not to become involved in earthly cares lest that day should take them by surprise. They should always be watchful, praying to escape all these things and to stand before the Son of Man.

22:1 Thus Jesus spent the days teaching in the Temple, while by nights he went out and lodged on the Mount of Olives. Now when Passover was near, Satan entered Judas Iscariot, one of the twelve, and he went to the high priests and magistrates to betray Jesus. They were glad and agreed to give him money. When the day came on which the Passover sacrifice was to be killed, Jesus sent Peter and John into the city where he said they would meet a man carrying a pitcher of water; they should follow him to the house he would enter and there ask the owner where the teacher was to eat the Passover meal. They did so, were shown the room, and prepared the meal.

When the hour came, he and the apostles lay down to dinner, 22:14 and he told them he had greatly desired to eat this Passover with them before his suffering, for he would not eat it again until it was fulfilled in the Kingdom of God. He said much the same thing over the first cup of wine when he blessed it. Then taking bread, he blessed it, broke it, and gave it to them, saying, "This is my body. But see, the hand of my betrayer is with me on the table, for the Son of Man goes, according to what is ordained, but woe to that man by whom he is betrayed." The apostles began to dispute as to which of them should do this, and there was rivalry among them as to which of them was greatest, but Jesus told them that the greatest should be their servant, as he was. "You," he said, "are those who have stayed with me in my temptations, and I make over to you, as my father made over to me, kingship, that you may eat and drink at my table in my Kingdom and sit on twelve thrones, judging the twelves tribes of Israel." "Simon, Simon," he exclaimed. "Satan has demanded to sift all of you like wheat, but for you I have prayed that your faith may not fail, and you, when you have repented, strengthen your brothers." Peter protested his faithfulness, but Jesus said, "I tell you that today before cockcrow you will thrice deny that you know me." And he said to them, "When I sent you out without purse or bag or shoes, did you lack anything?" They said, "Nothing." "But now," he said, "let him who has a purse take it, and likewise a bag, and whoever has no sword, let him sell his cloak and buy one. For I tell you that the prophecy, 'He was reckoned with the transgressors' must be fulfilled in me." They said, "Lord, here are two swords." He replied, "That is enough."

On leaving he went according to his custom to the Mount of 22:39 Olives, and the disciples followed him. When he came there, he said to them, "Pray not to come into temptation," and he went a stone's throw apart from them and knelt and prayed, "Father, if you will, take this cup from me. But not my will, but yours, be done." An angel from heaven appeared to him, strengthening him, and in agony he prayed harder, and his sweat was like drops of blood. When he finished praying, he came to the disciples and found them sleeping from sorrow, and said to them, "What are you doing asleep? Wake up and pray that you come not into temptation." While he was yet speaking, a crowd came up, with the aforesaid Judas leading them. He approached Jesus to kiss him. Jesus said to him, "Judas, do you betray the Son of Man with a kiss?" His followers, seeing what was about to happen, asked if they should use the swords, and one of them struck the slave of the high priest and cut off his right ear, but Jesus touched the ear and healed it, and he merely reproached the high priests, magistrates, and elders who were present for their cowardice in seizing him like a thief, by night, while they had not dared lay hands on him by day in the Temple. "But this," he said, "is your hour, and the realm of darkness."

22:54   He was taken to the house of the high priest. Peter followed from a distance and sat down with them by the fire in the court-yard. Presently he was noticed and thrice accused of being one of Jesus' followers, and thrice he denied it. Just as he was denying it for the third time, a cock crowed, and the Lord turned and looked at him. And Peter remembered what the Lord had said, and he went out and wept bitterly.

22:63   The men who were holding Jesus mocked and abused him during the night. When day came, the senate of the people—the high priests and scribes—assembled. Jesus was brought before it and asked if he were the Messiah. He replied, "If I tell you, you will not believe, and if I ask questions, you will not answer. But from now on the Son of Man will be sitting at the right hand of the Power of God." "You, then, are the Son of God." "You say that I am." They said, "What further need have we of testimony, after what we ourselves have heard from his own mouth?"

23:1   Thereupon they took him to Pilate and accused him of per-verting the people, forbidding the payment of tribute to the emperor, and declaring himself the Messiah, that is, a king. Pilate asked him, "Are you the King of the Jews?" He answered, "So you say." Pilate told the high priests and the crowds that he found nothing actionable in the case, but they insisted that Jesus had been stirring up the people, first in Galilee and then in Judea. Hearing the man was a Galilean, from Herod's territory, Pilate sent him to Herod, who was then in Jerusalem, and Herod was

glad to see him, for he had long wished to, and hoped to see him
do some miracle. Jesus, however, answered him nothing, so Herod
made a mock of him and sent him back in gorgeous clothing to
Pilate. Pilate then told the high priests and rulers that neither
he nor Herod had found any justification for the charges they
brought against Jesus and that he would therefore have him
whipped and release him. But they cried out all together, demanding that Jesus be killed and Barabbas, a murderer then in prison,
be released. Pilate twice again repeated his proposal to release
Jesus but was met always with the same reply. Therefore he
yielded, released the murderer, and gave over Jesus to their will.

As they led him off, a great crowd followed, the women wailing   23:26
for him. He turned around and told them to wail not for him but
for themselves and their children, since the disasters prophesied
of old were to come upon the city. Two criminals were taken out
for execution at the same time, and the three were crucified, with
him in the middle. He said, "Father, forgive them, for they do
not know what they are doing." They divided up his clothes and
cast lots for them, while the people stood around watching and
the rulers mocked him, saying, "He saved others, let him save
himself." The soldiers also mocked him, bringing him vinegar and
challenging him to save himself. There was also a sign over him :
"This is the King of the Jews." And one of the crucified criminals
joined in the mockery, but the other said, "Don't you fear God,
seeing that you are suffering the same punishment? And we
justly, for we're getting back the deserts of what we did. But this
man has done nothing wrong." And he said, "Jesus, remember
me when you come into your kingdom." And Jesus said, "I tell
you truly, today you will be with me in the garden of God."

When it was already noon, the sun was eclipsed, and there was   23:44
darkness over all the earth until three in the afternoon. Also, the
veil of the Temple was torn down the middle. And Jesus uttered
a great cry and said, "Father, into your hands I commit my
spirit." So saying he expired. The officer in charge, seeing what
had happened, glorified God, saying, "Truly, this man was
righteous." And all the crowds who had come for the spectacle,
seeing these happenings, went back beating their breasts. All his

acquaintances and the women who followed him from Galilee and stood a long way off, watching these things.

23:50   Now a pious man named Joseph went to Pilate and asked for the body of Jesus and, taking it down, wrapped it in a linen sheet and put it in a new, rock-cut tomb. This was Friday, and the Sabbath was about to begin. The women from Galilee followed and saw the tomb and saw that his body was put there. Then they returned and prepared perfumes and ointments. They rested on the Sabbath, according to the commandment, but on the first day of the week at the break of dawn they went to the tomb, taking the perfumes they had prepared. They found the stone rolled away from the tomb and, going in, did not find the body. While they were at a loss over this, two men in shining garments suddenly appeared to them. While the women were frightened and bowed their faces to the ground, the men said, "Why do you seek the living among the dead? Remember how he told you, already in Galilee, that the Son of Man must be given into the hands of sinful men and be crucified and rise on the third day." Thereupon they remembered his words, and returning from the tomb they reported these things to the eleven and all the rest, none of whom believed them.

24:13   Then two of the disciples on that same day were going to a village called Emmaüs, some seven miles from Jerusalem. Jesus joined them on the way, but they did not recognize him. They told him of what had happened in Jerusalem, of their disappointed hope that Jesus might be the destined liberator of Israel, and of the reports brought by the women. He rebuked them for their failure to believe the prophets and proved to them from Scripture that the Messiah had to suffer these things. When they reached the village, they persuaded him to stay with them, and when at dinner he broke the bread and gave it to them, they recognized him, and he vanished. Thereupon they returned at once to Jerusalem and found the eleven assembled and those with them, saying, "The Lord is risen indeed and has appeared to Simon." They then told also their adventures on the road and how he was recognized by them when he broke the bread.

24:36   While they were saying these things, he stood among them.

They were terrified and thought they were seeing a ghost, but he said to them, "Why are you frightened? See my hands and my feet, that it is I myself. Feel me and see, for a ghost does not have flesh and bones, as you see I do." When they still disbelieved from joy, he said to them, "Have you anything here to eat?" They gave him a piece of boiled fish, and he took it and ate before them. Then he told them again that everything that had happened was the fulfillment of the ancient prophecies—as he had explained while he was still with them—and he enabled them to understand the Scriptures and said to them: "Thus it is written that the Messiah should suffer and rise from the dead on the third day and that in his name repentance for the remission of sins should be preached to all peoples, beginning from Jerusalem. You are the witnesses of these things. Now behold, I send forth upon you what was promised by my Father. So stay in the city until you shall be clothed with power from on high." Then he led them out to the Mount of Olives, and lifting up his hands he blessed them, and while he was blessing them, he departed from them and was carried up into heaven. Then they returned with great joy to Jerusalem and were continually in the Temple blessing God.

XV. A SUMMARY OF

THE LIFE OF APOLLONIUS OF TYANA

BY PHILOSTRATUS

INTRODUCTORY

FLAVIUS PHILOSTRATUS, author of the following life of Apollonius of Tyana, was a member of a distinguished Greek literary family from the island of Lemnos in the northern Aegean. Born about A.D. 170, he studied at Athens and later went to Rome, where he became a member of the literary circle around Julia Domna, wife of Emperor (193–211) Septimius Severus. She was interested in theosophy, and when a *soi-disant* relative of Damis, the disciple of Apollonius, presented her with a document purporting to be Damis' notebook, she turned it over to Philostratus with the request that he write a life of Apollonius.

Such at least is Philostratus' story. But the *Life of Apollonius* was not published until after Julia Domna's death in 217, and the material Philostratus declares he derived from Damis is so often so obviously his own invention that there is grave doubt whether any document attributed to Damis ever existed at all. Perhaps the best ground for supposing its existence—if that is to be supposed—lies in the great difference between the *Life of Apollonius* and the rest of Philostratus' work, which shows comparatively little interest in theosophy or the East but is mainly concerned with glorification of the Greek tradition. This concern also appears in many details of the *Life of Apollonius* which show Philostratus' hand, but in the basic structure of the book these details are overshadowed and contradicted by the claims made for the sages of India. Apollonius, in spite of his Greek philosophy, must go to them for true wisdom. We have seen above that it was typical of aretalogies to represent the hero as instructed by the wise men of the East; the particular emphasis on this trait in the *Life of Apollonius* is less likely to have come from Philostratus than from his source, and it is fundamental to the work.

Judgment of the question is complicated, however, by the fact that Philostratus certainly used other sources besides the notes (if any) of Damis. He drew on letters and books attributed (often correctly) to Apollonius and on works of Apollonius' contemporaries in which the sage was mentioned. He also had at his disposal some earlier works about Apollonius and the oral traditions that lived on in various cities.

Material from these sources he supplemented from his general literary knowledge and his own imagination. Appealing to the interests of his time, he inserted large sections of fanciful geography and anthropology, much of it from sources of what was already classical antiquity. His Apollonius is entertained by the king of Babylon (long since a ruin), asks favors for the Eretrians (who had been carried into captivity by the Persians five hundred years before his time), and argues with an Indian king about the equally ancient Persian invasion of Greece. All this is peculiar to Philostratus, not part of the aretalogical pattern; in the following outline it has therefore been reduced to a minimum. So have the long insertions of material reflecting the esthetic and rhetorical interests of Philostratus himself and of the "second sophistic" school to which he belonged.

When these execrescences are cut away, the remaining material shows clearly the aretalogical character of the underlying tradition: the *Wunderkind*, the instruction in the wisdom of the East, the disjointed traditions of miracle stories and sayings, the contest with the tyrant, the ascent to heaven, the posthumous appearance to the disciples. In Apollonius' case this tradition certainly shaped not only the stories about him, but his own life. He himself wrote an aretalogical life of Pythagoras, of which one famous passage was a dramatic account of Pythagoras' supposed defiance of the tyrant Phalaris. There is no doubt whatever that he modeled his Pythagoras on himself, and vice versa. Therefore, it is particularly difficult to estimate the historical value of the aretalogical material concerning him.

Moreover, account must be taken of the influence of this and similar traditions not only on Apollonius but also on the world around him. Thus the story of his visit to the Egyptian gymnosophists is customarily taken as an invention to demonstrate the superiority of Neopythagoreanism over Cynicism; the gymnosophists are thought to be idealized representatives of the Cynic school of philosophy. There is no doubt that Philostratus has used the encounter for this purpose and has put a typical Cynic diatribe in the mouth of the leading gymnosophist. But there is also no assurance that the wilds of upper Egypt (which a hundred years later were to furnish an ideal refuge for Christian monasticism) may not have already sheltered one or more communities of pagan ascetics, like the Jewish ones described by Philo and discovered near the Dead Sea. So the story of Apollonius' visit to those regions must be taken with a heaping tablespoonful of salt but must not out of hand be wholly rejected.

Greater credit is due, of course, to those traits in Philostratus' story that accord neither with the aretalogical tradition nor with his own interests. Particularly important among these are the traces of Apollonius' magical practice. That he was famous as a magician is known from many sources. Local traditions about him lived on to medieval times in some of the cities where he had shown his powers, and peculiar objects were pointed out as magical talismans he had set up to protect the cities from earthquakes, hailstorms, mice, scorpions, and the like. Philostratus does his best to contradict this tradition of magical practice, which he regarded as unworthy of a holy man and which was evidently the main charge brought against Apollonius in the trial before Domitian. Therefore Philostratus has surrounded the trial with an elaborate Neopythagorean and Stoic framework to transform Apollonius from a magician defending himself into a philosopher defending civil liberty. And throughout the rest of the book he has been at pains to conceal or to deny the magical overtones of the actions he reports. When Apollonius raises Achilles from the dead, Philostratus makes him explain that he did so by philosophic prayer and not by any sacrifices like those offered by Ulysses (IV.16; such sacrifices were used in necromancy, and necromancy was criminal). Similarly, Apollonius' responsibility for the stoning of the old beggar in Ephesus (IV.10) is told without comment, and nothing is said directly of its legal consequences, though it evidently figured in his trial (VIII.7.ix) and was probably one of the main counts in the indictment against him. (Similarly, the carrying of swords by Jesus' disciples and their wounding the high priest's servant [Luke 22:50 and parallels] do not figure in the Evangelists' report of the trial but cannot have been passed over in the actual proceedings.)

In sum, Philostratus' *Life of Apollonius* shows at least three strata of material: initial reports of the sayings and actions of a man at once magician and philosopher, development of these by folkloristic and especially aretalogical traditions, and reworking of these traditions along with other material by Philostratus himself to suit his notion of what a holy man should be. It is the second of these strata that is of particular relevance to this book and that the following summary attempts to make clear, though the three strata are so often fused together that none can be completely or consistently isolated.

APOLLONIUS WAS OF TYANA [a Greek city in central Asia Minor] and was born into one of the oldest and wealthiest families of the city.

While his mother was pregnant with him, a god appeared to her. She asked him to what she would give birth, and he said, "To me." "And who are you?" she asked. "Proteus," he said, "the Egyptian God."

Later, when she was near the time of his birth, a dream told I.5 her to go into a certain meadow and pick flowers. When she came there, her maids attended to the flowers and were scattered about the meadow, but she fell asleep, lying in the grass. Now there were swans feeding in the meadow, and these, while she slept, formed a circle about her. Then, as a breeze passed over, they raised their wings and cried out all at once. She was startled by their song and gave birth. Just then a thunderbolt that seemed about to fall to earth shot upward into the air and disappeared on high.

Near Tyana there is a spring sacred to Zeus, the god of oaths, I.6 where the water rises cold but bubbling like a boiling kettle. This water is sweet and healthful to men who have not committed perjury but causes perjurers dreadful sufferings. The natives say that Apollonius was the son of this Zeus, but Apollonius referred to himself as the son of his human father (who was also called Apollonius).

When he reached the age for learning, he showed industry and I.7 a good memory and became able to speak classical Greek without any trace of the dialect of his native district. Since he was also conspicuously beautiful, all eyes were turned upon him.

When he was fourteen, his father took him to the city of Tarsus to study under the Phoenician Euthydemus, who was a good teacher of rhetoric. Apollonius· became attached to his teacher but thought the flippant temper of the city unsuited to study and therefore persuaded his father to transfer him and his teacher to the nearby town of Aegae, in which there was not only the quiet helpful to one who would live a philosophic life but also a temple of the healing god Asclepius in which the god himself appeared to men. Here Apollonius studied with representatives of the Platonic, Stoic, and Aristotelian schools of philosophy and even heard the lectures of an Epicurean, but with unspeakable wisdom he took to himself the doctrines of the Pythagoreans. The man who taught him these was an Epicurean in private life and merely parroted Pythagoreanism, but Apollonius decided to live in Pythagorean fashion.

I.8   When his teacher asked at which point he intended to begin, he said, "Where the doctors do, for they, by purging men's bellies, cure some and even prevent others from getting sick." So saying, he gave up eating flesh on the ground that it was unclean and made the mind gross. He lived on dried fruits and vegetables, saying that foods the earth itself provides are pure. He even said that wine was a pure beverage, since it came from a fruit so useful to men, but that it was hostile to the stability of the mind because it troubled the ether in the soul. After this purification of his diet he began to go barefoot and wear only linen clothes, avoiding animal products, and he let his hair grow and lived in the temple. This attracted considerable attention in the district, people came in droves to see him, and Asclepius was reported to have told the priest of his temple that he was happy to cure the sick with Apollonius as a witness.

I.9   Among the sick who had come to the temple in hope of cure was a young Assyrian who suffered from dropsy but nevertheless lived a luxurious life and was continually drunk. Accordingly, Asclepius paid no attention to him and did not visit him even in dreams. When he complained about this, the god appeared to him and advised him to frequent Apollonius, who in turn told him bluntly that the gods give health only to those who take care of themselves and that if he wanted to get better, he should practice austerity. He did so and recovered.

I.10   On another occasion, seeing expensive sacrifices and other offerings being brought to the temple, Apollonius asked why they were being given and was told that the donor had not yet been benefited by the god but was sending these in advance and promising more if his prayer should be granted. His prayer was that one of his eyes, which had gone blind, should be restored. On hearing this Apollonius, as he was accustomed to do when an old man, fixed his eyes on the ground and asked, "What is his name?" When he was told, he said, "It seems to me that this man should not be admitted to the temple, for he comes polluted by something and has been afflicted with his misfortune for some sinister reason. The very fact that he sacrifices at such expense before having received anything from the god shows that he is not merely sacrificing but trying to buy off the penalty of scandalous and savage deeds." That very night Asclepius appeared to the priest of the temple and ordered that the newcomer's gifts should be returned to him and that he should depart. On investigation it turned out that he had lost his eye by seducing his stepdaughter : his wife, catching the two in bed, had stabbed it out with a brooch-pin. After this and other episodes, Apollonius I.11 taught that since the gods are just and know mens' actions, they will reward the good with good things and will punish the evil. Therefore the good man, when he comes before them, should pray merely to be given his due.

While Apollonius was in Aegae, the fame of his beauty came to I.12 the ears of the governor of Cilicia, a violent man and one given to infamous passions. He came to the temple on pretense of being sick and, finding Apollonius walking alone, attempted to seduce him with the philosophical argument that the beautiful should share their beauty and not be grudging of their charms. When Apollonius replied not with counter arguments but with insults, the governor went on to threats, whereupon Apollonius laughed and cried out, "Oh, the day after next!" On the day after next the governor was executed for having intrigued with a local king against the Romans.

Shortly after this, when Apollonius was twenty, his father died, I.13 and he was for some time subject to a guardian, who allowed him to remain in Aegae and continue his study of philosophy. When he came to be his own master, his first concern was to persuade his elder brother to give up the life of dicing, drinking, and similar pleasures to which he was addicted. This he succeeded in doing by first giving him half his own share of the estate, so persuading him of his friendship, and then going on to good advice.

Thereafter he distributed most of the rest of his property to the needy among his relatives and so conciliated them.

As for marriage, he declared Pythagoras' teaching—that a man should have intercourse only with his own wife—was intended by Pythagoras for others, but that he himself would neither marry nor ever have any sexual relationships.

I.14   Asked why, although he spoke so well, he did not write, he replied, "Because I have not yet kept silence." And from then on he saw fit to cease speaking. But his eyes and mind went on storing his memory, which remained vigorous even till his hundredth year, so that he used to sing a hymn of his own composition to Memory, in which he said that all things are withered by time, but time itself is ageless and deathless in Memory.

During the period of his silence he was not unpleasant company; his eyes and his hand and the nod of his head responded to conversation. Nor was he unsmiling and morose; he retained his fondness for companionship and his cheerfulness. This way of life that he practiced for five whole years was, he later said, the most difficult of any he had undertaken, for he had to refrain from saying what he had to say.

I.15   He spent the years of silence traveling in southern Asia Minor and in spite of his silence exercised considerable moral influence. His mere appearance and gestures were often enough to quell public disturbances that had arisen about trivial matters. On one occasion he even put a stop to a food riot, when the populace were about to burn a governor alive because the rich of the district had bought up all the grain and were selling it abroad, and he forced the rich to release the grain for local sale. At this time, though he did not speak, he wrote the following note: "Apollonius to the grain merchants. Earth is the mother of all, for she is just, but you, being unjust, have acted as if she were the mother of yourselves alone. Unless you desist, I shall not let you remain upon her."

I.16   After his period of silence, he visited the great city Antioch, in north Syria, where he was shocked by the general neglect of philosophy and declared that the Greeks there had become barbarians. He lived a life apart in the temples of the shrine of Apollo in the suburb of Daphne.

During this period the pattern of his daily life was as follows : at sunrise he privately performed certain ceremonies that he revealed only to those disciplined by four years of silence. Thereafter, if he were in a Greek city and the sacred rites of the city's gods were familiar, he would call together the priests and philosophize concerning the gods, correcting them if they had changed anything of the prescribed rituals. If the local rites were non-Greek and peculiar, he learned who had established them and on what occasions, and made suggestions if he thought of any improvements. After this he turned to his followers and told them to ask such questions as they wished. For he said that philosophers of his school should converse at dawn with the gods, thereafter about the gods, and then about human affairs. When he had answered the questions of his followers, finally he went on to his public lecture, this not before noon but just when the day stood still. When he had lectured as long as he thought sufficient, he would be anointed and rubbed and plunge into cold water, for he said hot baths aged men prematurely, and when the government punished the people of Antioch by closing them, he said, "Since you are bad, the emperor has granted you longer lives." Again, when the people of Ephesus wanted to stone their governor because the baths were not heated, he said, "You blame the governor because you bathe badly, but I blame you because you bathe."

He practiced a form of speech not dithyrambic nor burdened I.17 with poetic terms and archaisms, nor did he indulge in subtleties nor speak for any great length of time nor practice irony or methodical arguments, but his replies were like oracular responses. "I know," he would say, and "It seems to me" and "It should be known." His maxims were short and to the point and had the cadence of royal decrees. When a certain quibbler asked him why he did not teach by questioning, he replied, "When I was a youth, I asked questions; now it is fitting for me not to question but to teach what I have learned." The wise man, he said, should teach "as a lawgiver, for it is the lawgiver's duty to lay down as rules

for the many those principles of which he is himself persuaded."
By this sort of teaching in Antioch he made followers of men
who had hitherto been indifferent to learning.

I.18   After this he decided to travel further afield, since he was
anxious to see Brahmans in India and the Magi in Babylonia and
Susa. He announced his decision to his seven disciples, and when
they tried to dissuade him, he said, "I have taken counsel with
the gods and have declared the decision. I was testing you to see
if you had sufficient strength to accompany me. Since you do not,
stay here and philosophize, but I must go where wisdom and
divinity lead me." So saying he set out from Antioch with two
slaves whom he had inherited from his father's estate, one of them
a stenographer, the other a calligrapher.

I.19   When he came to the ancient city of Nineveh, he found a new
follower, one Damis, of that city, who was willing to accompany
him in his journey. "Let us go, Apollonius," he said, "you following God, and I you. And indeed you may find me of considerable
worth. Even if I know nothing else, I have been to Babylon; I
know the cities and villages along the route and even the languages of the natives. Although there are a number of different
ones, I know them all." "And I, my friend," said Apollonius,
"understand all languages, though I have never learned a one.
But this is no marvel, for I know also what men do not say." The
Assyrian, when he heard this, worshiped him, thinking him a
supernatural being, and remained with him, increasing in wisdom
and memorizing what he could learn. Moreover, he kept a notebook in which he put down what he heard and saw, not in good
literary form but accurately. He tried to record in it even
Apollonius' passing and careless remarks, so that nothing about
him should be unknown. When a critic reproached him with col-
lecting trivialities and compared him to the dogs that feed on
the scraps fallen from the table, he answered, "If the table be
that of the gods, there must be servants who take care that even
the scraps of ambrosia be not lost."

I.20   Accompanied by Damis, Apollonius set off into Mesopotamia.
To the customs agent at the Roman frontier he stated that he
had nothing to declare except his virtues. While traveling through

the territory inhabited by Arabian tribes he learned from them
to understand the language of animals, a skill they themselves
acquire by eating either the hearts or the livers of snakes. When I.21
he reached the Babylonian frontier, his dried-up appearance
frightened the governor of the frontier post into fits. Here Apollonius at first refused to answer questions as to who he was or
where he came from, declaring that all the earth was his and he
could travel it as he pleased. When the governor threatened torture, he replied with taunts, and these so daunted the governor
that he repeated more politely his requests for information, and
Apollonius condescended to reply. Learning his identity the
governor supplied him with food and sent him on to the king.

On arriving at Babylon he refused to perform the prostration I.27
before the image of the king, which was required for admission
to the city, and on being brought before the authorities he de- I.28
clared that he had come to teach the king to practice virtue. This I.29
being announced, the king received him with honor, and he, for I.30
his part, showed his indifference to worldly things by paying no
attention to the wonders of the palace and conspicuously discussing Greek literature while he was being shown in. The king I.31
invited him to join in the sacrifice of a white horse, but he refused
to participate in the bloody rite and consented only to sacrifice
a handful of frankincense, with the prayer, "O Sun, send me over
so much of the earth as seems good to you and to me, and may I
make the acquaintance of good men but learn nothing of evil
ones, nor they of me." So saying he threw the incense into the
fire, watching how the smoke rose and curled and observing the
fire to see if the omen were favorable.

He stayed for some time at Babylon, not only displaying his I.26
virtues at the royal court but also visiting the Magi. He forbade
Damis to accompany him on these visits, which took place at
midday and midnight, and when Damis asked about the Magi,
he replied merely, "They are wise, but not about all things." Of I.34
the incidents of his stay at court we are told that he refused to
accept any gift from the king but did use his influence to secure I.35
favors for the descendants of the Greeks who had been carried
off by the Persians from the city of Eretria, five hundred years

I.36 before, and settled in the Mesopotamian plain. By arguing that to
live impotent and subject to lust would be a fate worse than death
he persuaded the king to pardon a eunuch who had been caught

I.37 lying with one of the royal concubines. He refused to participate
in the royal hunting parties. He advised the king that the most
secure policy of government was to honor many and trust few.
He persuaded the king to yield to the Romans in a border dispute
about two villages, arguing that even great issues were not worth

I.38 a war. He pooh-poohed the engineering skill shown in building a
tunnel under a river and in the fortification of Ecbatana. When
Ecbatana was referred to as the dwelling place of the gods, he
said, "The gods have no dwelling place whatever, and whether
this city is a dwelling place of men, I do not know. The
Lacedaemonians, O king, dwell in a city without fortifications."
He reproached the king for spending two days in hearing the
pleadings for a single law suit and advised him to put the royal

I.40 treasure back in circulation by spending it. At length he saw fit
to go on to India and thereupon requested the king to reward the
Magi for their kindness to him and consented to accept a guide,
camels, and provisions for himself, Damis, and his slaves. These
the king was happy to provide.

II.4   The trip to India was uneventful, save for one night's journey
when an evil spirit appeared to them. Apollonius recognized it
and drove it away by abusing it. Otherwise the time was passed in

II.5 the necessities of travel and in philosophic discourse. Apollonius
used the occasion of their crossing the Caucasus to prove that one
got no better knowledge of the gods by coming nearer the
heavens and to draw the conclusion that exact astronomical observations were useless for theology, by which he meant the
understanding of divine providence, of man's duties toward the

II.14 gods, and of the nature of the virtues. The sight of elephants
II.15 forming a line to cross a river was the occasion of a long discourse
II.7 proving the intelligence and natural affection of animals. The
Easterners' use of wine made from dates occasioned a lecture on
the reason for abstinence from wine—not because it comes from
the vine but because it intoxicates. (Therefore other intoxicants
are equally to be avoided. "However," said Apollonius, "I do not

wish to dissuade you, Damis, from drinking and would even permit you to eat meat, for I see that your abstinence from these
things leads to no end, whereas mine leads toward that philosophic goal I have pursued since childhood.")

At Taxila, the first large Indian city they reached, they were II.23
graciously received by the king, who himself had been a pupil of
the Indian philosophers. Apollonius was delighted to find a king II.26
who lived in modest quarters with few attendants, valued his
wealth as a means of helping his friends and buying protection
from the barbarians, drank no more wine than he poured out in
libations, was a vegetarian, exercised in Greek fashion, and II.27
limited his bath to a cold plunge. Best of all, these philosophic
achievements were crowned by a knowledge of Greek! This enabled him to discuss philosophical questions with Apollonius
directly, without the medium of an interpreter. In the course of
the discussions the king told the story of his life and training, while II.30
Apollonius contributed a long discourse directed against the use II.36
of wine or drugs to induce sleep. Among the evidence on which II.37
he laid most weight was the fact that dreams seen in sleep induced
by wine or drugs are useless for divination. He also helped the II.39
king to decide a difficult case : a treasure had been found in a
recently purchased field and was claimed both by the new purchaser and by the previous owner. Apollonius suggested that if
the religious observances of the two men were investigated, it
would be found that the previous owner had neglected to sacrifice
to the gods. This would explain why they had not revealed the
treasure to him but had given it to the purchaser, who would be
found to be devout. The investigation was made and confirmed
Apollonius' expectations, so the king decided the case according
to the will of the gods.

After some days the king provided Apollonius with fresh camels, II.40
a new guide, and a letter of introduction to the Brahmans, and
sent him and his party on their way, giving them provisions and
linen garments (which later Apollonius accepted because they
were like the cloaks worn by the ancient Athenians). The king
also offered them gold and precious stones. Apollonius, according
to his custom, refused the gold but took one of the stones, saying,

"O jewel, how opportunely have I found you, and how providentially!"—this, no doubt, because he perceived in it some secret and divine power. His followers also refused the gold but helped themselves to handfuls of the jewels, that on returning to their own land they might dedicate them to their gods.

II.43
III.4
III.5

After passing the monument marking the place where Alexander turned back, and crossing the mountain range that runs down the center of India, they came into the upper valley of the Ganges, where apparently was located the spur of rock on which

III.12 the Brahmans lived. Near this was a village where everyone spoke Greek, and here a messenger from the sages met them, addressed them by name, and ordered Apollonius to leave his companions

III.13 there and come on alone. This he did and with the messenger went up the mountain into the cloud with which the sages con-

III.16 ceal their dwelling. He was introduced to their assembly, acknowledged their superiority in wisdom, and was given clear proof of it. Not only was he told the content of the letter that he brought and also a slip of the pen that it contained, but also he was given

III.23 a complete account of his family and past life and was told—what he already knew—that in his last previous incarnation he had been the captain of an Egyptian merchant ship (an employ-

III.24 ment he in his present life considered disgraceful). The sages rebuked his pride in what he thought to have been the best achievement of that incarnation—his refusal on one occasion to

III.25 betray the ship to pirates. They pointed out that, contrary to Greek opinion, the mere avoidance of vice cannot be considered a virtue : one should not praise a slave—nor a Roman governor—

III.18 merely because he does not steal. Their own virtues were positive powers, achieved by philosophic training that began, for them, with the goal of Greek philosophy, self-knowledge. Knowing themselves to be good men they knew themselves to be gods, and knowing themselves to be gods they learned to exercise their divine powers.

III.50
III.34

With these divinities Apollonius passed four months, learning many things. Shortly after his arrival Damis was permitted to join him and recorded what he heard of the sages' teaching, as

III.25 well as what Apollonius told about his previous stay. Sometimes

the sages taught symbolically, by criticizing Greek myths, declaring it scandalous that the tyrant Minos should have been made one of the judges of the dead, or praising the hero Tantalus because he had sought to share with his friends the immortality given him by the gods. Not only did they deny that Tantalus had been punished by the gods, but they had a statue of him parting his cloak and holding forth a flask in which an unmixed beverage foamed but did not overflow. From this flask it was their custom to drink each night before retiring; every one stooped down and III.32 took his turn, for the stream flowed up plenteously, like a spring, and the drink was a draught of friendship. At other times the sages III.27 taught by example, as when a king came to inquire of them about affairs of state and they tacitly showed Apollonius how kings should be kept in their places. (With this king, who was an III.31 arrogant ass, Apollonius had a rather prickly discussion in which he refuted the charge that the Greeks had been subject to Xerxes, the Persian despot, and maintained that Xerxes would have been more fortunate had he not fled from Greece but stayed and fallen bravely, for then the Greek artists and poets would have given him a glorious immortality. Apollonius' arguments reduced the III.32 king to tears, and he excused his previous statements by saying that he had been misled by Egyptians, who frequently came to India and always spoke badly of the Greeks.) On yet other occa- III.34 sions the sages taught directly—that the universe was composed not only of earth, air, fire, and water but also of a fifth element, the ether, which was the breath of divine beings; that by consequence the universe was alive, and natural phenomena like droughts, which seemed to happen accidentally, were really expressions of its will, punishing the wicked; that the gods of myth- III.35 ology were minor divinities, the crew, so to speak, of this great ship of which the maker and steersman was the supreme being. Finally, the sages also taught by demonstrations of their power. III.39 From all the country round afflicted persons came to them for healing : the blind received their sight, the paralyzed the use of their limbs, the lame walked, and remedies were prescribed for recurrent afflictions. Among those who came was a mother whose III.38 son had for two years been possessed by a devil that drove him into desert places and, speaking through him but with its own voice (which was not like his), had threatened to kill him by throwing him down some steep place if his mother appealed to the sages. She was given a letter to the demon, ordering him to vacate her son.

III.41 Beside all this teaching, which Damis reported, there were some things the sages taught to Apollonius in secret. Damis, being excluded from this instruction, could report only its general content : astrology, divination, rules for sacrifice, and incantations. Apollonius himself later wrote books on astrology and on sacrifices. Damis says also that the sages gave Apollonius seven rings named after the seven planets [Moon, Mercury, Venus, Sun, Mars, Jupiter, Saturn], and Apollonius wore a different one each day,

III.42 according to the names of the days of the week. Divination was of especial interest to Apollonius, and the sages declared that it deified those who practiced it and was also of the greatest benefit

III.44 to mankind, especially because it was the basis of the science of medicine, since only supernatural foreknowledge could have taught men that certain drugs would counteract certain diseases.

III.45– After four months of such learning—interspersed with inci-
49 dental information about griffins, phoenixes, pygmies, magnets,
III.50 and other marvels of nature—Apollonius left the Brahmans, being
III.58 sent on by them to the Indian Ocean, whence he returned by ship to Babylon and thence by land to Antioch. Since the Antiochenes took no more notice of him now than they did before, he soon went on by way of Cyprus to the western coast of Asia Minor,

IV.1 where he was more successful in attracting attention. His success was due in part to his eloquence, impressive appearance, and peculiar costume and way of life, in part to the support given him by the oracles of Apollo and Asclepius along the Asia Minor coast, who sent on to him some of the men who came to them for healing or advice, and so gave divine sanction to his teaching. Not only did he get a hearing from the men of wealth and learning who customarily took an interest in philosophy, but also he drew even the artisans away from their work. Various cities sent delegations to him to confer upon him municipal honors or to ask him about civic regulations or the establishment of altars or images, and he was kept busy sending letters to some and visiting others.

His advice to the cities was shaped by the characteristics of his own life. He recognized that the extremes of his own philosophic practice were not for the common man, and he made no attempt to impose general vegetarianism or celibacy or abstinence from wine. But he demanded puritanical reforms of IV.2 city life and lost no opportunity to denounce drinking, dancing, pantomimes, and noisy public amusements, especially if they carried with them any suggestion of sexual license. This puritanism IV.21 he represented as a return to the original Greek way of life, and he urged the cities to preserve their peculiarly Greek civic traditions, which separated them both from their Roman rulers and from the non-Greek population of the surrounding countryside. He sharply rebuked the Ionian assembly because some of its mem- IV.5 bers bore Latin names, and he expelled from the group of his IV.12 followers a young man who claimed Trojan ancestry. Perhaps in IV.8 connection with this revival of Greek civic feeling he tried to strengthen the cities internally by praising both concord and party spirit. The curse of the Greek city-states had always been factionalism, and from time immemorial their factionalism had been aggravated by the constant conflict of interest between the rich and the poor. Apollonius therefore taught that factions should contend with one another only in their efforts to benefit the city, and he tried to diminish the conflict between rich and poor by urging the rich to use their wealth for the public's benefit.

This teaching was presented not merely as counsels of pru- IV.3 dence but as the expression of the will of the gods, and Apollonius' knowledge of the will of the gods was demonstrated not only by his own austerity and peculiar observances but also by his miracles. On one occasion, in the city of Ephesus, he was discoursing on the duty of all men in general to help each other and of the rich especially to share their wealth by supporting the poor. Suddenly a sparrow flew up, chirping, and thereupon all the birds that had been sitting silent in the trees around flew away. "See," said Apollonius, "in such-and-such a street a boy carrying a bowl full of barley slipped and spilled it. Then he went off, leav-

ing much of it scattered about. So this sparrow came as a messenger to tell the others of the find and to invite them to share in
the feast." At this most of his hearers ran off to see if his statements were true. When they returned full of astonishment, he
went on to use the example for his argument.

IV.10   On another occasion, when a pestilence ravaged Ephesus and
the population appealed to him for help, he led them to the
theater where, under the statue of Asclepius, they found an old
beggar whom Apollonius ordered them to stone. The old man
pleaded for mercy, and the crowd was divided, but Apollonius
insisted. Some of the crowd began to throw stones and hit the
beggar. He had hitherto kept his eyelids closed as if blind. Now,
suddenly, he looked at them with eyes full of fire. Thereupon the
Ephesians realized he was a demon and stoned him to death.
When they had done, Apollonius ordered them to remove the
stones. Beneath them they found not a man but a creature in the
form of a dog and the size of a great lion, beaten to a pulp by their
stones. Therefore the statue of the god who averts evil (Hercules)
has been set up at the spot where the monster was stoned.

IV.11   After this miracle Apollonius left Ephesus and went north to
Pergamum, where there was a great temple of Asclepius, the god
with whom he had been associated at the beginning of his career
and whose oracles had sanctioned his work in Asia Minor. Here
he advised the suppliants of the god as to how they might obtain
favorable dreams, and he himself healed many of them. Thence
he went on to Troy, where, as part of his revival of the Greek
tradition, he visited the tombs of the Greek heroes, made long
speeches from them, performed many bloodless and pure rites, and
finally ordered his companions to go back to the ship and
announced his intention of spending the night on the barrow in
which Achilles was buried. His companions tried to frighten him,
for Achilles was said to be terrible when he appeared (of this the
people living in Troy were convinced), but Apollonius said he
knew from Homer that Achilles was a friendly soul, terrible only
to the Trojans, and in any event, if Achilles should kill him, he
IV.12 would lie with the heroes fallen at Troy. Next morning when he
came down to the ship, he said nothing about his experiences

during the night but sent away the young man of Trojan
ancestry and said that Achilles had told him to do so.

From Troy they went on across the Aegean, accompanied by IV.13
many people who wished to travel with Apollonius because the
autumn was now at hand and they thought him capable of pre-
venting storms. They sailed first to the mainland opposite the
island of Lesbos, for Apollonius said Achilles had told him that
the hero Palamedes, another of the Greeks who had sailed against
Troy, was buried there and that a statue of him was to be found
buried beside his tomb. Tomb and statue were found as predicted,
and Apollonius erected the statue, consecrated an area around it
large enough to hold some ten people in a funerary meal, and
prayed the divine Palamedes—who had been unjustly put to
death by the Greeks—to forget his wrath against them and grant
that they might become many and wise.

Hence the company set out across the Aegean Sea towards IV.15
mainland Greece. Most of Apollonius' companions questioned
him about the islands they passed, shipbuilding, sailing, and
similar matters, but Damis cut short some questioners and would
not permit others even to begin. When Apollonius asked him the
reason for his behavior, he explained that he was impatient to
learn what had happened during the night on the barrow of
Achilles. Apollonius therefore gave a full account :

"It was not by any bloody sacrifice, like that of Ulysses, that I IV.16
was enabled to speak with Achilles, but by such prayers as the
Indians say should be offered to heroes. 'O Achilles,' I prayed,
'men say you are dead, but I do not agree, nor did Pythagoras.
If we are right, show us your form, and use me as a witness to
prove that you still live.' At this the earth quaked, and a youth
about seven feet tall and wearing a Thessalian cloak emerged,
terrible but brilliant in appearance. His beauty was indescribable,
even Homer's praise of it seemed mere slander. As I watched, he
increased in size until he was about eighteen feet tall, and his
beauty increased with his size. He told me he had never cut his
hair but had kept it inviolate for the river Spercheus, that was
the first river he had consulted as an oracle. His cheeks had the
first down of a beard. He spoke to me, saying he was glad I had

come, for he had long needed such a man. The Thessalians had been neglecting their sacrifices to him, and he did not wish to destroy them by his wrath. Therefore he would send me to warn their assembly not to be found worse than the Trojans, who, although they lost so many men to him, still sacrifice to him and offer him their first fruits and beseech him to turn from his wrath, though he will not do so. I promised to go as his envoy in order to save the Thessalians, and I besought him to answer some of my questions about the Trojan war. He consented to answer five. I asked first whether he had been buried as the poets say. 'I lie here,' he answered, 'as was most pleasant to me and to Patroclus, for we came together as mere youths, and a single golden jar holds the remains of us both, as if we were one. The Muses have never lamented at our tomb, but the goddesses of the sea still visit it.' Next I asked if Polyxena had been killed over his tomb, and he said she had, but not by the Greeks—she killed herself. My third question was whether Helen had really been taken to Troy; he said the Greeks had long believed she was there, and when they learned she was really in Egypt, they continued their efforts to take Troy so as not to go away in disgrace. As a fourth question I said I marveled that Greece had produced at a single time so many great men as Homer brought together against Troy, but Achilles replied that even the barbarians then were almost the equals of the Greeks; that time was the flowering of the earth. Finally I asked why Homer did not mention Palamedes; he replied that Homer did not wish to refer to the fault of Ulysses, who had caused Palamedes' death, but that I should care for the tomb of Palamedes and set up his statue, which was fallen. He told me where to find the tomb and also warned me against the youth of Trojan ancestry whom I have since sent away. Then with a flash of lightning he departed, for already the cocks were beginning to crow."

IV.17　　When they landed at the port of Athens and walked up to the city, they met many students of philosophy coming down to the sea, some of them taking the sun, others reading or rehearsing their speeches or arguing. None of them passed by Apollonius. All turned to welcome him, and some even claimed to have been

on the point of setting out to Asia Minor to visit him there. He
in return greeted them all. But when he presented himself for   IV.18
initiation in the Eleusinian mysteries, that were then being celebrated, the hierophant refused to initiate him, declaring him a
magician and impure. "But my chief fault," said Apollonius, "is
to have presented myself for initiation to a man who knows less
about the mysteries than I do." This daring won the crowd over
to his side, and the hierophant thereupon offered to initiate him,
but Apollonius refused, saying he would be initiated at a later
time and by another man, whom he named. Four years later this
man became, in fact, the successor of the hierophant and did
initiate Apollonius.

As a consequence of this incident, Apollonius began his lectures   IV.19
at Athens with a discourse on religious rites, explaining—as he
later did in his book on the subject—the times and ways appropriate for the worship of each god. Thus he tacitly refuted the
charges of the hierophant, for who could think impure a man
who thus philosophized? During one of these lectures a young   IV.20
debauché who happened into the audience laughed at his teaching. Looking at him, Apollonius said, "It is not you who mis-
behave thus, but the demon who compels you without your knowing it." And, in fact, though nobody had realized it, the young
man had long been possessed by a demon, for he used to laugh
when nobody else did, and then suddenly he would weep without cause, and he talked and sang to himself. In all this, as in his
excesses, he had been merely the instrument of the demon, who
now uttered through him such cries as one hears from men being
burned or tortured, and swore to leave him and never attack any
other man. Apollonius rebuked the demon as a master would a
dishonest slave and commanded him to prove that he had left
the youth by throwing down a statue that stood nearby. When
the statue first tottered, then fell, the applause of the crowd was
indescribable. The young man, as if awaking, rubbed his eyes and
was embarrassed to find everybody looking at him. From then on
he was again himself and no longer lived licentiously, but turned
to philosophy and became a follower of Apollonius.

Such displays of power gave credit to Apollonius' moral and   IV.21

religious teaching, in which he undertook to reform the abuses of the Athenians. He rebuked them particularly for celebrating the festivals of Dionysus with obscene dances and luxurious garments
IV.22 such as, he said, the old Athenians never wore, and for using condemned criminals for gladiatorial games in the theater below the
IV.23 Acropolis. He also went as envoy for Achilles to the Thessalians and persuaded them to resume their sacrifices to the hero. On the way he visited the site of the battle of Thermopylae and
IV.24 praised the men who had fallen there. Later he visited the major Greek oracles and corrected the rites practiced at their shrines. He prophesied that the Isthmus of Corinth would be "cut, or rather, not cut," which happened later, when Nero began but did not complete a canal through it.
IV.25   In Corinth Apollonius won the admiration of a philosopher named Demetrius, of the Cynic school. Demetrius urged his own followers to go to Apollonius. One of them was a young man named Menippus, who had an extraordinarily beautiful body and was thought to be the lover of a beautiful and wealthy foreign lady. This lady was really a demon in disguise. Apollonius, when he saw Menippus, realized what was happening and attempted to warn him, but Menippus would not listen and went forward with his plan to marry his beloved. Therefore Apollonius went to the marriage feast that was provided by the bride and denounced her. At his denunciation the vessels of gold and silver turned light as air and vanished before the eyes of the guests, the cooks and waiters disappeared, and the demon was forced to confess her true nature and her intention, which had been to eat Menippus after their marriage. This story became the most famous of all those about Apollonius.
IV.26   At this same period he had a difference with Bassus of Corinth, who claimed to be a wise man and had an unbridled tongue. Apollonius both in lectures and in open letters attacked him as a parricide, and his attacks were generally believed, for it was thought that such a man as he would not stoop to slander nor say what was not so.
IV.27   On his way from Corinth to Olympia he was met by a delegation from Sparta, asking him to visit their city. The men of the

delegation were so luxurious and effeminate that he sent back a message to the Spartans which shocked them into restoring their ancient austerity.

Looking at the famous statue of Zeus in Olympia he said, "Hail, IV.28 O good Zeus, who art so good that thou dost share thine own nature with men." Here too he explained the allegorical signific- ance of the details of the ancient statues and praised the care IV.29 with which the rites were conducted by those in charge. A young IV.30 rhetorician who asked him to attend the reading of an encomium on Zeus got a sharp rebuke for attempting a subject too great for human powers, and the crowds at the festival were harangued on IV.31 the various virtues. These discourses so pleased the now reformed Spartans that they were ready to worship him, but from this Apollonius dissuaded them for fear of envy.

He did, however, consent this time to visit Sparta, and while there he gave a number of laconic answers to the questions the Spartans asked him : How should the gods be served? "As lords." How should heroes be served? "As fathers." How should men be served? "That is not a Spartan question." What did he think of the Spartan laws? "They are the best of teachers, and the teachers will be famous if the pupils are not lazy." What is your advice about courage? "Show it." This last advice he soon had IV.33 occasion to interpret in connection with a specific incident, for a letter came from the emperor accusing the Spartans of taking ad- vantage of their liberty. They were divided as to how they should reply, some holding that they should take a lofty tone, others that they should try to placate the emperor. In this situation Apollonius' advice was, "Palamedes discovered writing not only that men should write but also that they should know what should not be written." In private matters he was no less prudent : one IV.32 young Spartan had developed a shipping business and was neg- lecting public affairs. Some of his compatriots therefore brought suit against him as an offender against the national customs. Apollonius, meeting him when he was worried about the suit, persuaded him that shipmen were a godless, mercenary lot and that it was a disgrace for a citizen of Sparta to concern himself with business. These arguments reduced the young man to tears;

he sold his ships, and Apollonius succeeded in getting the case against him dismissed.

IV.34 After spending the winter in Sparta Apollonius prepared to set out for Rome, but he then dreamed that a very large and elderly lady embraced him and besought him to visit her before sailing to Italy. She said she was the nurse of Zeus, and she wore a wreath containing all the products of earth and sea. Apollonius took this as an indication that he must visit Crete, which was said to be the birthplace of Zeus, and accordingly he sailed thither as soon as he could find a ship large enough to hold his "community"—for so he called his companions and their slaves. At Cnossus he would not visit the Labyrinth which is shown to tourists there, but he permitted his companions to visit the place, which bears witness to the crime of Minos. He himself visited the shrine of Gortyna and Mount Ida and other shrines of the island. Here on one occasion when he was lecturing, there was an earthquake which he explained by saying that the sea had given birth to land. A few days later travelers arrived and reported that just at that time an island had risen from the sea between Crete and Thera.

IV.35 From Crete Apollonius went on to Rome, where Nero suspected philosophers of being magicians in disguise, was extremely unfriendly to them, and had thrown a number into prison.

IV.36 Others had left the city, and one of these, Philolaus, attempted to dissuade Apollonius from visiting it, but Apollonius declared that the spectacle of an emperor making himself contemptible was so fine an occasion for philosophic reflections that it should

IV.37 not be missed. Philolaus' warnings, however, frightened away many of Apollonius' companions; from thirty-four they were

IV.38 reduced to eight, among whom Damis and Menippus were the most prominent. With these Apollonius went forward to the city, partly, he said, to exercise the virtue of bravery, partly to have a closer view of that strange monster the tyrant, which, although it inhabits the hearts of cities, is more savage than any beast of the mountains or forests.

IV.39 When they came to the gates of Rome, the wardens asked them no questions, although their peculiar dress attracted considerable

attention, for it resembled priestly garments and was not at all
like that of wandering beggars. They put up at an inn near the
gates and were having supper when a drunken singer came up
and sang them some of the compositions of Nero. They listened
without enthusiasm, and he thereupon accused them of *lèse
majesté,* but the matter ended when Apollonius paid him for his
performance and told him to go sacrifice to the Muses of Nero.
Next day Apollonius was called before one of the consuls and IV.40
questioned about his costume and the content of his teaching.
He explained the costume as determined by his concern for
purity, which dictated the avoidance of products derived from
mortal animals. As for his wisdom, he said it was an inspiration
that taught how men should sacrifice and pray to the gods. He
himself prayed, he said, that justice might be done, that the laws
might not be broken, that the wise might be poor and the rest of
mankind rich but honest; and he summed up all these requests in
the single prayer that the gods might give him what he deserved.
The consul was so much impressed by these answers that he gave
Apollonius permission to visit all the temples, live in such as he
chose, and reform the rituals as he saw fit. Moreover, he promised
to write to the priests in charge, ordering them to accept both
Apollonius and his reforms. Apollonius took advantage of this
permission to live now in one temple, now in another, so as to
pay his respects to all the gods. His preaching in Rome produced IV.41
a revival of religious observance and was particularly popular
because he did not reserve it for either rich or poor, but made it
public and talked with all who came to him.

Presently, however, Demetrius the Cynic, who in Corinth had IV.42
become a follower of Apollonius, came to Rome and there made
himself conspicuous by attacking the Romans for their luxury
and especially their baths—this at a time when Nero was trying
to make himself popular by building new and more luxurious
baths. The government, therefore, banished Demetrius from
Rome and had Apollonius watched as suspect of sedition. The IV.43
suspicion was increased when he interpreted an ominous clap of
thunder during an eclipse as indicating that "something great
will and will not occur." And shortly after this prophecy, Nero

IV.44 narrowly escaped being struck by a thunderbolt. Next came an epidemic of sore throat, and the temples were full of people supplicating the gods because Nero's voice was affected. Apollonius denounced the folly of the crowd but made no attack on anyone in particular and even rebuked Menippus when he spoke bitterly of what was going on, urging him to pardon the gods if they were amused by the antics of buffoons. When this saying was reported to the authorities, Apollonius was charged with impiety towards Nero. When the trial came, however, and the document containing the charge was presented to the court, it was found to be blank. This persuaded the judge that he was dealing with a supernatural being, so he questioned Apollonius in private, asking him who he was and to what end he used his wisdom. Apollonius declared his father's name and his native country and said that he used wisdom to know the gods and to live with men, since to know another man is even more difficult than to know oneself. He further said that he dealt with evil spirits merely as he would with evil men, and he maintained that he was not a prophet but had interpreted the thunder clap as he did by means of the wisdom revealed to wise men by the gods. He admitted that he did not fear Nero but excused himself by saying that bravery had also been given him by the gods, and maintained that he respected Nero more highly than did the officer questioning him. "For you," he said, "think him fit to sing, but I think him fit to keep silent." This answer so impressed the officer that he offered to release Apollonius if someone would put up bond for him. To this Apollonius asked, "Who will go bond for a body no one can bind?" And this question so frightened the officer that he let him go without any guarantees.

IV.45 There is also a story of a miracle Apollonius did in Rome. A girl had died, so it seemed, just before her marriage, and the bridegroom was following her bier lamenting, and Rome lamented with him, for she had been of a great family. Apollonius, meeting the funeral procession, said, "Put down the bier, for I will put a stop to your tears for the girl." Thereupon he asked her name. The crowd thought he was going to deliver a funeral oration, but he merely touched her and said something secretly over her and thus awoke her from her seeming death. She then went back to her father's house. When her relatives offered a great sum to Apollonius, he told them to give it to her as a dowry.

At this time, too, Apollonius corresponded with the philosopher IV.46 Musonius, who had been imprisoned by Nero. At Musonius' request Apollonius did not himself go to visit him, which would have been dangerous, but Menippus and Damis often went to the prison. Four brief letters from the correspondence have been preserved; they show Apollonius offering to help Musonius and the latter insisting that he is sufficient to himself.

Eventually Nero issued a proclamation that no one should IV.47 teach philosophy publicly in Rome. This decided Apollonius to go to the extreme west of the empire, since he wished to see the tides of the ocean and also had heard that some men in the west had made great advances in theology. On this journey he was followed by all his pupils. He rewarded them by explaining the V.2 cause of the tides—undersea gasses, by a sort of breathing of the earth, periodically force the ocean out of submarine caverns and then permit it to return—and by explaining the writing on certain V.5 ancient pillars in a shrine at Cadiz, after he found that the priests there were unable to explain it. He declared that these pillars had been inscribed by the Egyptian Hercules in the house of the Fates and set up as bonds to unite earth and ocean and to prevent any discord from arising between the elements.

While in Spain Apollonius gave much freer vent to his V.7 criticisms of Nero than he had in Rome. The main point of his criticism was that Nero neglected the proper dignity and power of his position by condescending to appear as an actor and contestant in the Greek games. Apollonius may even have gone so V.10 far as to intrigue against the emperor with one of the Spanish governors, who came with a few intimate friends to see him and spent three days with him in private. Whether or not anything came of this intrigue, a number of revolts broke out at this time V.11 [68 A.D.], Nero committed suicide, and Apollonius could only predict that the throne would fall into the hands "of many Thebans"—a prediction in which the piety of his disciples later saw a prognosis of what did happen.

V.13   Somewhat later, as he was returning from Spain, a woman in Sicily gave birth to a three-headed child, which was publicly exposed so that it could be seen by those who knew how to interpret portents. Apollonius sent Damis to look at it, and from his report he declared, "The three heads are three emperors of Rome, whom I formerly referred to as 'Thebans,' but none will succeed in establishing his rule. Two will hold power over Rome itself, one over neighboring countries, but all three will perish more quickly than the tyrants of stage tragedies." This prophecy was fulfilled exactly, the emperors being Galba, Otho, and Vitellius, who all arose and perished within a single year [68–69 A.D.].

V.14   While in Sicily they passed by Mount Etna, where the people told them that the fire of the volcano was breathed out by a giant who had once taken part in a revolt against the gods and whom Zeus had pinned down beneath the mountain. This led Apollonius to attack the blasphemous stories the poets told about the gods and to praise by contrast the fables of Aesop, as simple, healthful food seasoned with good advice as to what should be done. Further, he said, Aesop has the honesty to make no pretence that the events told in his stories actually happened. Moreover, he teaches children to be fond of animals and to think of them as having characters of their own.

V.15   "My mother," he said, "when I was a little boy, used to tell me a myth about Aesop's wisdom. It seems Aesop was once a shepherd and pastured near a temple of Hermes. He was also a lover of wisdom and prayed to Hermes for it. Many other men, asking the same gift, resorted to the god, one bringing gold, another silver, another a herald's staff of ivory, or the like. Aesop had none of these things, but he saved up of what he had and used to pour out to Hermes for a libation as much milk as a ewe would give in one milking or to bring to the altar as much honeycomb as he could hold in his hand. And he took thought to bring myrtles for the god's banquets, adding a very few roses or violets. 'For why, O Hermes,' he said, 'should I plait wreaths and neglect my sheep?' So when they came to the day set for giving out wisdom, Hermes, who is the god both of wisdom and of business, said to the one who had given most, 'You take philosophy.' And to the next, 'And you go into rhetoric. And you, astronomy, and you, music,' and so on. Thus, although most learned, he used up all the branches of learning and didn't notice that he was over-looking Aesop. When he realized his mistake, he remembered that the Seasons, by whom he had been brought up on the peaks of Olympus, used to tell him, when he was still a baby, a story about the cow and how she talked to man about herself and the earth. Thus they taught him to love the cattle of Apollo. Accordingly, he gave Aesop storytelling, as the only thing left in the house of wisdom, saying, 'You may have what I first learned.' "

When he finished his story, Apollonius apologized for having V.16 turned aside to praise fables (of the sort told by Aesop) when he had meant to discredit the blasphemous myths invented by the poets and then go on to a physical explanation of volcanoes, as V.17 resulting from the penetration of gases into deposits of sulphur and asphalt. In conclusion, however, he said he would not dis-credit the story that in one eruption the streams of lava had miraculously parted to spare a group of men trying to rescue their parents. "For we should consider that to those whose actions are holy all the earth is safe and the sea, too, is easily crossed, not only when they sail but even when they try to swim." (He always ended his discourses with some useful exhortation.)

After his stay in Sicily Apollonius went on to Greece, stopping V.18 at Leucas to change ships, since he knew it would not be well to travel further with the one in which he had set out (it sank a few days later). In Athens he was initiated into the Eleusinian V.19 mysteries by the hierophant of whom he had prophesied this. He V.20 spent the winter in the temples of Greece, and in the spring after generally lecturing the Greek cities, he set out for Egypt.

The master of the first ship he approached would not take him and his company aboard. It seems the ship was to carry a cargo of statues of deities for sale in Ionian ports, and the merchant did not want them polluted by the sort of company and conduct likely to be met with on shipboard. Apollonius replied by accus-ing him of superstition and impiety : superstition because the gods had gone aboard the ships of the ancient Athenian navy without fear of pollution (how much more fitting, then, to carry with them philosophers, men in whom the gods especially rejoice); impiety because he made a business of the gods' statues, taking them around like slaves to be sold in the market places (whereas the piety of ancient times had provided that men should contribute only labor, tools, and raw materials to the temples, and the statues of the gods should be made in the temple precincts).

V.21 On arriving in Chios, without even setting foot on land he jumped from the boat in which he had come to that next to it. His companions jumped after him without saying a word, for he taught them to imitate him in whatever he said or did. The new boat took them to Rhodes, where he dismissed the Colossus with the comment that it was not so great as a true philosopher, lec-
V.22 tured a flute player on the technique of his art, and called down a rich young man for spending more on his mansion than on his
V.23 education. Here, too, he had an encounter with a young glutton who was proud of his notoriety and had the impertinence to compare it with Hercules' reputation for feats of eating and drinking. "But he," said Apollonius, "was Hercules. As for you, you garbage can, your only means to get attention is to burst."

V.24 In Alexandria he was expected with eagerness, for his fame had preceded him. When he went up from the ship into the city, men gazed at him as if he were a god and made way for him in the streets as they do for those carrying the holy objects in a religious procession. While he was thus escorted, he encountered twelve men being led to execution as brigands. Looking at them he declared that one was innocent and told the public executioners who were in charge to proceed as slowly as possible and to kill that one last, since it would be a holy action to spare him for at least a short part of the day. He enlarged on this theme at unaccustomed length, and his purpose soon became evident, for when eight had been killed, a horseman dashed up with orders to spare the man Apollonius had designated : he had inculpated himself from fear of being racked, but had been proved guiltless by the evidence obtained from others under torture. This miracle secured Apollonius the admiration of all Egypt.

V.25 When he went up to the temple, he declared that its orderliness and the account of it [given by the guide] were religious and wisely composed, but he did not approve the animal sacrifices nor consider them fit for the repasts of the gods. When the priest asked him what authority he had for refusing to sacrifice thus, he asked the priest what authority he had for thus sacrificing. "Who," said the priest, "is so skilled in religious matters as to correct the practices of the Egyptians?" "Any sage," said Apollonius, "if he come from India." He went on to ridicule the notion that the gods lived on the smoke of burning bulls, and to offer them instead the smoke of a burning frankincense image of a bull. When the priest said he saw nothing in such an ·offering, Apollonius reproached him for his ignorance of divination by fire, which had been practiced by many Greek oracles and enabled the sage to see the things revealed in the disc of the sun at its rising. Not content V.26 with rebuking the priest, he went on to compose and deliver in the temple a rhetorical denunciation of the Alexandrians because their fondness for horse racing had led to riots between backers of opposing teams, and some individuals had been killed. He called down fire on the wicked city full of bloodshed and the cries of the oppressed.

Vespasian [the Roman general in command of the army sup- V.27 pressing the Jewish revolt in Palestine] was planning at this time to seize power. With this in mind he advanced into Egypt [where he was hailed in 69 as emperor], and all the city—priests and civil officials and philosophers and scholars—went out to welcome him. Apollonius, however, busied himself in the temple. Vespasian, after greeting the dignitaries courteously but briefly, asked whether Apollonius were in the city. "Yes," they said, "he's improving us." Thereupon Vespasian asked his whereabouts and, on learning that he was in the temple, set out thither to reverence the gods and meet the philosopher. (This gave rise to the story that earlier, when he was besieging Jerusalem and first had the idea of seizing power, he sent for Apollonius, but the latter refused to enter a land whose inhabitants had polluted it both by what they had done and by what they had suffered.) After arriving V.28 at the temple and sacrificing to the gods, Vespasian turned to Apollonius and, as if imploring him, said, "Make me emperor." Apollonius answered, "I have already done so, for when I prayed for an emperor righteous and noble and temperate and gray-haired and the father of legitimate sons, I was asking the gods for you." This delighted Vespasian, and the crowd in the temple cheered in agreement. Apollonius then went on to criticize the rule of Nero as immoderate and to recommend moderation in all things. Vespasian replied with the wish that he might rule wise men and be ruled by them, and he promised the assembled

V.29 Egyptians that they might draw on him as on the Nile. As they left the temple, he grasped Apollonius by the hand and took him along to the palace, while explaining to him his motives for attempting to seize power. This he did with the expressed hope that Apollonius would defend him to the public and that, knowing the will of the gods, he would tell him whether or not they

V.30 favored his enterprise. Apollonius in return gave him his approval, prayed that Zeus Capitolinus would preserve him, and prophesied that he would rebuild the Capitoline temple (though the news of its burning had not yet reached Alexandria). Therewith Apollonius took his leave, explaining that he had some Indian customs that he must follow at noon.

V.31   Next morning at dawn he went to the palace and asked the guards what the emperor was doing. They said he was up long since and answering letters. Hearing this Apollonius went off with the remark, "This man will reign." He came back about sunrise and found two other philosophers, Dion and Euphrates, waiting for admission. To them he summarized Vespasian's defence of his actions, then on being admitted to the imperial presence he recommended them to the emperor and secured their admission

V.32 Vespasian asked them all to advise him how he should rule.

V.33 Thereupon Euphrates advised him not to rule but to restore democratic government to the Roman state. Dion seconded this but with the reservation that the Romans might by this time have become incapable of self-government. He therefore advised Vespasian to let the Romans choose between democratic and auto-

V.35 cratic rule. This advice was followed by a silence during which Vespasian's face revealed his disappointment.

Apollonius then told his colleagues that their advice was silly. Such philosophic precepts might be listened to by a philosopher, but a practical man, accustomed to rule, could not be expected to deny himself and his sons the fruits of victory or to expose himself and them to the ruin that would certainly follow if he fell from power. As for democracy: "To me," Apollonius said, "no constitution is a matter of concern, for I live under the guidance of the gods. However, I do not think it right that the human herd should perish for want of a just and temperate herdsman. And as a single man of pre-eminent capacities transforms democracy so that it seems the rule of the one best man, thus the rule of one man, when it always looks ahead for the common good, is democracy." From these principles and from the fact that Vespasian had already taken the decisive step and had been proclaimed emperor, Apollonius concluded that the proposal to restore democracy was unimportant and impracticable.

The emperor heard him gladly, expressed his complete agreement, and asked him now to go on to the question of how the good ruler should rule. Apollonius told him to consider as wealth, not treasure lying idle nor that extorted from unwilling taxpayers, but money put in use to help the poor and to secure the rich in their possession of their property. He advised him to fear the temptations of power; to prevent revolt by destroying not the great but the hostile; to be ruled by the laws; to serve the gods; to attend to matters of government as a king, but to his body as a private citizen; to keep a tight rein on his sons and warn them that unless they were worthy, they would not succeed to the throne; to moderate little by little the pleasures of Rome; to teach imperial slaves and freedmen appropriate humility; and to send out as governors men who at least knew the languages of the territories they were to govern. This last point Apollonius emphasized by saying that when he was in the Peloponnesus, Greece was governed by a man who knew no Greek. Since the Greeks knew no Latin, the governor was at the mercy of his associates, who made their control of his judgments a source of profit. These, Apollonius said, were all the precepts he could think of at the time; if later he thought of any more, he would come back. So saying he made his departure, followed by his students.

Euphrates and Dion, who remained behind, made their peace V.37

V.36

with Vespasian and accepted his rule without further dispute. Dion, in fact, being a person of charm and a skillful speaker, retained some influence. But the emperor was particularly attached to Apollonius and listened untiringly to his accounts of India and his reports of the will of the gods. When Vespasian had settled the affairs of Egypt and was about to depart, he urged Apollonius to accompany him, but the latter refused, for he wished to see more of Egypt and then to go on to Ethiopia and visit the gymnosophists, to compare their wisdom with that of the Indians.

V.38   Vespasian then offered him gifts, but he refused them, urging him, however, to give something to Euphrates and Dion. When the emperor consented, Dion asked merely that a friend of his might be released from military service to go on with his study of philosophy, but Euphrates had in readiness a whole letter full of requests, some for friends, some for himself, and all financial. The emperor humiliated him by reading this out in public. Thereupon Apollonius laughed and said, "So you advised the restoration of democracy while planning to ask all this from the emperor!"

V.39   This was the beginning of the quarrel between Apollonius and Euphrates. Later, when the emperor had departed, they publicly attacked each other, Euphrates using angry abuse, Apollonius philosophic rebuke. His accusations of Euphrates for conduct unbecoming a philosopher can be learned from his numerous letters. On at least one occasion the two almost came to blows.

V.41   Apollonius went no further in his friendship with Vespasian because the latter, after his departure from Egypt, restored Greece to the Roman provincial system, taking away the freedom Nero had bestowed on the country. Of this Apollonius disapproved; therefore he replied to the emperor's repeated invitations only with curt notes of refusal, taxing him with the enslavement of Greece and comparing him unfavorably in this respect with Nero. Beyond this, however, his hostility did not go, and he was delighted by the excellence of Vespasian's government in other respects.

V.42   Another story told of Apollonius' stay in Egypt concerns a man who had a tame lion, so tame it was allowed to beg for food even in the temples. When it came to Apollonius, he recognized it as a reincarnation of Amasis, the great sixth-century king of Egypt. The beast wept piteously when its identity was revealed. Apollonius therefore arranged for its acceptance as a sacred animal by the temple at Leontopolis, and the priests from that shrine came out and sacrificed to it and decorated it and led it home in procession with pipes and hymns.

Now Apollonius was ready to set out for Ethiopia and the gymnosophists. To keep an eye on Euphrates he left Menippus in Alexandria and with him some twenty students either unfit or disinclined for the trip. With the remaining ten he set out south by camel back and boat, stopping at every shrine by the way to learn its legend. V.43

At the border of Ethiopia [i.e., Nubia, northern Sudan] they came on uncoined gold and linen and an elephant and various herbs and myrrh and aromatics lying unguarded in the road. This is a market to which the Ethiopians bring their goods and leave them; the Egyptians take them away and bring in return Egyptian goods of equal value. Apollonius understood the practice and praised it by contrast with the Greek habit of bargaining and trying to make a profit on everything. It would be well, he said, if wealth were honored less and equality more; then we might have peace and the whole earth would seem one. VI.2

In Ethiopia they acquired as guide a young Egyptian named Timasion, who had fled from his father's house because his mother-in-law attempted to seduce him and, when he refused her, accused him to his father of homosexuality. He judged Apollonius' party to be philosophers by their cloaks and the books they were studying, and he asked if he might accompany them. Apollonius consented, and while the young man was coming (for he had hailed them from another boat), told the company his story. When he arrived, he was asked to tell his story, which proved to be just what Apollonius had foretold. Apollonius praised him particularly because, in spite of his rejection of his stepmother's advances, he recognized the power of Aphrodite, the goddess of love, and sacrificed to her daily. "For it is the part of moderation," Apollonius said, "to speak well of all the gods, VI.3

and this especially at Athens, where altars are erected even to
unknown divinities."

VI.4   With Timasion as guide they visited the famous statue of
Memnon,[1] where they sacrificed, as the priests advised, to the Sun
of Ethiopia and to Memnon of the Dawn. Hence they went on
VI.5 towards the land of the gymnosophists [i.e., "naked sages"]. On
their way they passed a man wandering about aimlessly, and
Timasion explained that he was one who had killed another by
accident and must now wait until the gymnosophists would
purify him of the pollution of manslaughter, before he could
return to his home. This man had now been kept waiting seven
months. Apollonius said this showed the ignorance of the gymnosophists, since the man had killed one who was thirteenth in
descent from an Egyptian who had laid waste their country. They
should therefore have rewarded the killer, even if he had acted
deliberately. So saying, since he himself could not speak to one
defiled by blood, he told Timasion to tell the man to come to him,
and when he came, he purified him according to the rites of
Empedocles and Pythagoras and told him to go home, since he
was now clean.

VI.6   Next day before noon they came to the gymnosophists, who
VI.7 live on a little hill a short distance from the Nile. Here they met
with a cool reception, for Euphrates had sent one of his friends
ahead of them to tell the gymnosophists that Apollonius was coming and would give them no little trouble, since he admired himself even more highly than he did the Indian sages (whom he was
always praising); he would try to trick them in any number of
ways, and he reverenced neither sun nor heaven nor earth, for he
VI.8 claimed to move these about as he wished. The gymnosophists
were taken in by these stories, and therefore when Apollonius
arrived, although they did not refuse to receive him, yet they
pretended to be busy with important things and asked by messenger why he came and what he wanted. The messenger also

----

[1] Memnon was an Ethiopian hero mentioned in *Odyssey* 11.522. In classical
times a statue of Pharoah Amenhotep III (d. 1370 B.C.) at Thebes was supposed
to be a statue of Memnon and to utter a sound at dawn, greeting the rising sun.
Thebes was in Roman territory, not in Nubia.

brought word that Apollonius and his party might stay in the porch the community had built for its guests (the gymnosophists themselves had no houses). Apollonius replied that in their country anybody could live without clothing and shelter and that the Indians had not needed to ask him questions. The rest VI.9 of that day he spent in discussion with his disciples. Meanwhile, however, Timasion, who had long been acquainted with the gymnosophists, found out what the trouble was and persuaded them to meet Apollonius on the next day.

When the meeting took place, after the customary greetings VI.10 the eldest of the gymnosophists delivered a discourse in which he compared Indian and Egyptian wisdom to the disadvantage of the former. "The Indians," he said, "are masters of magical tricks but servants of their desires. They use their supernatural powers to provide themselves with bodily luxuries. But the Egyptians' powers are equal to the Indians' "—to prove this point he ordered a neighboring elm tree to greet Apollonius, which it did with a voice like that of a woman. "And the Egyptians," he went on, "have such control of their passions that they have no need to use their powers for base purposes. They sleep on the earth, they eat what the earth naturally provides them, they have no need of houses or clothing. This is the true wisdom, that which was taught by the simplicity of the Delphic oracle, that which surpasses the wisdom of India as the Olympic contest of naked athletes does the Pythian games tricked out with theatrical performances. The choice between Indian and Egyptian wisdom is like the famous choice of Hercules between the strumpet life of ignominious pleasure and the chaste life of austere, laborious virtue. You, Apollonius, should choose as did Hercules."

Apollonius asked him politely if he had nothing more to say. VI.11 "Nothing," he said, "I have spoken." "And the others?" "You have heard them all through me." Apollonius paused for a moment and then pointed out that he had long since made the choice of Hercules by choosing the austerities of Pythagorean philosophy. By adherence to Pythagorean practices he had become what a philosopher should be, and by studying the question of the origin of philosophy he had come to realize that it must have originated among men extraordinarily gifted in things divine, men who most carefully studied the soul, of which the deathless and unbegotten elements are the sources of existence. Philosophy, therefore, could not have originated among the Athenians, since they had rejected the teachings of Plato. Consequently, one should ask what the city is where not one or another individual but all citizens hold the same beliefs as to the soul. When he came to this question, he thought of going to Egypt, but his teacher told him that the Indians were the true fathers of philosophy. Apollonius found this opinion confirmed by the facts that the Indians are of finer intelligence because they live in purer sunlight, and they hold truer opinions concerning nature and the gods because they are closely related to the gods and live near the edge of the hot, life-producing substance. When he visited them he found his expectations surpassed by the actuality. They dwell on the earth, yet not on it; they are protected as by fortifications, though unfortified; they have nothing but have all things. As for you—he told the gymnosophists—you are merely degenerate Indians, who have tried to rid yourselves of the signs of your Indian origin in order to be spared the embarrassment of the contrast. Therefore you pretend to be Egyptians, though you are really Ethiopians come from India. And as for your famous simplicity, it is not justified by the Delphic oracle, for the god made his shrine the patron of all the arts of Greece. The very existence of the arts is for the purpose of adornment; ornament is proper to majesty, and luxury to the banquets of the gods. And as for miracles, those men who desire to hymn the sun worthily must rise from the earth and soar aloft with the god. This all men wish, but only the Indians can.

VI.12   This exchange of courtesies was followed by a rather acrid
VI.13   conversation in which it came out that the Egyptians' attack on Apollonius had been motivated by Euphrates' report that Apollonius had been attacking them. Apollonius thereupon taunted them for their lack of perspicacity, which had made it possible that they should be deceived by slander. At length, however, both parties agreed to drop their differences and discuss more profit-
VI.14   able matters. Thereupon Nilus, the youngest of the gymnosophists, who had been much impressed by the speech of Apollonius,

begged him to tell them of his studies in India. The other gymnosophists seconded his request, so Apollonius complied and spoke
on the subject until noon, when both he and the gymnosophists
turned to their customary religious observances.

When it came time for the afternoon meal, Nilus arrived, bring-   VI.15
ing gifts of vegetables and bread and dried fruits, and took the
opportunity to sit down beside Apollonius and hear more of his
conversation. This so enchanted him that when the dinner ended,   VI.16
he declared his determination to leave the gymnosophists and
become a follower of Apollonius. Apollonius warned him that his
former teachers would blame him for the choice, but he persisted
and explained that it was not really a change of purpose. His
father had been a captain in the shipping trade between Egypt
and India and had brought home stories of the Indian sages and
also the report, now confirmed by Apollonius, that the gymnosophists were merely colonists sent out from India. Therefore,
Nilus said, when he grew up, he gave away his inheritance and
betook himself to the gymnosophists, hoping to learn from them
the wisdom of the Indians. Disappointed in this, he found in the
coming of Apollonius the means of fulfilling his lifelong desire.
This explanation contented Apollonius, and he made only the   VI.17
proviso that Nilus should not annoy his former teachers by trying
—as he at first proposed—to persuade them too to become
Apollonius' disciples. Nilus consented to this, and after some more   VI.18
talk they fell asleep in the grass.

Next morning after their accustomed prayers they rejoined the
gymnosophists, and this time it was the turn of the latter to ex-
pound their wisdom. Apollonius was told to ask what questions he   VI.19
would and began by asking why the gymnosophists encouraged
the Egyptians to worship gods in animal forms, a ridiculous
practice. Their spokesman replied by attacking the Greek practice
of using images of the gods, since these could not be likenesses.
Apollonius maintained that the gods were properly represented
by images, understood as works of imagination, then he returned
to his attack on the theriomorphic cults. The Egyptian defended
these as symbolic, and Apollonius replied that the symbols were
contemptible and occasions of scandal; it would be better to use

none at all. The Egyptian appealed to Socrates' practice of swearing by the dog or the goose; Apollonius replied that Socrates did

VI.20 so because he did not wish to swear by the gods. The Egyptian thereupon, as if changing the subject, began to ask about the Spartan practice by which citizens were ceremonially whipped in the festival of Artemis till their blood ran out on the altar. Apollonius did his best to defend this but was reduced to pleading that it was a Scythian practice prescribed by oracles, and he had not been able to change it when he was adviser to the Spartans, since it would be madness to make rules contrary to the expressed will of the gods. "Just so," replied the Egyptian, "and what I have been saying was not so much against the Spartans, Apollonious, as against you. For if we are to examine critically customs so ancient that they cannot be understood, and are to cross-question the gods on why they rejoice in such things, a great many very strange arguments will emerge in this branch of philosophy. For we could ask about the Eleusinian initiation and the mysteries of Samothrace and the Dionysiac rites and the phallus and the image in Cyllene,[2] and before we were through, we should be finding fault with everything. Therefore let us turn to some other topic. It is best to keep silent about such things as these."

VI.21   To this Apollonius consented and turned to the question of justice. Here the Egyptian agreed with and developed the Indians' view that a man is not to be called just merely because he refrains from acting unjustly. Moreover, he went beyond this to define the just man as one who takes the initiative in acting justly and

VI.22 who inspires others to do likewise. To this Apollonius agreed. They had further discussions concerning the soul and concerning nature, in which they arrived at conclusions like those of Plato in the *Timaeus*; they also discussed Greek laws. Then Apollonius expressed his desire to go on to the sources of the Nile, and the gymnosophists sent Timasion with him as a guide. Nilus too went with him after having a private discussion with his former colleagues.

    [2] A mountain in Arcadia, where Hermes was worshipped in the form of an erect phallus.

The trip to the sources of the Nile (they turned out to be the VI.23
cataracts rather than the sources) was uneventful save for the VI.24
sights by the way—marvels of nature and strange animals and
peoples. On the way back Apollonius helped the inhabitants of VI.27
a village plagued by a satyr that not only attacked the women
but also killed them. The gymnosophists had long been trying
to prevent the monster's outbreaks but had not been able to.
Apollonius resorted to the method of [the legendary king] Midas
and filled the village drinking trough with wine; then he called
the satyr, using some secret threat. The satyr did not appear
visibly, but the wine sank as if being drunk. When it had disappeared, Apollonius led the villagers to a nearby cave of the
Nymphs, where he showed them the satyr asleep and told them
not to beat or abuse him, for from then on he would be tame.

When Apollonius returned to Alexandria, his quarrel with VI.28
Euphrates reached its height, because of daily arguments, but
these he left to Menippus, for he himself was giving his attention
to Nilus. About this time [70 A.D.] Titus [Vespasian's elder son] VI.29
captured Jerusalem with great slaughter. The neighboring peoples
sent him crowns of victory, but he declared himself unworthy of
these, saying he had merely put his forces at the service of the
wrath of God. This judgment pleased Apollonius, who sent him
a letter saying he did well not to accept a crown for war
and bloodshed, but he deserved the crown of moderation, since
he knew for what things a man should be crowned. This profoundly gratified Titus, who replied that he had captured
Jerusalem, but Apollonius him.

When he was called to Rome to rule jointly with his father VI.30
[in 71], he asked Apollonius to meet him on the way at Tarsus.
When they met, he told Apollonius that Vespasian had written
him of the assistance which Apollonius had given their house.
Consequently, he wished to ask Apollonius' advice, for he was
scarcely thirty years old, and he feared that he might not yet be fit
to rule. Apollonius stroked his neck, which was strong as
any weight lifter's, and said, "Who can force under the yoke a
bull with so strong a neck?" "He who raised me from a calf," said
Titus. Apollonius praised his intention to follow his father's

directions and said that the rule of an old and a young man acting in harmony should have the advantage of both energy and
VI.31 discretion. His father, therefore, should be his example in ruling,
but to supplement this example Apollonius promised to give him
his friend the cynic philosopher, Demetrius, who would advise
him on what a good ruler should do. This gift Titus accepted with
some hesitation, yielding only to Apollonius' insistence and urging Apollonius himself to come with him to Rome—a request to
which Apollonius replied that he would come when it was best for
VI.32 them both. Titus then dismissed the other persons present and
asked Apollonius privately concerning the safety of his life and
what persons he should fear. Apollonius, gazing into the sun,
swore by it that even had Titus not asked this question, he would
have told him, for the gods had ordered that he should be told
to beware, while his father was alive, his father's bitterest enemies,
but after his father's death his own closest relations. He would
die as Ulysses died; his death would come from the sea. (Damis
thought Titus fulfilled this prophecy by dying of poisonous fish,
at the hand of his brother Domitian). After this private conversation they embraced each other in public, and Apollonius,
departing, said, "Conquer, O King, your enemies by your arms
VI.33 and your father by your virtues." Apollonius, then, as he had
promised, wrote Demetrius to advise Titus on conduct befitting
a ruler.

VI.34   This visit was the occasion of Apollonius' reconciliation with
the people of Tarsus. They had formerly detested him because
he had rebuked them sharply, but now they were so taken by the
man that they reckoned him as the founder and supporter of the
city. It seems that they had asked Titus for great favors, and Titus
had said he would ask his father. Then Apollonius came to him
and said, "If I should prove to you that some of these men were
hostile to you and your father and had incited the Jewish revolt
and were hidden allies of your most open enemies, what would
be their punishment?" "Death," said Titus, "what else?" "But
isn't it shameful," said Apollonius, "to demand penalties immediately but put off benefactions, and to punish on your own
authority but to make benefactions wait for consultation?" Titus

replied, delighted, "I grant the gifts, for my father will not be angry at me for having been conquered by the truth and by you."

After his return from Ethiopia Apollonius visited no more VI.35 exotic countries but traveled continuously through the lands around the eastern Mediterranean, from northern Egypt through Palestine, Syria, Cilicia, the Ionian coast and southern Greece, and as far west as Italy. Throughout these journeys he remained the same (as the wise man should), and many stories are told of events in his travels.

There was a young man, himself uneducated, who devoted VI.36 himself to training birds to speak. Apollonius told him he was doubly spoiling them, first because he denied them their own musical utterance, secondly because he taught them his own vile accent. Further, he strongly urged him to learn to speak well—not merely to speak with a good accent but to argue cogently and to speak in public—because this was the only way in which he could hope to protect himself from false accusers who, if he could not defend himself, would threaten him with one lawsuit after another and have to be bought off again and again, until he was left penniless.

Of two sayings current in Sardis, that the river Pactolus had VI.37 brought gold dust to [the Lydian king] Croesus and that trees were older than the earth, Apollonius approved the first, for he said that the gold might have been washed down from the neighboring mountains, where gold had at one time been found, but he ridiculed the second, saying he had never yet heard that the stars were older than the sky.

When an earthquake occurred in Antioch at a time when the VI.38 city was torn by factional strife, he interpreted the occurrence as a god-sent punishment and so succeeded in reconciling the parties.

A certain man sacrificed to the Earth, asking to find a treasure, VI.39 and also prayed to Apollonius to the same end. Apollonius accused him of being over anxious to get rich, but he replied that he had only twenty thousand drachmas [about $10,000] and had four daughters to marry off; if he gave them each five thousand, they would have little, and he nothing. Apollonius pitied him and said, "The Earth and I will take care of you." He then went out to the suburbs as if to buy fruit, and seeing a field with good olive trees and a garden in it and a bee hive and flowers, he went into the garden and said a prayer to Pandora and returned to the city. There he found the owner of the field (a rich man who had got his wealth by nefarious means) and persuaded him to sell it to the poor man for twenty thousand drachmas. The poor man found a treasure hid in his field and made money on the olive crop besides.

VI.40   There was a man in Cnidus who fell in love with the naked statue of Aphrodite there and wanted to marry it. The Cnidians were not unfavorable to his proposal—he had made large gifts to the temple and promised more, and they said the goddess would be more famous if she had a lover. Apollonius, however, told the man that mixed marriages between gods and men or men and animals could not turn out happily. He reminded him of Ixion [who tried to have connection with the goddess Hera and was therefore racked by Zeus] and thus frightened him so that he gave up his plan and sacrificed instead to ask pardon for having thought of it.

VI.41   When the cities on the left side of the Hellespont were struck by earthquakes, Egyptians and Chaldeans wandered around them to collect money for sacrifices costing ten talents [about $30,000] to Earth and Poseidon. Apollonius, however, drove them out of the cities as profiteering on other men's misfortunes, and himself calculating the causes of the divine wrath and sacrificing as was appropriate to each, he averted with small expense the visitation, and the earth stayed still.

VI.42   When Domitian [emperor, 81–95] prohibited the making of eunuchs and also the planting of vineyards and ordered existing vineyards cut down, Apollonius, who was then in Ionia, said, "These laws are nothing to me, for I, perhaps alone of all men, need neither wine nor genitals, but this amazing legislator does not realize that he is sparing men yet castrating the earth." This saying encouraged the Ionians to send an embassy protesting the laws against vineyards.

VI.43   This story is told in Tarsus : a boy was bitten by a mad dog and consequently behaved like a dog himself, barking and howling and going on all fours. When he had been sick for thirty days, Apollonius, who had just arrived at Tarsus, met him and ordered the dog that had bitten him to be found. But no one, not even the boy, knew what dog it was. Apollonius, on reflection, bring it, which Damis did merely by telling it that Apollonius was able to describe it and say where it was, and he sent Damis to ordered it to come. When it came, Apollonius made it lick the bite, which cured the boy, and then swim a stream, which cured the dog.

[After the death of Titus in 81, when his brother, Domitian, VII came to the throne, relations between the emperor and the Senate so disintegrated that during the last years of his reign, from 93 to 96, Domitian ruled by terror and was himself in constant fear of the assassination which eventually overtook him. During the whole of his reign it was a matter of considerable danger to criticize the government even indirectly.] Nevertheless, Apollonius VII.4 went around the provinces, preaching the love of liberty and telling of the heroic deeds of the tyrannicides of old. And he left little doubt as to the reference of his stories. In the midst VII.5 of a crowded theater at Ephesus he applied to Domitian the lines of Euripides declaring that tyrants whose power has been long in growing are tripped up by little things. When it was reported VII.6 that Domitian had condemned three priestesses of the goddess Vesta to death for unchastity, Apollonius prayed in public that the sun might be purified because of the unjust murders it beheld throughout the world. When Domitian executed his relative VII.7 Sabinus and married Julia, wife of the deceased and his own niece, Apollonius interrupted the sacrifices for prosperity of the marriage, at Ephesus, with the regret that it would not be altogether like the marriage of the Danaïdes, [legendary ladies who were forced to marry their cousins and murdered their bridegrooms on the wedding night].

Beside these public expressions of disapproval Apollonius in- VII.8 trigued secretly with important Romans, especially Nerva [a prominent lawyer], whom he thought most suitable to succeed Domitian. He did not correspond with them, since informers were everywhere and men were often betrayed by their wives or slaves, but he sent his trusted companions to them with secret messages. Domitian exiled the ringleaders of the group before the plot matured, and Apollonius, on learning of their exile, discoursed in VII.9 Smyrna on the Fates and necessity. Since he foreknew that Nerva would soon become emperor, he declared in his discourse that tyrants could not change the decrees of the Fates, and he apostrophized a bronze statue of Domitian that stood near by, saying, "You fool, even if you should kill the man who is destined to rule after you, he would rise from the dead."

This was reported to Domitian by Euphrates, but no one knew which of the banished men Apollonius had been talking about. Domitian therefore decided to kill them all, but to have an excuse for this action he sent for Apollonius to answer charges concerning his secret messages, reasoning that if he came, he would be convicted and so, through him, would the others, while if he did not VII.10 come, his flight would serve as proof for their conviction. Apollonius, foreknowing this plan, set out for Italy while the letter ordering his arrest was still on its way.

At Dicaearchia [a city just above Naples] they met Demetrius the Cynic, who was thought the most courageous of the philoso-VII.11 phers because he lived the least distance from Rome. He did his best to deter Apollonius from going thither, telling him that Nerva and his associates had now been accused of treason and that he (Apollonius) was charged with having fomented the plot and having sacrificed a boy in order to divine the future by inspection of the entrails. Contributing to the charge, he said, were Apollonius' peculiar costume and way of life and the fact that some VII.12 people worshiped him. Therefore he urged Apollonius to flee to some remote part of the empire and live in obscurity, for if he went to Rome, Domitian would certainly have him executed.

VII.13 Damis, who was present at the conversation, seconded this advice.

VII.14 But Apollonius pointed out that to run away would brand him as a coward and his friends as guilty; therefore his conscience compelled him to go to Rome.

VII.15 Accordingly, after saying good-bye to Demetrius he and Damis continued on their journey. At his orders Damis disguised himself,

replacing his Pythagorean costume by ordinary linen clothes and
having his hair cut, so that he would not look like a philosopher.

When they arrived, Apollonius was arrested and brought be- VII.17
fore [the official whom the emperor had apparently ordered to
take cognizance of the case], the Praetorian Prefect, Aelian.
Aelian had made the acquaintance of Apollonius some twenty- VII.18
five years before, when as a young man he went to Egypt in the
train of Vespasian. At that time Apollonius, taking a fancy to him,
had told him his name and history and also foretold his future
life, including the office he now held. He, therefore, had used his VII.16
influence to discredit the accusations brought against Apollonius,
and now when Apollonius was brought before him, he took him VII.17
into his private office, told him of their previous meeting, and VII.18
assured him of his friendship, while explaining that he could not
safely let it be known. Apollonius praised him for his frankness VII.19
and explained that, as for himself, he could have run away, but for
the sake of his own reputation and of those involved in the charges
with him he had come to make his defense. Therefore he asked
Aelian to tell him precisely what the charges were.

"The charges are numerous and varied," Aelian replied. VII.20
"Your dress, your conduct, that some people have worshiped
you, that in Ephesus you gave an oracle about a famine, that
you spoke against the emperor privately and publicly, and pretended that some of the things you said had been told you by the
gods. The thing most implausible to me (for I know that you do
not permit bloodshed, even for sacrifices) is that which seems
most plausible to the emperor : they say you met Nerva in the
country and there cut up an Arcadian boy for him when he was
offering sacrifices for the overthrow of the emperor, and you encouraged him by these rites. These things are said to have been
done at night, when the moon was on the wane. This should be
considered the main charge; the others merely go to confirm and
explain it. So you see what you have to defend yourself against.
And make sure that your speech is not contemptuous of the
emperor."

Apollonius assured him that he would behave as desired, both VII.21
for his own sake and for his friends'. Aelian admired his *sang-froid*

and terminated the interview. Then, pretending to be angry at him, he ordered him held until the emperor should examine him.

While he was being held, a tribune who knew him well taunted him by asking for what crime he was in danger. When Apollonius replied that he did not know, the tribune said, "But I know. The way people worshiped you has led to the accusation that you think yourself an equal of the gods." "Who worshiped me?" said Apollonius. "I did as a boy in Ephesus, when you cured us of the pestilence." "You were lucky," said Apollonius, "both you and the city of Ephesus, which was saved." "Therefore," said the other, "I have prepared a defense for you that will free you of the accusation. Let us go outside the city, and if I cut off your head with my sword, the charge will be refuted and you will be free, but if you frighten me and I let go of the sword, you will have to be thought divine and be judged as truly accused." This he said with a grimace and a guffaw, but Apollonius, as if he did not hear, was talking with Damis about the delta of the Nile.

VII.22   Aelian had Apollonius consigned to that prison in which the prisoners were not chained. Here he was kept, awaiting the emperor's leisure, for the emperor wished to talk with him privately before the trial. When Apollonius arrived in the prison, he proposed to discourse on philosophy to the other prisoners, since he thought they would need such consolation. But Damis, who still accompanied him, wanted to hear what had happened in his interview with Aelian, so Apollonius gave him an account of it. Damis thereupon thanked the gods, who had not left them without some hope of escape. But Apollonius reminded him that the wise man had nothing to fear, "for wisdom astounds whatever meets with her, but is herself astounded by nothing." "But," said Damis, "we have come to one who cannot have any meeting with wisdom and therefore will not be astounded." "Don't you realize, Damis, that he is puffed up with pride and behaving stupidly?" "Of course I realize it. How could I not?" "Accordingly," said Apollonius, "you should despise the tyrant more, the more you know him."

VII.23   While they were talking, another prisoner came up and began to tell them his story. He was in prison because of his wealth, which was so great that he had been accused as one who might finance an attempt at revolution. He remembered wistfully how, when a poor man, he had been free, but then as his wealth accumulated, he had become tributary to more and more leeches and parasites—false accusers and government officials and relatives and slaves and self-styled friends—all of whom he had to satisfy for his own safety. And in spite of his efforts to satisfy them he had finally ended in prison. Apollonius comforted him by saying that his wealth, which had got him into this fix, would also get him out; by giving it up he would free himself not only from prison but also from his swarm of hangers-on.

Another man said he was being prosecuted because, when VII.24 sacrificing in the city of which he was governor, he had not added to the public prayers the statement that Domitian was the child of Athena. "You perhaps thought," said Apollonius, "that Athena, being ever virgin, would not give birth. I suppose you did not know that this goddess once did give birth, at Athens, to a snake."

In all there were about fifty men in the prison, some of them VII.26 sick, most dejected, some resigned, others lamenting their fate. Apollonius therefore returned to his purpose to comfort them by a philosophic discourse. Having called them together he reminded them that they were making matters worse for themselves by anticipating misfortunes that might not overtake them. Rather they should try to bear their present misfortune with patience. If they were imprisoned justly, they should lament not their imprisonment but the crimes that led to it; if unjustly, the knowledge of their innocence should give them courage. If they thought imprisonment a misfortune, they should be comforted by the reflection that it is the universal fate of man. "The whole world is the prison of the men who live in it : the body is the prison of the soul; to live in a house is a second imprisonment; cities are common gaols; the nomads are the prisoners of their plains; the earth itself is chained in by ocean; and ancient legends tell us of the imprisonments of the gods." By these observations he so cheered up the inmates that most of them consented to take food and stopped crying, with the hope that they would suffer nothing while he was with them.

VII.27   Next day while he was talking in the same vein, a spy who pretended to be a prisoner was sent in by Domitian. Apollonius, however, saw through him and therefore talked about rivers and mountains and wild animals and trees, by which the true prisoners were amused but the informer was not aided. When he tried to draw him into abuse of the tyrant, Apollonius replied, "You say whatever you please, for you will certainly not be accused by me, but whatever faults I may find with the emperor I shall tell him myself."

VII.28   On the evening of the fifth day of his imprisonment someone of Greek speech who claimed to have been sent by Aelian came to the prison and told Apollonius that the emperor would talk with him next day. He said, too, that the man in charge of the prison had been ordered to give him any assistance he might want. Apollonius thanked him but said, "I lead the same life here as I do outside, for I discourse on whatever topics arise, and I am in need of nothing." "Not even of someone to advise you as how you should speak with the emperor?" "That I need," he said, "provided he does not persuade me to flatter." "What if he should persuade you not to show contempt?" "He would be giving excellent advice, and that is just what I have decided to do." "This was what I came for," said the visitor, "and I am glad to find you sensibly disposed. Besides this you must be prepared for the way the emperor speaks and for the unpleasantness of his face. He speaks in a deep voice, even if he is talking mildly. His eyebrows overhang the sockets of his eyes, and his cheeks are bloated with bile. This is what is most noticeable. So do not be frightened by these things. They are natural to him and always the same." "Ulysses," said Apollonius, "on his arrival in the cave of [the man-eating monster] Polyphemus, had not heard in advance how big he was or what he ate or how his voice thundered, but he found courage to deal with him, even though he was afraid at the beginning, and he behaved like a man and escaped from the cave. It will be enough for me to get out, saving myself and my companions, for whose sake I am running this risk." Having had this conversation and reported it to Damis he lay down to sleep.

At dawn a clerk came from the imperial court and told Apol- VII.29
lonius he was to come to the palace during the forenoon, not to
make his official defense but to undergo a private, preliminary
interview. Apollonius asked whether arrangements had been
made to enable him to leave the prison and go to the court, and
on being assured of this he again lay down to sleep, explaining VII.30
to Damis that he had been kept awake during the previous night
by trying to remember certain things he had been told in India.
Damis marveled that he was not going to use the remaining time
to prepare himself for the interview but intended to risk his life
on extempore answers. "Yes, indeed, Damis," he said, "I live extempore. But you may find it helpful if I tell you what I remembered. It was that tame lions should not be beaten, because they
bear grudges, nor spoiled, because that makes them insolent, but
should be stroked while being threatened. Now, the Indians were
not concerned with animal training; when they spoke of lions,
they meant tyrants." "Their advice was excellent," said Damis,
"but I remember also that of Aesop's fox, who would not go into
the cave where the lion was because he saw no tracks left
by animals coming out." "He would have been wiser," said Apollonius, "had he known how to go in and come out again."

So saying he snatched a brief nap, then at dawn he made his VII.31
prayer to the sun as best he could in prison and discussed whatever questions were put to him until the clerk arrived to take
him to the court, whereupon he went at once, accompanied by
four guards. Damis, although fearful, followed him. Apollonius'
costume made him conspicuous, and his appearance was super-
naturally striking. Moreover, the fact that he had come to risk his
life for other men won over at this time even those formerly envious
of him. Seeing the crowds going into and coming out of the palace
he said, "Damis, this place is like a bath; those inside are trying
to get out, those outside in, like the washed and the unwashed."
He made some further philosophic comments on the foolishness
of courtiers and finally rebuked Damis for his evident fear, saying
that after living with him so long he should have learned to be
prepared for death, since a major concern of philosophy was to
choose the right time and way to die, as he himself had done.

VII.32   When he was sent in to the emperor, Damis was not permitted
to follow. Domitian accused him of conspiring with Nerva and
VII.33 others. Apollonius denied the charge and asserted their innocence.
Domitian told him the formal accusation would prove the
charge, since he knew the oaths taken and their purpose and time
and what was sacrificed. Apollonius told him that it was shameful
VII.34 of a judge to form on opinion before hearing the case. Domitian
thereupon ordered his beard and hair cut off and had him chained
in the prison reserved for the worst criminals. "I did not realize,
your Majesty," Apollonius said, "that I was risking my hair."
And as for the chains : "If you think me a magician, how can you
chain me? And if you chain me, how can you say I am a
magician?" "And I shall not let you go," said the emperor, "until
you turn into water or some animal or a tree." "I should not do
so even if I could," Apollonius replied, "so as not to betray those
who are quite unjustly in danger. But such as I am, I shall submit
myself to whatever you may do to this body, until I may speak in
defense of these men." "And who will speak in defense of you?"
"Time," Apollonius said, "and the holy spirit and the love of
wisdom, with which I live."

VII.36   When he had been in chains for two days, one of Domitian's
creatures came to see him, pretending to have bought his way
into the prison in order to advise him as to how he might save his
life. He harped on Apollonius' misfortunes in the hope of leading
him to abuse the emperor, but Apollonius turned aside his remarks, and as for the discomfort of his chained leg, he said he
wasn't thinking about it. "Then what are you thinking about?"
"Not thinking about it." The informer revenged himself for this
snub by telling Apollonius that the emperor had received from
a prominent man in Ionia further accusations against him concerning what he had said there. Apollonius promptly identified
his accuser as Euphrates but said that Euphrates had played him
a worse trick before by slandering him to the Egyptian gymnosophists. "You think," said the amazed informer, "that to be
slandered to those naked Egyptians was a worse thing than to be
accused to the emperor?" "Of course," said Apollonius, "for
there I went to learn; here I came to teach." "Teach what?"

"That I am a good man; the emperor does not yet know this."
"There are some things you could teach him that would resolve
your difficulties, and if you had said those before coming here,
you might not have been imprisoned." Apollonius perceived that
he was being pushed toward what the emperor wanted him to
say, and fearing that out of weariness of his bonds he might say
something false against his friends, he said, "My good man, if I
was imprisoned when I told the truth to Domitian, what would
happen to me if I didn't tell the truth? Truth seems to him to
deserve imprisonment; falsity, to me." At this his interlocutor gave VII.37
up and went off baffled.

Damis, however, was almost in despair. A little before noon he VII.38
said to him, "O man of Tyana"—for Apollonius particularly
liked this form of address—"what is going to happen to us?"
"What has happened," Apollonius answered, "and nothing more.
Nobody is going to kill us." "Who is so invulnerable?" said Damis.
"And will you ever be set free?" [Apollonius answered,] "By the
one who will judge me, today; and by myself, now." So saying he
took his leg out of the chain and said to Damis, "I have given you
a demonstration of my freedom, so take heart." Damis says this
was the first time he clearly understood that Apollonius' nature
was divine, for without any sacrifice or prayer or spell he made
a mock of the chain and then, putting his leg back in it, resumed
the role of a prisoner.

At noon a messenger arrived saying that the emperor on the VII.40
advice of Aelian had ordered Apollonius released from his chains
and returned to his former prison pending his trial, which would
probably take place on the fifth day thereafter. When he returned
to his former prison, he was welcomed with astonishment by the
prisoners, who had regarded him as a father. Next day he told VII.41
Damis that his trial would take place as scheduled and ordered
him to go by foot to Dicaearchia and greet Demetrius and then
to go to the seaside by the island of Calypso, "for there you shall
see me appear." "Living?" said Damis. "Or how?" Apollonius
laughed and said, "As I myself believe, living; but as you believe,
risen from the dead." Damis says that he went away unwilling,

and neither despairing of Apollonius as of one certain to perish nor having any great hope of his not perishing. Three days thereafter he arrived at Dicaearchia and heard there of the damage done to the shipping by the storm that had raged during those days. He then understood why Apollonius had ordered him to go by foot.

VII.42   Apollonius, remaining in prison, made the acquaintance of a beautiful young man from Arcadia who had come to Rome to study law, attracted the attention of Domitian, and been jailed because he would not comply with the emperor's wishes. Apollonius reminded him that continued refusal might cost him his life, but he declared himself ready to die rather than yield, and Apollonius praised him for his resolution. As matters turned out, he escaped death and returned to Arcadia, where everyone marveled at his strength of character.

VIII.2   When the day came for his trial, Apollonius nonchalantly went off to the court with the remark that both he and the emperor were up for judgment. He refused to set any time limit for his speech, since he could not speak long enough to set forth the justification of his actions nor briefly enough to dismiss the charges with the contempt they deserved. When the clerk reminded him that Socrates had been put to death for similar contempt of court, Apollonius answered, "He did not die; the Athenians merely VIII.3   thought he did." When another clerk told him that he must go into court without anything on him, Apollonius said, "Am I going to be tried or bathed?" The clerk explained that he meant without any papers, and Apollonius exchanged abuse with his accuser, who had suggested this ruling to the emperor. One of Euphrates' freed men was also present, sent by Euphrates to report on Apollonius' lectures in Ionia and to bring a gift of money to the accuser.

VIII.4   The courtroom was full. All the most prominent people were there, since the emperor wanted as many witnesses as possible to Apollonius' conviction, as a step toward that of the other conspirators. Apollonius did not even look at the emperor, and when the accuser berated him for his disrespect and bade him look to the god of all mankind, Apollonius looked at the ceiling as if trying to look to Zeus.

The accuser completed his speech by demanding that Apollonius answer specifically each item in a written list of charges that he presented. The emperor agreed to this request in VIII.5 principle but threw out as trivial all charges except four. On these he questioned Apollonius one by one. "For what reason do you wear not the same dress as other men but a peculiar and individual garb?" "Because," Apollonius replied, "the earth that feeds me also clothes me, and I will not levy on the unfortunate animals." "For what reason do men call you a god?" "Because any man thought to be good is honored with that apellation." "What motivated or suggested your prediction of the plague in Ephesus?" "Since, your Majesty, I live on a more meager diet than other men, I was the first to perceive the danger. If you wish, I shall go on to state the causes of plagues." This would have given him occasion to mention, as causes of plagues, injustice and incestuous marriages and other topics about which the emperor was sensitive, so the latter replied, "I do not need any such answer as that." He then went on after some reflection to the fourth question. "Tell me," he said, "when you went out on such and such a day and went into the country, for whom did you sacrifice the boy?" Apollonius answered as if rebuking a child, "Do not be abusive. If I went out, I might have gone to the country. And if this, I might have sacrificed. And if I sacrificed, I might also have eaten of the victim. Let these things be attested by persons worthy of confidence." This answer brought more applause than is permitted in an imperial court, and the emperor, judging that the persons present had borne witness to the victory of Apollonius, acquitted him of the charges against him but ordered him to remain for private examination [most likely, torture]. Apollonius replied, "I thank your Majesty. But through the work of these accursed accusers the cities of the empire have gone to ruin, the islands are full of exiles, the mainland of lamentation, the army camps of cowardice, and the Senate of suspicion. If you see fit, give me time to speak, and if not, send someone to take my body, for you cannot take my soul. Indeed, you shall not even take my body, 'for you shall not kill me, for I am not mortal.' "³ So saying he vanished.

VIII.6   Apollonius composed an oration that he intended to deliver in
VIII.7.i court, but he was not permitted to. It began with a reminder to
the emperor of the risk he ran in trying a philosopher (think how
the Athenians disgraced themselves by condemning Socrates!)
and went on to a denunciation of the Emperor's sycophants.

ii Then it turned to Apollonius' record, his support of Vespasian,
and the latter's consultation of him. Vespasian would never have
iii consulted a magician, and anyhow all magicians were after
money, to which Apollonius was indifferent, as shown especially
by his having given away his inheritance.

iv   Apollonius' costume and diet were not his own inventions but
were those prescribed by Pythagoras, who learned of them from
the Egyptians, who learned of them from the Indians. By avoiding the impurity of animal food and clothing, Pythagoras had
profited in many ways, above all, he had attained immortality
by attaining consciousness of his own soul, a consciousness that
continued uninterrupted through its various incarnations. Apollonius had never made a nuisance of himself by criticizing other
people's clothing and diet; it was therefore unfair that he should
v be prosecuted because of his own. Finally, to those who sleep
under linen rather than wool, dreams speak more truly.

vi   As for long hair, it might be a sign of guilt in effeminate young
men, but in Apollonius' case it was a perpetuation of the manly
Spartan custom and a sign of the holiness of the head, which as
seat of the senses and source of speech should not be desecrated by
the touch of iron. [The ancient philosopher] Empedocles wore
long hair and proclaimed himself a god and was not called into
court for either of these actions.

vii   The charge that Apollonius was worshiped as a god should
have been accompanied by an account of the reasons for which
men prayed to him. For he never discussed among the Greeks
the forms from or into which his soul changed, nor did he dis-
seminate rumors about himself nor give oracular responses like

³ *Iliad* 22.13; in the *Iliad* the line is spoken by the god Apollo when threatened
by Achilles.

persons inspired, and there was no city in which the residents voted to sacrifice to Apollonius, although he conferred on them the great benefits for which they besought him—that the sick might be cured, that initiations and sacrifices might be performed in more holy ways, that arrogance might be cut off and the laws be strengthened. By performing these benefits Apollonius improved the cities and therefore acted in the interest of the emperor. Had the cities believed him a god, his action would have been the more effective and the belief would therefore have been to the emperor's advantage. "But they believed rather that there is some relationship between man and the gods, as a result of which man is the only animal to have knowledge of the gods and philosophize about his own nature and how he participates in divinity. Further, they said that even the form of man is like that of God, as the practice of making images and paintings shows, and it is believed that virtues come from God to man and that those who participate in them are demigods and divine." These opinions derive not only from the Athenian practice of calling men by such divine titles as "just" and "Olympian" but also are sanctioned by the Delphic oracle, which hailed [the Spartan lawgiver] Lycurgus as a god, and by the Spartans, who accepted the oracle's judgment. Moreover, they are justified by the philosophy of the Indians and the Egyptians, who agree in teaching that God is the creator of all things, that all things are therefore related, and that consequently good men have something of God. Now, as the visible world depends on the creator, so there is a world that depends on the good man. This is the world of sick and disordered souls that only he, having become a god by wisdom, can restore to order.

As for Ephesus, to have saved that city from a plague was a viii feat that should not require defense. The accusation, therefore, ix specified only foreknowledge of the plague as a proof of magical practice. But similar foreknowledge of natural phenomena is reported of other Greek philosophers, who were not accused of magic on that account. And as for Apollonius, his peculiar diet kept his senses so clear that he could perceive not only present events but those about to occur. Moreover, the fact that he set

up a statue of Hercules to commemorate the event proved that
he was not a magician, for a magician would have sought to take
the credit for himself or at least would have tried to attribute it
to one of the gods of the underworld.

x   The accusation concerning sacrifice was utterly incredible because Apollonius never tolerated bloody sacrifices of any sort. Had
he participated in one, his power of foreknowledge would have
left him, and so long as he had this power of foreknowledge—
shown in the case of Ephesus—he had no need to sacrifice in
order to foretell the future. Nor would he, certainly, have con-
spired with Nerva, who was a sick man scarcely able to manage
his own affairs, let alone those of the empire, nor with the others
accused as parties to the plot, who were good men but too slug-
xi gish for conspirators. Moreover, Apollonius had no motive to
participate in any such conspiracy, for he wanted none of the
rewards its success could have brought him. Proof of this was the
fact that during the reigns of Vespasian and Titus he had never
asked for money or office, though he might have had them for
the asking.

xii   The accusation concerning the sacrifice was elaborated in a
story which declared that the victim was an Arcadian boy of good
family. But this story was unsupported either by witnesses or by
any details concerning the boy. His name, his family, his city,
xiii how he was got to Italy—none of these were specified. It is true
that Apollonius was in Rome at the time, but so was the emperor
xiv and so were myriads of other men. Moreover, Apollonius spent
that night at the bedside of a sick pupil whom even his prayers
could not save. This he substantiated by producing witnesses, a
friend of the dead man and two doctors who attended him (the
dead man's family had gone back to his native island for the
xv funeral and were therefore not available). Further, the charge
was wholly implausible because human beings are not suitable
victims for divinatory sacrifices. Unlike animals, they are aware
of what is about to be done to them, and their fear of death dis-
turbs their entrails so as to make them useless for divination (this
is why they were never sacrificed by the famous diviners of old,

though these were often employed by kings, who could have provided human sacrifices).

Having thus disposed of the charges of his principal accuser xvi
(an Egyptian) Apollonius' speech went on to those made by
Euphrates. Those concerned what he had said against the emperor in Ionia, and especially in his discourse on the Fates and
necessity. In that he had referred to the emperor merely because
imperial matters were the greatest of human affairs, and his statement that one destined to succeed the emperor would, even if
killed, rise from the dead, was a hyperbole : he had in mind the
stories of ancient rulers who had ordered the destruction of persons destined to succeed them and believed their orders had been
carried out when actually they had not; in such stories the
destined successor always reappears, as if from the dead, and
succeeds. He could, however, have used the example of
Vitellius, who at one time thought he had Domitian in his power;
thanks to fate, Domitian had escaped and eventually succeeded
to the throne. This example, however, Apollonius had not used
because it smacked of flattery and because he was not concerned
with current events but exclusively with the question of the Fates
and necessity, a theme tolerated, as appears in Homer, by the
gods themselves. The Fates have decreed transience for all things
human; therefore the emperor should resign himself to their
decree, practice philosophy, put an end to his purges, which
filled the empire with grief, and pay no more attention to the
sycophants who slandered all men to him and him to all men.

Such was Apollonius' written speech, but it contained also, as VIII.8
a conclusion, the statements with which he had ended his remarks
in court, including the assertion of his immortality.

Apollonius disappeared from the court before noon. About VIII.10
evening he appeared in Dicaearchia to Demetrius and Damis.
They had gone to the seashore, as Apollonius ordered, and were VIII.11
sitting in a grotto sacred to the Nymphs and talking almost in
despair of Apollonius' chances of escape. Damis said, "Shall we VIII.12
ever see again, O gods, our noble and good companion?" At this
Apollonius, who was standing beside him, answered, "You shall
see him, or rather you have seen him." "Alive?" said Demetrius.

"For if dead, we have not yet ceased to lament you." Thereupon Apollonius, stretching out his hand, said, "Take hold of me, and if I am intangible, I am an image come to you from Persephone, such as the gods of the underworld send to those who are despondent in grief. But if I prove solid when you grasp me, persuade Damis that I am alive and have not abandoned the body." They were no longer able to disbelieve but, jumping up, embraced the man and kissed him and asked about the defense. Apollonius replied, "I have made my defense, gentlemen, and we have won. I spoke today, not long ago, for it went on till nearly noon." "How then," said Demetrius, "did you come so long a distance in so short a time?" To this question Apollonius said only that he had come with divine aid, but to the flood of questions about his trial, which followed, he replied, while the three of them were walking back to the city, with a full account of the

VIII.13 proceedings. When they reached the city, he said he was tired, made a prayer to Apollo and to the sun, went into the house where Demetrius was living, washed his feet, told Damis and his companions to eat dinner, since he saw they had been fasting, threw himself into bed and went off to sleep.

VIII.14 Demetrius was on tenterhooks, fearing pursuit, but the next morning Apollonius assured him there would be no pursuit. To Demetrius' question where he would go, he said he was going to Greece, and since a ship was sailing for Sicily that morning, he

VIII.15 and Damis went aboard and sailed to Syracuse and thence in early autumn to the Peloponnesus, where he went to stay in the temple of Zeus at Olympia. The unhoped for news of his coming spread like wildfire over Greece, and crowds came from every city

VIII.16 to see him and hear of his escape. Not all were absolutely friendly; there was one young man of Athens who was so impertinent as to declare that Athena was particularly concerned for the well-being of Domitian and rightly so, since Domitian had been elected chief magistrate of her city. Apollonius told him not to slander the goddess at the shrine of her father, Zeus, nor to disgrace the Athenians by reporting that they had forgotten

VIII.17 [the tyrannicides] Harmodius and Aristogeiton. By contrast to this young gentleman the great majority of the visitors were enthusiastically on the side of Apollonius, and the authorities of Olympia so far shared these sentiments that the priest of the temple actually provided him with funds from the treasury of Zeus. Apollonius in return discoursed on the natural advantages VIII.18 of Olympia which made it suitable as a center for Greek festivals.

After forty days' stay at Olympia Apollonius went on to VIII.19 Lebadea, a town in Boeotia, to visit [in the underworld] the hero Trophonius. There, however, the priests refused him admission [to the sacred cave], telling the crowds that they would never permit a magician to inspect the shrine, while to Apollonius they alleged that the god had given them inauspicious and unfavorable responses. He, therefore, during the day lectured on the origin and procedure of the oracle and at evening went with his young followers to the mouth of the cave (which lay outside the temple) and pulled up four of the iron posts by which it was fenced and went down into the cave just as he was [without the prescribed ritual preparation or costume]. This action pleased Trophonius, who appeared to his priests to rebuke them for their treatment of Apollonius and send them to Aulis, where the marvelous man would emerge from the earth. Apollonius stayed down for seven days—longer than anyone else had ever visited the oracle—and came up bringing a book that answered the question he had put to the oracle when he went in. For he had said, "Which, O Trophonius, do you think to be the most suitable and purest philosophy?" And the book contained the tenets of Pythagoras, as evidence that the oracle too agreed with this wisdom. (This book, with some of Apollonius' letters, eventually VIII.20 came into the possession of Emperor [117–38] Hadrian and was preserved in his palace at Antium on the west coast of Italy.)

After this episode Apollonius' following was increased by VIII.21 many disciples from Ionia, whom the mainland Greeks called "Apollonians," and his popular success was so great that even the study of rhetoric was generally neglected for that of his philosophy, which he made freely available to all comers, answering questions on all subjects. He encouraged his disciples to avoid VIII.22 governors and suchlike officials and to withdraw from the world to live in tranquillity. When someone joked about the way he drove off his sheep if he heard rhetoricians were coming, he said, "I do, indeed. I don't want the wolves to attack the flock." His dislike of rhetoricians was due not only to their concern for money but also to their huckstering hatreds and especially to their role as false accusers, for though he had always disliked them, his experience with the Roman prisons and the prisoners there made him so hostile that he blamed all those miseries more on the rhetoricians than on the tyrant, and he sharply rebuked those who associated with them.

VIII.23   At about this time a remarkable sign appeared in the heavens, an iridescent wreath around the sun that diminished its light. Everyone realized that this portended some revolution. The governor of Greece called Apollonius from Boeotia to Athens and said to him, "I hear you are wise in supernatural matters." "I hope you hear that I am also wise in human ones." "I do," said the governor, "and I agree." "Since you agree, do not pry into the plans of the gods; this is the counsel of human wisdom." But he besought Apollonius to give him his opinion, saying he feared the world might be returning to night. "Don't be afraid," said Apollonius. "From this night will come light."

VIII.24   After spending two years in Greece Apollonius, with his following, went on to Ionia and philosophized especially in Smyrna and Ephesus, though he visited the other cities, too, and was well received everywhere.

VIII.25   At this time [Sept. 18, 96] occurred the assassination of Domitian that had been heralded by the portent described above.[4] The assassin bandaged his left arm as if broken and hid a sword in the bandage. He then pretended to have information about a plot, so got a private interview with the emperor and stabbed him in the thigh. Domitian was 45 and vigorous; he threw his assailant to the ground and gouged out his eyes, but then he fainted and was himself dispatched by his guards.

VIII.26   While this was being done in Rome, Apollonius saw it in Ephesus. It happened while he was lecturing, and he at first lowered his voice as if afraid, then spoke absently like those who are watching something else while speaking, then stopped alto-

---

[4] The assassin was named Stephanos, which in Greek means "wreath."

gether. Staring terribly at the earth and taking a few steps forward he shouted, "Strike the tyrant, strike him!" Not like those who see the image of some object in a mirror, but as if he saw the thing itself and thought he was taking part in what was done. The whole city of Ephesus was astounded, for everybody had been present at his lecture. He paused as if to watch the outcome of something, then said, "Take courage, gentlemen, for the tyrant has been killed today. Why should I say, 'today'? Now! By Athena, now! At the time when I stopped speaking!" The Ephesians thought this lunacy, wished it truth, and feared the danger that having heard it might entail. Apollonius said, "I am not surprised at those who do not accept the news which not even the whole of Rome knows. But see, it is learning; the news spreads; already myriads believe, and twice as many jump for joy, and twice as many yet, and four times, and all the people there. The news will come here, too, and you should put off your sacrifices of thanksgiving until these things will be officially announced, but I must go pray to the gods for what I have seen." When the news did VIII.27 arrive, it confirmed Apollonius' vision, even to the hour of the day.

Thirty days later Nerva wrote him that by the counsels of the gods and of Apollonius he had secured control of the empire and would retain it more easily if Apollonius would come to advise him. Apollonius sent back at once the following note: "Your Majesty, we shall be together a very long time, when we shall neither rule others, nor others us." No doubt he referred to the fact that both he and Nerva were soon to depart this life. But lest he VIII.28 should seem neglectful of a friend, a good man, and a ruler, he composed a letter of advice for rulers and sent it to him by Damis. And he persuaded Damis to take the letter so as to get him out of the way. For one of his constant sayings had been, "Live without being noticed, but if you can't do that, depart from life without being noticed." Therefore, when Damis was leaving, Apollonius said none of those things that people commonly say when they shall never see each other again, but he did tell him, "O Damis, if you ever philosophize on your own, keep me in mind."

VIII.29   This concludes the work of Damis, who says nothing of Apollonius' death nor even of how old he was. Reports of his age vary
from eighty to more than a hundred, but all agree that as an old
and wrinkled man he was sound of body, erect in carriage, and
VIII.30   extraordinarily beautiful. Some say he died in Ephesus under the
tendance of two female slaves, of whom he freed one and told
the other that it would be better for her to be a slave to her former
companion. (Her companion, after his death, sold her to a slave-
merchant, who sold her to a wealthy man, who fell in love with
her—although she wasn't pretty—and made her his lawful wife.)
Others say Apollonius died in Lindus [in Rhodes] : he entered
the temple of Athena there and disappeared. Others say that he
died in the temple of Dictynna on the northwest coast of Crete.
He came to the temple late at night, but the savage dogs that
guarded it fawned on him and did not even bark. However, the
custodians of the temple, supposing him a magician and a robber
and claiming he had doped the dogs, seized him and put him in
bonds. But when midnight came, he released himself and, having
called those who bound him, that he might not act without witnesses, ran to the doors of the temple, which opened for him and
closed again after he entered. Then from the temple came the
sound of maidens singing, and their song was, "Go from the
earth; go into Heaven; go."
VIII.31   Even after this he proved the immortality of the soul by ap-
pearing to a young man at Tyana who denied immortality
because he had prayed to Apollonius for nine months to prove
it and had got no answer. Shortly thereafter Apollonius appeared
to him in a dream and rebuked him so vividly as to remove his
doubts. There is no tomb of Apollonius in any country, but there
is a temple to him in Tyana, built by imperial funds, for the emperors have not denied him that deification of which they themselves were thought worthy.

INDEX

From the Country
of Nevermore

From the Country
of Nevermore

Selected Poems of Jorge Teillier

Translated and with an Introduction by Mary Crow

NE *Wesleyan University Press*
Published by University Press of New England
Hanover and London

The University Press of New England

is a consortium of universities in New England dedicated to publishing scholarly and trade works by authors from member campuses and elsewhere. The New England imprint signifies uniform standards for publication excellence maintained without exception by the consortium members. A joint imprint of University Press of New England and a sponsoring member acknowledges the publishing mission of that university and its support for the dissemination of scholarship throughout the world. Cited by the American Council of Learned Societies as a model to be followed, University Press of New England publishes books under its own imprint and the imprints of Brandeis University, Brown University, Clark University, University of Connecticut, Dartmouth College, University of New Hampshire, University of Rhode Island, Tufts University, University of Vermont, and Wesleyan University.

Copyright © 1990 by Jorge Teillier
Translation and Introduction copyright © 1990 by Mary Crow

Most of the poems in *From the Country of Nevermore* were translated from *Muertes y maravillas,* © 1971, by permission of Editorial Universitaria. "Not a Sign of Life" and "Story about a Branch of Myrtle" were translated from *Cartas de reinas de otras primaveras,* © 1985 by Jorge Teillier.

Some of these translations appeared in these magazines: *The American Poetry Review, The Black Warrior Review, George Washington Review, Ground Water Review, International Poetry Review, Mississippi Valley Review, New Letters, New Mexico Humanities Review, Nimrod, The Poetry Miscellany, Southern Humanities Review, Willow Springs, Wooster Review,* and *Xavier Review.*

Library of Congress Cataloging-in-Publication Data

Teillier, Jorge.
From the country of Nevermore : poems / by Jorge Teillier : translated by Mary Crow. — 1st ed.
p. cm.
Translated from Spanish.
ISBN 0–8195–2176–0 — ISBN 0–8195–1178–1 (pbk.)
1. Teillier, Jorge—Translations, English. I. Crow, Mary. II. Title.
PQ8098.3.E4A17 1990
861—dc20   89–28425
                                  CIP

PQ
8098.3
.E4
A17
1990

Printed in the United States of America

5   4   3   2   1

Wesleyan Poetry in Translation

Contents

III. The Land of Night

IV. I Would Give All the Gold in the World

Introduction

Jorge Teillier, who has been called the most important Chilean poet of his generation, was born in 1935 in Lautaro, in the south of Chile. Author of twelve collections of poems, he has also written short stories and essays, and edited literary magazines. But even though his poetry has been the subject of many articles, including a number in the United States, and Hispanic scholars have been discussing it for some years, his work has not been available to the general reader of poetry in English because of the lack of translation.

Teillier has a contemporary voice, influenced by the French Symbolists, by Edgar Allan Poe, and by his nostalgia for North American memorabilia of the twenties and thirties—old songs like "Paper Moon" and old-fashioned singers like Al Jolson. Typically, a Teillier poem is inhabited by Chile's southern countryside and its persistent rainy days, by the beliefs and superstitions of country people, by the sad sound of passing night trains on their way, perhaps, to happiness, and by death in its many incarnations. Yet, in spite of such imagery, Teillier's poems stop short of sentimentality through his use of simple matter-of-fact conclusions and by the exclusion of self-pity. If self-pity creeps in, it is accompanied by a saving self-mockery.

There is no other voice in contemporary poetry quite like Teillier's, which has been accorded a recognition in Chile and Latin America that it deserves to receive in other countries. His reputation has begun to spread around the world, and some of his poems are being translated into French, Italian, Swedish, Czechoslovakian, Russian, Rumanian, and Polish, as well as English. The translations of his work into English have, until now, appeared only in literary magazines, in translations by Miller Williams, Margaret Sayers Peden, John Upton, and Carolyn Wright; in *Anthology of Magazine Verse and Yearbook of American Poetry*, 1987; and in a broadsheet.

Jorge Teillier began writing poems when he was twelve. At that time he loved to read fiction, especially Jules Verne and other "fairy tales," and such books influenced his poetry. One of his earliest and most persistent favorites among poets was Edgar Allan Poe; Teillier's mature work retains more than a trace of Poe's nostalgia and mystery. His first book, *Para angeles y gorriones* (For Angels and Sparrows), appeared when he was twenty-one. By then he was interested in the work of Paul Verlaine, Rubén Darío, Vicente Huidobro, Teófilo Cid. As he read, he says, he began to wonder: What does *Chilean* mean? "Poetry," he concluded, "is universality. . . . The death before us is the death of the lutist of ancient Egypt, is also the death of Rilke, death is great and we belong to death, and the same snow is remembered in Villon and is like the solitude in Rilke, and time is a river in Heraclitus and Jorge Manrique." So, he says, he took the train back from Santiago, back to the provinces, to the rain and snow, the silence, solitude, and deserted stations of Chile's lovely South, full of snow-capped volcanoes, rivers, and lakes, small villages with plazas and patios. In those years of his development, his hero was Pablo Neruda, who lamented that young men were reading his Surrealist and literary *Residencia en la tierra* (Residence on Earth) instead of the simple words of his social-protest poems. Teillier, however, did not find that writing political poems came naturally to him, in spite of his sympathy with Neruda's complaint. His poems focus, instead, on the politics of the psyche or on poor, lovely, but ill-fated dreams of happiness.

Although Jorge Teillier studied history education at the University of Chile, he taught only one year. He then joined the editorial staff of the university's *Bulletin,* and eventually became its editor.

Among his books of poetry are *Para angeles y gorriones, El cielo cae con las hojas, El árbol de la memoria, Poemas del país de nunca jamás, Los trenes de la noche y otros poemas, Poemas secretos, Crónica del forastero, Muertes y maravillas, Para un pueblo fantasma,* and *Cartas para reinas de otras primaveras.* He has also published two collections of essays: *Romeo Murga, poeta adolescente* and *Actualidad de Vicinte*

Huidobro. In addition to his extensive writing for newspapers and literary magazines, he has translated poems from French into Spanish, and his poetry has appeared in magazines and anthologies throughout Latin America.

In 1986, in the introduction to *Cartas para reinas de otras primaveras,* fiction writer Jorge Edwards said, "In Teillier's poetry a mythical South exists, the same rainy and forested frontier of Pablo Neruda, but in this case made unreal, changed into a pretext for a verbal creation where trees, mountains, provincial plazas, are colored by innumerable references to contemporary literature, as if literary and natural space were interwoven. The phantasmagorical House of Usher, that in the story of Poe was brought down on top of his dream, floats in the verses of Teillier in a ghostly South, and the poet William Gray is cured of his delirium tremens in a clinic on the outskirts of Santiago."

Even now, Teillier lives in a timeless place of literature, dividing his days between a house in Santiago and a nearby country estate with an old wooden mill.

A Note on the Translation

It has been a pleasure to help introduce the poems of Jorge Teillier to English-language readers and to give Teillier the chance to join the "congregation of voices" of world literature. I used two premises. First, each translation into English must be a poem. To be a poem, the translation needs to achieve natural English that moves rhythmically. Second, each translation must keep as close as possible to the original, respecting the author's style, punctuation, lines—in short, everything—unless this results in awkward phrasing or syntax in English where there was no awkward phrasing or syntax in Spanish.

If the first is not achieved, there would be little reason to read the translations; after all, a book of translations is a book for readers of English. Given this constraint, I have tried to stay as close to my understanding of the author's intent as I could, while reproducing line and phrasing as far as possible. Of course, some effects are inevitably lost—alliteration, assonance and consonance, double meanings, and the range of connotations embedded in the phrasings Teillier uses. Other effects are gained.

Luckily for me, Teillier writes poetry that is highly translatable into English. This is partly because his poems are so image-laden and partly because the Poesque atmosphere will be familiar to readers of English.

In a few instances, a translation includes something not in the original. These are Teillier's changes; he asked me to include, for example, the words "in memoriam" in a dedication to a person who died after the poem's original publication. There are also a few old-fashioned English usages. These reflect allusions to a literary work translated into English, as in the case of "the snows of yesteryear" from François Villon, and quotations from an earlier period, such as the now archaic "nevermore" from Poe's "The Raven."

Most of the poems in this collection are from *Muertes y maravillas*

(Editorial Universítaria, 1971), a volume that collects a large body of Teillier's poetry. In my opinion, that is the strongest of his books. I have also chosen a few poems from his most recent book, *Cartas para reinas de otras primaveras* (Ediciones Manieristas, 1985), to demonstrate the range and variety of his writing.

I would like to express my gratitude for a Fulbright research grant, which took me to Chile in 1982 and led me to the poetry of Jorge Teillier. I would also like to thank Colorado State University, for a grant that allowed me to return in 1986, and Patsy Boyer, for her generous help and support in the revision of these translations.

I
Letter of Rain

Nieve nocturna

¿Es que puede existir algo antes de la nieve?
Antes de esa pureza implacable,
implacable como el mensaje de un mundo que no amamos
pero al cual pertenecemos
y que se adivina en ese sonido
todavia hermano del silencio.
¿Qué dedos te dejan caer,
pulverizado esqueleto de pétalos?
Ceniza de un cielo antiguo
que hace quedar solo frente al fuego
escuchando los pasos del amigo que se va,
eco de palabras que no recordamos,
pero que nos duelen como si las fuéramos a decir de nuevo.

¿Y puede existir algo después de la nieve,
algo después de la última mirada del ciego a la palidez del sol,
algo después que el niño enfermo olvida mirar la nueva mañana,
o, mejor aún, despúes de haber dormido como un convaleciente
con la cabeza sobre la falda
de aquella a quien alguna vez se ama?
¿Quién eres, nieve nocturna,
fugaz, disuelta primavera que sobrevive en el cerezo?
¿O qué importa quién eres?
Para mirar la nieve en la noche hay que cerrar los ojos,
no recordar nada, no preguntar nada.
desaparecer, deslizarse como ella en el visible silencio.

Night Snow

Can something exist before snow?
Before this implacable purity,
implacable as the message of a world
we don't love but belong to
and which can be divined in that sound,
still a brother of silence.
What fingers drop you,
pulverized skeleton of petals?
Ash of an ancient sky
that makes one remain alone before the fire
listening to the steps of the friend who leaves,
echo of words we don't remember, but that hurt us
as if we were going to say them once more.

And can something exist after snow?
Something after the last glance of the blind man at the sun's pallor,
something after the sick child forgets to look for the new morning,
or, more exactly, after a sleep like the sleep of a convalescent
with his head in the lap
of the woman he once loved?
Who are you, night snow?
Fleeting, dissolved spring that survives in the cherry tree?
Or does it matter who you are?
To look at the snow in the night one has to shut his eyes,
remember nothing, ask nothing,
disappear, slip away like snow into the visible silence.

Otoño secreto

Cuando las amadas palabras cotidianas
pierden su sentido
y no se puede nombrar ni el pan,
ni el agua, ni la ventana,
y ha sido falso todo diálogo que no sea
con nuestra desolada imagen,
aún se miran las destrozadas estampas
en el libro del hermano menor,
es bueno saludar los platos y el mantel puestos sobre la mesa,
y ver que en el viejo armario conservan su alegría
el licor de guindas que preparó la abuela
y las manzanas puestas a guardar.

Cuando la forma de los árboles
ya no es sino el leve recuerdo de su forma,
una mentira inventada
por la turbia memoria del otoño,
y los días tienen la confusión
del desván a donde nadie sube
y la cruel blancura de la eternidad
hace que la luz huya de sí misma,
algo nos recuerda la verdad
que amamos antes de conocer:
las ramas se quiebran levemente,
el palomar se llena de aleteos,
el granero sueña otra vez con el sol,
encendemos para la fiesta
los pálidos candelabros del salón polvoriento
y el silencio nos revela el secreto
que no queríamos escuchar.

Secret Autumn

When the loved daily words
lose their meaning
and bread cannot be named,
or water, or window,
and all dialogue has proven false
that wasn't with our own desolate image,
when you can still look over the tattered pictures
in your kid brother's book—
then it's good to greet the cloth and the dishes arranged on the table,
good to see that the cherry liqueur grandmother made
and the apples put by for safekeeping
conserve their happiness in the old sideboard.

When the form of trees
is merely the slight memory of their form,
a lie invented
by autumn's turbid memory,
and days have the confusion of the attic
no one climbs up to,
and the cruel whiteness of eternity
makes light flee from itself—
then something reminds us of the truth
we love even before we know it:
branches snap lightly,
the pigeon coop is filled with fluttering,
the granary dreams again of the sun,
we light for the party
pale candelabras in the dusty parlor,
and silence reveals to us the secret
we didn't want to hear.

Para hablar con los muertos

Para hablar con los muertos
hay que elegir palabras
que ellos reconozcan tan fácilmente
como sus manos
reconocían el pelaje de sus perros en la oscuridad.
Palabras claras y tranquilas
como el agua del torrente domesticada en la copa
o las sillas ordenadas por la madre
después que se han ido los invitados.
Palabras que la noche acoja
como a los fuegos fatuos los pantanos.

Para hablar con los muertos
hay que saber esperar:
ellos son miedosos
como los primeros pasos de un niño.
Pero si tenemos paciencia
un día nos responderán
con una hoja de álamo atrapada por un espejo roto,
con una llama de súbito reanimada en la chimenea,
con un regreso oscuro de pájaros
frente a la mirada de una muchacha
que aguarda inmóvil en el umbral.

To Talk with the Dead

To talk with the dead
you have to choose words
they can recognize as easily
as their hands recognized
their dog's fur in the darkness.
Words clear and calm
as the water of the torrent tamed in a cup
or the chairs rearranged by a mother
after all the guests have gone.
Words that night welcomes
as swamps welcome will-o'-the-wisps.

To talk with the dead
you have to know how to wait;
they are fearful
as the first steps of a child.
But if we have patience
one day they will answer us
with a poplar leaf trapped in a broken mirror,
with a flame that suddenly flares in the fireplace,
with a dark return of birds
before the glance of a girl
who waits motionless on the threshold.

Alegría

Centellean los rieles
pero nadie piensa en viajar.
De la sidreria viene olor
a manzanas recién molidas.
Sabemos que nunca estaremos solos
mientras haya un puñado de tierra fresca.

La llovizna es una oveja compasiva
lamiendo las heridas
hechas por el viento de invierno.
La sangre de las manzanas
ilumina la sidrería.

Desaparece la linterna roja
del último carro del tren.
Los vagabundos duermen
a la sombra de los tilos.
A nosotros nos basta mirar
un puñado de tierra en nuestras manos.

Es bueno beber un aso de cerveza
para prolongar la tarde.
Recordar el centelleo de los rieles.
Recordar la tristeza
dormida como una vieja sirvienta
en un rincón de la casa.
Contarles a los amigos desaparecidos
que afuera llueve en voz baja
y tener en las manos
un puñado de tierra fresca.

Happiness

The train tracks flash
but no one thinks of traveling.
Smell of apples recently crushed
comes from the cider press.
We know we will never be alone
so long as there's a handful of fresh earth.

The drizzle is a forlorn sheep
licking wounds
made by the winter wind.
Blood of the apples
lights up the cider press.

The red lantern
of the caboose disappears.
Tramps sleep in the shade of linden trees.
It's enough for us to look at
a handful of earth in our hands.

It's good to drink a glass of beer
to prolong the afternoon.
To remember the flash on the tracks.
To remember sadness
asleep like an old servant
in a corner of the house.
To tell our missing friends
that outside it is raining in a whisper
and to hold in our hands
a handful of fresh earth.

La llave

Dale la llave al otoño.
Háblale del río mudo en cuyo fondo
yace la sombra de los puentes de madera
desaparecidos hace muchos años.

No me has contado ninguno de tus secretos.
Pero tu mano es la llave que abre la puerta
del molino en ruinas donde duerme mi vida
entre polvo y más polvo,
y espectros de inviernos,
y los jinetes enlutados del viento
que huyen tras robar campanas
en las pobres aldeas.
Pero mis días serán nubes
para viajar por la primavera de tu cielo.

Saldremos en silencio,
sin despertar al tiempo.

Te diré que podremos ser felices.

The Key

Give the key to autumn.
Speak to it of the mute river in whose depth lies
the shadow of wooden bridges
gone for many years.

You haven't told me any of your secrets.
But your hand is the key that opens the door
of the ruined mill where my life sleeps
between dust and more dust,
and between ghosts of winters
and the mourning riders of the wind
who flee after stealing bells
in the poor towns.
But my days will be clouds
to travel through the spring of your sky.

We leave in silence,
without waking time.

I tell you we can be happy.

Estas palabras

Estas palabras quieren ser
un puñado de cerezas,
un susurro—¿para quién?—
entre una y otra oscuridad.

Sí, un puñado de cerezas,
un susurro—¿para quién?—
entre una y otra oscuridad.

These Words

These words want to be
a handful of cherries,
a whisper—for whom?—
between one darkness and another.

Yes, a handful of cherries,
a whisper—for whom?—
between one darkness and another.

Carta de lluvia

Si atraviesas las estaciones
conservando en tus manos
la lluvia de la infancia que debimos compartir
nos reuniremos en el lugar
donde los sueños corren jubilosos
como ovejas liberadas del corral
y en donde brillará sobre nosotros
la estrella que nos fuera prometida.

Pero ahora te envío esta carta de lluvia
que te lleva un jinete de lluvia
por caminos acostumbrados a la lluvia.

Ruega por mí, reloj,
en estas horas monótonas como ronroneos de gatos.
He vuelto al lugar que hace renacer
la ceniza de los fantasmas que odio.
Alguna vez salí al patio
a decirles a los conejos
que el amor había muerto.
Aquí no debo recordar a nadie.
Aquí debo olvidar los aromos
porque la mano que cortó aromos
ahora cava una fosa.

El pasto ha crecido demasiado.
En el techo de la casa vecina
se pudre una pelota de trapo
dejada por un niño muerto.
Entre las tablas del cerco
me vienen a mirar rostros que creía olvidados.
Mi amigo espera en vano que en el río
centellee su buena estrella.

Letter of Rain

If you cross the seasons
holding in your hands
the rain of your childhood we should have shared
we will meet again in the place
where dreams run joyously
as sheep freed from the corral
and where the star we were promised
will shine above us.

> *But now I send you this letter of rain*
> *that a rider of rain carries to you*
> *by roads accustomed to rain.*

Pray for me, clock,
in these hours monotonous as the purring of cats.
I have returned to the place
where the ash of ghosts I hate
is born again.
Once I went out to the patio
to tell the rabbits
love had died.
When I am here I shouldn't remember anyone.
When I am here I ought to forget the aromatic trees
because the hand that cut them
now digs a grave.

The pasture has grown too high.
On the roof of the neighboring house
a ball made of rags rots,
left there by a dead child.
Through the poles of the fence
faces I thought I'd forgotten come to look at me.
My friend waits in vain for his lucky star
to flash on the river.

Tú, como en mis sueños vienes
atravesando las estaciones,
con las lluvias de la infancia
en tus manos hechas cántaro.
En el invierno nos reunirá el fuego
que encenderemos juntos.
Nuestros cuerpos harán las noches tibias
como el aliento de los bueyes
y al despertar veré que el pan sobre la mesa
tiene un resplandor más grande que el de los planetas enemigos
cuando la partan tus manos de adolescente.

Pero ahora te envío una carta de lluvia
que te lleva un jinete de lluvia
por caminos acostumbrados a la lluvia.

You—as if in my dreams—
come crossing the seasons,
with the rains of childhood
in your cupped hands.
In the winter the fire we light together
will unite us.
Our bodies will make nights warm
as the breath of oxen
and on waking I will see that the bread on the table
has a greater dazzle than enemy planets
when your young hands break it.

But now I send you a letter of rain
that a rider of rain carries to you
by roads accustomed to rain.

II

When Everyone Leaves

Cuando todos se vayan

a Eduardo Molina Ventura

Cuando todos se vayan a otros planetas
yo quedaré en la ciudad abandonada
bebiendo un último vaso de cerveza,
y luego volveré al pueblo donde siempre regreso
como el borracho a la taberna
y el niño a cabalgar
en el balancín roto.

Y en el pueblo no tendré nada que hacer,
sino echarme luciérnagas a los bolsillos
o caminar a orillas de rieles oxidados
o sentarme en el roído mostrador de un almacén
para hablar con antiguos compañeros de escuela.

Como una araña que recorre
los mismos hilos de su red
caminaré sin prisa por las calles
invadidas de malezas
mirando los palomares
que se vienen abajo,
hasta llegar a mi casa
donde me encerraré a escuchar
discos de un cantante de 1930
sin cuidarme jamás de mirar
los caminos infinitos
trazados por los cohetes en el espacio.

When Everyone Leaves

To Eduardo Molina Ventura
in memoriam 1913–1986

When everyone leaves for other planets
I will stay behind in the abandoned city
drinking a last glass of beer,
and then I will return to the town to which I always return
as the drunk returns to his tavern
and the child comes back to straddle
a broken crossbeam.

And in the town I'll have nothing to do,
except put fireflies in my pockets
or walk on the edge of rusty rails
or sit down on the dilapidated store counter
to talk with old pals from school.

Like a spider that travels over and over
the same threads of its net
I will walk slowly through streets
invaded by thickets
looking at the pigeon coops
that are falling down,
until I get to my house
where I will shut myself up to listen
to records of a singer from the thirties
never caring to watch
the infinite roads
traced by rockets in space.

Cuento de la tarde

Es tarde,
El tren del norte ha pasado.
En tu casa la cena se enfría,
las madejas ruedan
desde la falda de tu madre dormida.
He estado inmóvil mientras hablabas.
La palabras no son nada
junto a la hoja que resucita al pasar frente a tu cara,
junto al barco de papel
que me enseñaste a hacer.
No he mirado sino tu reflejo en el estanque.

Es tarde.
Las horas son madejas rodando
desde la falda de tu madre dormida.
Volvamos al pueblo.
Las ranas repiten inútilmente su mensaje.
Te ayudo a saltar un charco, te muestro un vagabundo
encendiendo fuego en un galpón abandonado.
Estrellas irreales hacen extinguirse
las miedosas sonrisas de los tejados rojizos.
Nada debe existir.
Nada sino nuestros inmóviles reflejos
que aún retiene el estanque
y esas hojas
a veces resucitadas al pasar frente a tu cara.

Story of the Afternoon

It is late.
The train to the north has gone by.
In your house supper is getting cold,
skeins fall
from the lap of your sleeping mother.
I have kept still while you talked.
Words are nothing
beside the leaf that comes to life when it passes before your face,
beside the paper boat
you taught me to make.
I have looked only at your reflection in the pool.

It is late.
The hours are skeins falling
from the lap of your sleeping mother.
Let's go back to town.
The frogs uselessly repeat their message.
I'll help you jump a puddle, I'll show you a tramp
lighting a fire in an abandoned shack.
Unreal stars extinguish
the frightened smiles of the red roofs.
Nothing ought to exist.
Nothing but our unmoving reflection
still retained by the pool
and those leaves that sometimes come to life
when they pass before your face.

La última isla

De nuevo vida y muerte se confunden
como en el patio de la casa
la entrada de las carretas
con el ruido del balde en el pozo.
De nuevo el cielo recuerda con odio
la herida del relámpago,
y los almendros no quieren pensar
en sus negras raíces.

El silencio no puede seguir siendo mi lenguaje,
pero sólo encuentro esas palabras irreales
que los muertos les dirigen a los astros y a las hormigas,
y de mi memoria desaparecen el amor y la alegría
como la luz de una jarra de agua
lanzada inútilmente contra las tinieblas.

De nuevo sólo se escucha
el crepitar inextinguible de la lluvia
que cae y cae sin saber por qué,
parecida a la anciana solitaria que sigue
tejiendo y tejiendo;
y se quiere huir hacia un pueblo
donde un trompo todavía no deja de girar
esperando que yo lo recoja,
pero donde se ponen los pies
desaparecen los caminos,
y es mejor quedarse inmóvil en este cuarto
pues quizás ha llegado el término del mundo,
y la lluvia es el estéril eco de ese fin,
una canción que tratan de recordar
labios que se deshacen bajo tierra.

The Last Island

Again life and death get mixed up
as in the courtyard of the house
the entry of the carts
mixes with the noise of the bucket in the well.
Again heaven remembers with hate
the lightning wound,
and the almond trees don't want to think
about their black roots.

Silence can't go on being my language,
but I can find only those unreal words
the dead address to stars and ants,
and love and happiness disappear from my memory
like light from a pitcher of water
thrown uselessly against the darkness.

Again you can hear only
the inextinguishable pattering of rain
that falls and falls without knowing why,
just as the lonely old woman goes on
weaving and weaving;
and you want to run away to a town
where a top still doesn't stop whirling,
waiting for me to pick it up,
but wherever you put your feet,
the roads disappear,
and it is better to remain motionless in this room,
since maybe the end of the world has come,
and the rain is the sterile echo of that end,
a song that a mouth decomposing in the earth
is trying to remember.

Carta

Cuando al fin te des cuenta
que sólo puedo amar los pueblos
donde nunca se detienen los trenes,
ya podrás olvidarme
para saber quien soy de veras.

Sabrás quien soy de veras
y los anillos de la corteza del árbol
serán señal de nuestros desposales,
y podrás entrar al bosque
donde te hallé antes de conocerte.

Y el bosque donde te hallé sin conocerte
se llenará con las hojas de mis palabras.
La noche será luminosa de ojos de caballos
que vienen a beber las aguas del recuerdo
para que siempre haya un amor que no muere.

Porque siempre hay en mí un amor que no muere
y eso te lo dirán los pueblos donde el tren no se detiene,
y el guitarrista ebrio
que entona la canción que te escribí
hará detenerse el remolino de las calles
para mostrarte el camino hacia el bosque.

Letter

When at last you realize
I can love only those towns
where the trains never stop,
then you will be able to forget me
in order to know who I truly am.

You will know who I truly am
and rings made from tree bark
will be the token of our wedding vows,
and you will be able to enter the forest
where I found you before I met you.

And the forest where I found you without knowing you
will fill up with the leaves of my words.
Night will be luminous with the eyes of horses
come to drink the waters of memory
so there will always be a love that doesn't die.

Because there is always in me a love that doesn't die
and the towns where the train doesn't stop
will tell you this, while the drunk guitar player
who croons the song I wrote you
will have to stop the whirling of the streets
to show you the road into the forest.

Camino rural

Solitario camino rural
a fines del verano.
¿Qué puedo hacer
troncos podridos sobre el charco?

Temo llegar al pueblo
cuando la niebla se desprende de la tierra.
Temo llegar al pueblo
porque a otro esperan allí
las mujeres que duermen en montones de heno.
Para otro van a amasar pan las hermanas esta noche.
Para otro contarán historias
los que encienden hogueras en los barbechos.

Aparecen lejanas luces
como débiles tañidos de guitarras.
Las perdices silban
llamando a sus parejas.
El pozo se aniega de hojas de castaños.
Alguien cierra las ventanas
para no sentir el cruel olor
a glicinas de otro verano.
Salen estrellas desesperadas
como abejas que no pueden hallar el colmenar.

¡Adiós, troncos podridos sobre el charco!
Voy hacia un pueblo donde nadie me espera
por un solitario carmino rural
a fines del verano.

Country Road

Lonely country road
at the end of summer.
What can I make
of rotten trunks over the puddle?

I am afraid of arriving at the town
when mist is rising from the earth.
I am afraid of arriving at the town
because there women who sleep on piles of hay
wait for someone else.
For someone else, the sisters are going to make bread tonight.
For someone else, those who light bonfires in the fallow fields
will tell stories.

Distant lights appear
like the weak strumming of guitars.
Quails whistle,
calling to their mates.
The well is drowning in chestnut leaves.
Someone closes the windows
to keep from smelling the cruel odor
of wisterias from another summer.
The desperate stars come out
like bees that can't find their hive.

Good-bye, rotten trunks over the puddle!
I am headed for a town where nobody waits for me
by way of a lonely country road
at the end of summer.

Después de todo

Después de todo
nos volveremos a encontrar.
El verano tenderá sus manteles en el suelo
para que dispongamos nuestras provisiones
y tú seguirás bella
como la canción *El Vino de Mediodía*
que el loco tocaba en la leñera.

Después de todo
hay tantas y tantas tierras.
Yo no me impaciento.
Tenemos todos los años del mundo para recorrerlas
hasta que de nuevo estemos juntos
y tú me contarás
que una vez me conociste
en un pequeño planeta que yo no recuerdo
un planeta llamado Tierra
y vas a hablarme
de casas visitadas por la luna,
billetes de apuesta a los hipódromos,
nuestras iniciales dibujadas con tiza blanca en un muro en demolición.

Equivoquémonos todo lo que queramos.
La tierra del desamor no existe
ante el gesto tuyo de mostrar las magnolias de una plaza de barrio,
tu cabeza en mi hombro,
la clara música nocturna de tu cuerpo.
Un gesto rehace todo:
Cuando la casa se incendia
su vida sigue entera
en la hoja chamuscada de un cuaderno,
el alfil sobreviviente del ajedrez.

After All

After all
we will meet again.
Summer will spread its tablecloth over the ground
so we can set out our provisions
and you will still be as beautiful
as the song "Noon Wine"
the crazy man used to play in the woodshed.

After all
there are so many, many lands.
I'm not feeling impatient.
We have all the years of the world to travel them
until we will be together again
and you will tell me
you knew me once
on a little planet I don't remember,
a planet called Earth,
and you will speak to me
of houses visited by the moon,
betting at the racetracks,
our initials drawn with white chalk on a wall being torn down.

Let us make as many mistakes as we like.
The land of love-no-more doesn't exist
before your gesture as you point out magnolias in a neighborhood
        plaza,
your head on my shoulder,
the clear nocturnal music of your body.
A gesture mends everything:
When the house burns up
its life continues whole
in the singed leaf of a notebook,
the surviving bishop of the chess set.

En otro lugar,
lejos de esta tierra y de su tiempo
espero tu rostro
donde se reúnen todos los rostros que he amado,
y comenzaremos a ser otra vez los desconocidos
que hace años se miraban y miraban
sin atreverse a decir que iban a amarse.

In another place,
far from this earth and from its time,
I wait for your face
where all the faces I have loved will meet,
and we will begin again to be strangers
who years ago gazed at each other and gazed
not daring to say they were about to fall in love.

Andenes

Te gusta llegar a la estación
cuando el reloj de pared tictaquea,
tictaquea en la oficina del jefe-estación.
Cuando la tarde cierra sus párpados
de viajera fatigada
y los rieles ya se pierden
bajo el hollín de la oscuridad.

Te gusta quedarte en la estación desierta
cuando no puedes abolir la memoria,
como las nubes de vapor
los contornos de las locomotoras,
y te gusta ver pasar al viento
que silba como un vagabundo
aburrido de caminar sobre los rieles.

Tictaqueo del reloj. Ves de nuevo
los pueblos cuyos nombres nunca aprendiste,
el pueblo donde querías llegar
como al niño el día de su cumpleaños
y los viajes de vuelta de vacaciones
cuando eras—para los parientes que te esperaban—
sólo un alumno fracasado con olor a cerveza.

Tictaqueo del reloj. El jefe-estación
juega un solitario. El reloj sigue diciendo
que la noche es el único tren
que puede llegar a este pueblo,
y a tí te gusta estar inmóvil escuchándolo
mientras el hollín de la oscuridad
hace desaparecer los durmientes de la vía.

Platforms

You like to get to the station
when the wall clock ticktocks,
ticktocks in the office of the stationmaster.
When the afternoon shuts its eyelids
like a tired traveler
and the tracks get lost
beneath the soot of darkness.

You like to stay in the empty station
when you can't obscure memory
the way clouds of steam
obscure the outline of locomotives,
and you like to see the wind pass
whistling like a tramp
bored with walking the rails.

Ticktock of the clock. You see again
the towns whose names you never learned,
the town at which you wanted to arrive
as a boy longs to reach the day of his birthday,
and the trips returning from vacations
when you were—for the relatives who waited for you—
only a student, flunking, reeking of beer.

Ticktock of the clock. The stationmaster
plays solitaire. The clock goes on saying
night is the only train
that can arrive at this town,
and it pleases you to stand still listening to it
while the soot of darkness
makes the ties disappear from the track.

III
The Land of Night

Cuento sobre una rama de mirto

Había una vez una muchacha
que amaba dormir en el lecho de un río.
Y sin temor pascaba por el bosque
porque llevaba en la mano
una jaula con un grillo guardián.

Para esperarla yo me convertía
en la casa de madera de sus antepasados
alzada a orillas de un brumoso lago.
Las puertas y las ventanas siempre estaban abiertas
pero sólo nos visitaba su primo el Porquerizo
que nos traia de regalo
perezosos gatos
que a veces abrian sus ojos
para que viéran os pasar por sus pupilas
cortejos de bodas campesinas.
El sacerdote había muerto
y todo ramo de mirto se marchitaba.

Teníamos tres hijas
descalzas y silenciosas como la belladona.
Todas las mañanas recogían helechos
y nos hablaron sólo para decirnos
que un jinete las llevaría
a ciudades cuyos nombres nunca conoceríamos.

Pero nos revelaron el conjuro
con el cual las abejas
sabrían que éramos sus amos
y el molino
nos daría trigo
sin permiso del viento.

Nosotros esperamos a nuestros hijos
crueles y fascinantes
como halcones en el puño del cazador.

Story about a Branch of Myrtle

Once upon a time there was a girl
who loved to sleep in the bed of a river.
And she went rambling fearless through the forest
because she carried in her hand
a guardian cricket in a cage.

Waiting for her I changed myself
into the wooden house of her ancestors
high on the shores of a misty lake.
My doors and windows were always open
but the only one who visited us was her cousin Swineherd,
who brought us a gift of lazy cats
which sometimes opened their eyes
so we could see
the processions of country weddings
passing across their pupils.
The priest had died
and every branch of myrtle withered.

We had three daughters
barefoot and silent as belladonna.
Every morning they gathered ferns
and only spoke to us to say
a rider would carry them off
to cities whose names we'd never know.

But they revealed the spells to us
that would teach the bees
we were their masters
and make the mill
give us wheat
without the wind's permission.

We waited for our children,
cruel and fascinating
as falcons on the hunter's fist.

Bajo un viejo techo

Esta noche duermo bajo un viejo techo,
los ratones corren sobre él, como hace mucho tiempo,
y el niño que hay en mí renace en mi sueño,
aspira de nuevo el olor de los muebles de roble,
y mira lleno de miedo hacia la ventana,
pues sabe que ninguna estrella resucita.

Esa noche oí caer las nueces desde el nogal,
escuché los consejos del reloj de péndulo,
supe que el viento vuelca una copa del cielo,
que las sombras se extienden
y la tierra las bebe sin amarlas,
pero el árbol de mi sueño sólo daba hojas verdes
que maduraban en la mañana con el canto del gallo.

Esta noche duermo bajo un viejo techo,
los ratones corren sobre él, como hace mucho tiempo,
pero sé que no hay mañanas y no hay cantos de gallos,
abro los ojos, para no ver reseco el árbol de mis sueños,
y bajo él, la muerte que me tiende la mano.

Under an Old Roof

Tonight I sleep under an old roof,
mice run over it as they did long ago,
and the child who lives in me is reborn in my dreams,
breathes again the odor of oak furniture,
and looks toward the window full of fear,
since he knows no star ever comes back to life.

That night I heard the walnuts fall from the tree,
I listened to the advice of the grandfather clock,
I learned that the wind tips the sky's cup over,
shadows spill out
and earth drinks them without loving them,
but the tree of my dreams bore only green leaves
that grew in the morning when the rooster crowed.

Tonight I sleep under an old roof,
mice run over it as they did long ago,
but I know there are no mornings and no roosters crowing.
I open my eyes, in order not to see the tree of my dreams withered,
and under it, death holding out her hand to me.

La tierra de la noche

No hablemos.
Es mejor abrir las ventanas mudas
desde la muerte de la hermana mayor.

La voz de la hierba hace callar la noche:
Hace un mes no llueve.
Nidos vacíos caen desde la enredadera.
Los cerezos se apagan como añejas canciones.
Este mes será de los muertos.
Este mes será del espectro
de la luna de verano.

Sigue brillando, luna de verano.
Reviven los escalones de piedra
gastados por los pasos de los antepasados.
Los murciélagos no dejan de chillar
entre los muros ruinosos de la Cervecería.
El azadón roto
espera tierra fresca de nuevas tumbas.
Y nosotros no debemos hablar
cuando la luna brilla
más blanca y despiadada que los huesos de los muertos.

Sigue brillando, luna de verano.

The Land of Night

Let's not talk.
It's better to open windows
mute since the death of the oldest sister.

The voice of the grass makes night hush:
It hasn't rained for a month.
Empty nests fall from the vine.
The cherry trees go out like vintage songs.
This month will be for the dead.
This month will be for the ghost
of the summer moon.

Shine on, summer moon.
Stone stairs worn down
by the steps of ancestors come alive.
Bats don't stop chittering
among the crumbling walls of the Brewery.
The broken hoe
waits for fresh earth from new graves.
And we shouldn't speak
when the moon shines
whiter and more merciless than the bones of the dead.

Shine on, summer moon.

Sentados frente al fuego

Sentados frente al fuego que envejece
miro su rostro sin decir palabra.
Miro el jarro de greda donde aún queda vino,
miro nuestras sombras movidas por las llamas.

Esta es la misma estación que descubrimos juntos,
a pesar de su rostro frente al fuego,
y de nuestras sombras movidas por las llamas.
Quizás si yo pudiera encontrar una palabra.

Esta es la misma estación que descubrimos juntos:
aún cae una gotera, brilla el cerezo tras la lluvia.
Pero nuestras sombras movidas por las llamas
viven más que nosotros.

Si, ésta es la misma estación que descubrimos juntos:
—Yo llenaba esas manos de cerezas, esas
manos llenaban mi vaso de vino—.
Ella mira el fuego que envejece.

Sitting in Front of the Fire

Sitting in front of the fire that is growing old
I look at her face without saying a word.
I look at the cup in which wine still remains,
I look at our shadows moved by flames.

This is the season we discovered together,
in spite of her face before the fire
and our shadows moved by flames.
Perhaps if I could find a word. . . .

This is the season we discovered together:
a drizzle still falls, the cherry tree shines through rain.
But our shadows moved by flames
are more alive than we are.

Yes, this is the season we discovered together—
I filled those hands with cherries,
those hands filled my glass with wine.
She looks at the fire that is growing old.

Puente en el sur

Ayer he recordado un día de claro invierno. He recordado
un puente sobre el río, un río robándole azul al cielo.
Mi amor era menos que nada en ese puente. Una naranja
hundiéndose en las aguas, una voz que no sabe a quién llama,
una gaviota cuyo brillo se deshizo entre los pinos.

Ayer he recordado que no se es nadie sobre un puente
cuando el invierno sueña con la claridad de otra estación,
y se quiere ser una hoja inmóvil en el sueño del invierno,
y el amor es menos que una naranja perdiéndose en las aguas,
menos que una gaviota cuya luz se extingue entre los pinos.

Bridge in the South

Yesterday I remembered a day of clear winter. I remembered
a bridge over the river, a river stealing blue from the sky.
On that bridge my love was less than nothing: an orange
sinking in the water, a voice that doesn't know whom it calls,
a gull whose shine dissolved among the pines.

Yesterday I remembered one isn't anyone on a bridge
when winter dreams of the clarity of another season,
and one wants to be a still leaf in winter's dream,
and love is less than an orange sinking in the water,
less than a sea gull whose light goes out among pines.

Día de feria

a Jorge Aravena Llanca

Día de feria
frente a las figuras de greda:
frente a esas luces
encendidas por dedos morenos que cambiaban por ellas
la sopa caliente, el pedazo de pan.
Y en el día de feria
estas figuras de greda
están mucho más vivas
que las miradas impasibles de quienes no las comprenden,
que las vanas monedas, que las campanadas que cruzan la plaza.
Viven hechas sangre en nuestra sangre, como el vaso de vino tinto,
la charla de invierno junto a los rescoldos,
—eso que está en nosotros
más que el miedo en la noche.

Yo había conocido antes esta certeza,
esta alegría humilde,
sí: unas flores silvestres creciendo entre los rieles,
bautizos donde los padrinos
no tenían dinero que lanzar al aire.
Pero sólo ahora sé
que he crecido para ellas:
manos de campesinos, terrones pardos y fecundos
para que el oro vuelva a su lugar
y el hierro no sea más una herramienta de sepultureros.
Y entre la multitud del día de feria respiro un aire puro
libre de cánticos para muertos.

Fair Day

To Jorge Aravena Llanca

Fair day
in front of the clay statues:
in front of these candles
lit by dark fingers that gave up
hot soup, a piece of bread, to light them.
And on fair day
these figures of clay are much more alive
than the impassive glances of people
who don't understand them,
than useless coins, than bells tolling across the plaza.
They live blood in our blood, like red wine,
winter conversation beside the embers—
whatever is greater in us
than fear of the dark.

I had known this certainty before,
this humble happiness,
yes: some wild flowers growing between the rails,
baptisms where the godparents
didn't have money to toss into the air.
Only now do I know
I have grown up for these things:
peasant hands, dark and fertile clods of soil,
so that gold may return to its place
and iron be only a gravedigger's tool.
And among the multitude on fair day I breathe a pure air
free of canticles for the dead.

Sin señal de vida

¿Para qué dar señales de vida?
Apenas podría enviarte con el mozo
un mensaje en una servilleta.

Aunque no estés aquí.
Aunque estés a años sombra de distancia
te amo de repente
a las tres de la tarde,
la hora en que los locos
sueñan con ser espantapájaros vestidos de marineros
espantando nubes en los trigales.

No sé si recordarte
es un acto de desesperación o elegancia
en un mundo donde al fin
el único sacramento ha llegado a ser el suicidio.

Tal vez habría que cambiar la palanca del cruce
para que se descarrilen los trenes.
Hacer el amor
en el único Hotel del pueblo
para oír rechinar los molinos de agua
e interrumpir la siesta del teniente de carabineros
y del oficial del Registro Civil.

Si caigo preso por ebriedad o toque de queda
hazme señas de sol con tu espejo de mano
frente al cual te empolvas
como mis compañeras de tiempo de Liceo.

Not a Sign of Life

Denmark is a prison.
—Hamlet

Why give signs of life?
I could hardly send you a message
in a napkin with the waiter.

Even though you aren't here.
Even though you are shadow years away,
I love you suddenly
at three in the afternoon,
the hour when madmen
dream of being scarecrows dressed in sailor suits
frightening clouds in the wheatfields.

I don't know if remembering you
is an act of despair or elegance
in a world where at last
suicide has become the only sacrament.

Perhaps I would have to throw the switch at the crossing
to derail the trains.
To make love
in the only Hotel in town
in order to hear the water mills grind
and interrupt the nap of the police lieutenant
and the clerk at the Civil Registry.

If I land in jail for drinking or breaking the curfew,
send me sun signs with the hand mirror
you use when you powder your face
as my girlfriends from high-school days once did.

Y no te entretengas
en enseñarle palabras feas a los choroyes.
Enséñales sólo a decir Papá o Centro de Madres.
Acuérdate que estamos en un tiempo donde se habla en voz baja,
y sorber la sopa un día de Banquete de Gala
significa soñar en voz alta.

Qué hermoso es el tiempo de la austeridad.
Las esposas cantan felices
mientras zurcen el terno único
del marido cesante.

Ya nunca más correrá sangre por las calles.
Los roedores están comiendo nuestro queso
en nombre de un futuro
donde todas las cacerolas
estarán rebosantes de sopa,
y los camiones vacilarán bajo el peso del alba.

Aprende a portarte bien
en un país donde la delación será una virtud.
Aprende a viajar en globo
y lanza por la borda todo tu lastre:
Los discos de Joan Baez, Bob Dylan, los Quilapayún,
aprende de memoria los Quincheros y el 7° de Línea.
Olvida las enseñanzas del Niño de Chocolate, Gurdgieff o el Grupo Arica,
quema la autobiografía de Trotzki o la de Freud
o los 20 *Poemas de Amor* en edición firmada y numerada por el autor.

Acuérdate que no me gustan las artesanías
ni dormir en una carpa en la playa.
Y nunca te hubiese querido más
que a los suplementos deportivos de los lunes.

And don't waste time
teaching dirty words to the parrots.
Teach them only to say "Papa" or "The Mothers' Club."
Remember we live in a time when you must speak in a whisper,
and sipping soup one day at the Awards Banquet
means to dream aloud.

How beautiful is the time of austerity.
Wives sing happily
while they darn the only suit
owned by their unemployed husbands.

Nevermore will blood run through our streets.
The rats are eating our cheese
in the name of a future
where all the pots and pans
will be overflowing with soup,
and the trucks will wobble under the weight of dawn.

Learn how to behave well
in a country where denunciation will be a virtue.
Learn how to travel in a balloon
and toss all your ballast overboard.
Learn by heart the records of Joan Baez, Bob Dylan,
the Quilapayún, the Quincheros, and the 7th Regiment.
Forget the teachings of Chocolate Boy, Gurdjieff, or the Arica Group,
burn the autobiographies of Trotsky and Freud
and *Twenty Love Poems* in an edition
signed and numbered by the author.

Remember I don't like handicrafts
or sleeping in a tent on the beach.
And never could I have loved you more
than the Monday sports supplement.

Y no sigas pensando en los atardeceres en los bosques.
En mi provincia prohibieron hasta el paso de los gitanos.

Y ahora
voy a pedir otro jarrito de chicha con naranja
y tú
mejor enciérrate en un convento.
Estoy leyendo *El Grito de Guerra* del Ejército de Salvación.
Dicen que la sífilis de nuevo será incurable
y que nuestros hijos pueden soñar en ser economistas o dictadores.

And don't go on thinking about afternoons in the forest.
In my part of the country they have forbidden the gypsies even
        to pass through.

And now
I'm going to order another cup
of *chicha* with orange juice

and you'd
better close yourself up in a convent.
I'm reading *The War Cry* of the Salvation Army.
They say syphilis will again be incurable,
and our children can dream of becoming economists or dictators.

IV

I Would Give All the Gold
in the World

Daría todo el oro del mundo

Daría todo el oro del mundo
por sentir de nuevo en mi camisa
las frías monedas de la lluvia.

Por oír rodar el aro de alambre
en que un niño descalzo
lleva el sol a un puente.

Por ver aparecer
caballos y cometas
en los sitios vacíos de mi juventud.

Por oler otra vez
los buenos hijos de la harina
que oculta bajo su delantal la mesa.

Para gustar
la leche del alba
que va llenando los pozos olvidados.

Daria no sé cuánto
por descansar en la tierra
con las frías monedas de plata de la lluvia
cerrándome los ojos.

I Would Give All the Gold in the World

I would give all the gold in the world
to feel the cold coins of rain
again on my shirt.

To hear the rolling of the wire hoop
in which a barefoot child
carries the sun to a bridge.

To see
horses and kites appear
in the wide-open places of my youth.

To smell once more
the good offspring of the flour
who hides the table under her apron.

To taste
the milk of dawn
gradually filling forgotten wells.

I would give I don't know how much
to lie down on the ground
with the cold silver coins of rain
closing my eyes.

Regalo

Un amigo del sur
me ha enviado una manzana
demasiado hermosa
para comerla de inmediato.
La tengo en mis manos:
es pesada y redonda
como la Tierra.

Gift

A friend from the South
has sent me an apple
too beautiful
to eat right away.
I hold it in my hands:
It is heavy and round
like the Earth.

Poema de invierno

El invierno trae caballos blancos que resbalan en la helada.
Han encendido fuego para defender los huertos
de la bruja blanca de la helada.
Entre la blanca humareda se agita el cuidador.
El perro entumecido amenaza desde su caseta al témpano flotante de
     la luna.

    Esta noche al niño se le perdonará que duerma tarde.
    En las casa los padres están de fiesta.
    Pero él abre las ventanas
    para ver a los enmascarados jinetes
    que lo esperan en el bosque
    y sabe que su destino
    será amar el olor humilde de los senderos nocturnos.

El invierno trae aguardiente para el maquinista y el fogonero.
Una estrella perdida tambalea como baliza.
Cantos de soldados ebrios
que vuelven tarde a sus cuarteles.

    En la casa ha empezado la fiesta.
    Pero el niño sabe que la fiesta está en otra parte,
    y mira por la ventana buscando a los desconocidos
    que pasará toda la vida tratando de encontrar.

Winter Poem

Winter brings white horses that skid on the ice.
Someone's lit a fire to protect the gardens
from the white witch of ice.
Among white puffs of smoke the caretaker frets.
From his doghouse, the numb dog menaces the floating drum
     of the moon.

    Tonight the child will be pardoned for sleeping late.
    In the house the parents are celebrating.
    But the child opens the windows
    to see the masked riders
    who wait for him in the forest
    and he knows his destiny will be
    to love the damp odor of night paths.

Winter brings *aguardiente* for the machinist and the stoker.
A lost star reeling like a buoy.
Songs of tipsy soldiers
returning late to their barracks.

    In the house the party has begun.
    But the child knows the party is somewhere else
    and he looks out the window searching for the strangers
    he will spend his whole life trying to find.

Fin del mundo

El día del fin del mundo
será limpio y ordenado
como el cuaderno del mejor alumno.
El borracho del pueblo
dormirá en una zanja,
el tren expreso pasará
sin detenerse en la estación,
y la banda del Regimiento
ensayará infinitamente
la marcha que toca hace veinte años en la plaza.
Sólo que algunos niños
dejarán sus volantines enredados
en los alambres telefónicos,
para volver llorando a sus casas
sin saber qué decir a sus madres
y yo grabaré mis iniciales
en la corteza de un tilo
pensando que eso no sirve para nada.

Los evangélicos saldrán a las esquinas
a cantar sus himnos de costumbre.
La anciana loca paseará con su quitasol.
Y yo diré: »El mundo no puede terminar
porque las palomas y los gorriones
siguen peleando por la avena en el patio«.

End of the World

The day of the end of the world
will be as clean and orderly
as the notebook of the best student.
The town drunk
will sleep in a ditch,
the express train will go by
without stopping at the station,
and the Regimental band
will practice infinitely
the march it played in the plaza twenty years ago.
Only, some children
will leave their tangled string
in the telephone wires
to run home crying
without knowing what to say to their mothers,
and I will carve my initials
in the bark of a linden
thinking it will do no good.

The evangelicals will come out to the corners
to sing their usual hymns.
The crazy old lady will parade with her parasol.
And I will say: "The world can't end
because the pigeons and sparrows
are still fighting for oats in the patio."

Imagen para un estanque

Y así pasan las tardes:
silenciosas, como gastadas monedas
en manos de avaros.
Y yo escribo cartas que nunca envío
mientras los manzanos se extinguen
víctimas de sus propias llamas.

Hasta que de lejos
vienen las voces
de ventanas golpeadas por el viento
en las casas desiertas,
y pasan bueyes desenyugados
que van a beber al estero.
Entonces debo pedirle al tiempo
un recuerdo que no se deforme
en el turbio estanque de la memoria.

Y horas que sean
reflejos de sol
en el dedal de la hermana,
crepitar de la leña
quemándose en la chimenea
y claros guijarros
lanzados al río por un ciego.

Image for a Pool

And so the afternoons pass:
silent, like worn coins
in misers' hands.
And I write letters I never send
while the apple trees die out,
victims of their own flame.

Until from far away
voices come
from windows in deserted houses
battered by wind,
and oxen pass unyoked,
going to drink at the water hole.
Then I should ask of time
one recollection that isn't deformed
in the murky pool of memory.

And hours may be
reflections of sun
on my sister's thimble,
cracklings of wood
burning in the fireplace,
and shining pebbles
skipped on the river by a blind man.

Edad de oro

Un día u otro
todos seremos felices.
Yo estaré libre
de mi sombra y mi nombre.
El que tuvo temor
escuchará junto a los suyos
los pasos de su madre,
el rostro de la amada será siempre joven
al reflejo de la luz antigua en la ventana,
y el padre hallará en la despensa la linterna
para buscar en el patio
la navaja extraviada.

No sabremos
si la caja de música
suena durante horas o un minuto;
tú hallarás—sin sorpresa—
el atlas sobre el cual soñaste con extraños países,
tendrás en tus manos
un pez venido del río de tu pueblo,
y Ella alzará sus párpados
y será de nuevo pura y grave
como las piedras lavadas por la lluvia.

Todos nos reuniremos
bajo la solemne y aburrida mirada
de personas que nunca han existido,
y nos saludaremos sonriendo apenas
pues todavía creeremos estar vivos.

Golden Age

One day or another
we will all be happy.
I will be free
of my shadow and my name.
The one who was afraid
will hear in his own footsteps
the steps of his mother,
the face of the loved one will be forever young
in the reflection of old light from the window,
and the father will find his flashlight in the pantry
so he can search for the hidden pocketknife
in the patio.

We won't know
if the music box
plays for hours or a minute;
you will discover—without surprise—
the atlas that made you dream of strange countries,
you will hold in your hands
a fish pulled from the river in your hometown,
and She will open her eyes wide
and be once again pure and grave
as stones washed by rain.

We will all be reunited
beneath the solemn and bored gaze
of people who have never existed,
and we will greet each other barely smiling,
because we will still believe we are alive.

Despedida

... el caso no ofrece
ningún adorno para la diadema de las Musas.

—*Ezra Pound*

Me despido de mi mano
que pudo mostrar el paso del rayo
o la quietud de las piedras
bajo las nievas de antaño.

Para que vuelvan a ser bosques y arenas
me despido del papel blanco y de la tinta azul
de donde surgían los ríos perezosos,
cerdos en las calles, molinos vacíos.

Me despido de los amigos
en quienes más he confiado:
los conejos y las polillas,
las nubes harapientas del verano.

Me despido de las Virtudes y de las Gracias del planeta:
Los fracasados, las cajas de música,
los murciélagos que al atardecer se deshojan
de los bosques de las casas de madera.

Me despido de los amigos silenciosos
a los que sólo les importa saber
dónde se puede beber algo de vino,
y para los cuales todos los días
no son sino un pretexto
para entonar canciones pasadas de moda.

Me despido de una muchacha
que sin preguntarme si la amaba o no la amaba
caminó conmigo y se acostó conmigo
cualquiera tarde de esas que se llenan
de humaredas de hojas quemándose en las aceras.

Good-bye

... the case presents
No adjunct to the Muses' diadem.
—*Ezra Pound*

I say good-bye to my hand,
which could move as fast as lightning
or lie still as stones
beneath the snows of yesteryear.

So they can become forests and sands again,
I say good-bye to white paper and blue ink
from which lazy rivers used to grow,
pigs in the street, empty mills.

I say good-bye to the friends
I've trusted most:
rabbits and moths,
tattered clouds of summer.

I say good-bye to the Virtues and Graces of this planet:
failures, music boxes,
bats that defoliate the forests
of wooden houses at dusk.

I say good-bye to silent friends,
those who only want to know
where we can go to drink some wine,
and for whom every day
is nothing but a pretext
for crooning songs long out of fashion.

I say good-bye to a girl
who never asked me whether I loved her or not
but walked with me and went to bed with me
on any of those afternoons filled
with the smoke of leaves burning on the sidewalk.

Me despido de una muchacha
cuya cara suelo ver en sueños
iluminada por la triste mirada
de linternas de trenes que parten hacia la lluvia.

Me despido de la memoria
y me despido de la nostalgia
—la sal y el agua
de mis días sin objeto—

y me despido de estos poemas:
palabras, palabras—un poco de aire
movido por los labios—palabras
para ocultar quizás lo único verdadero:
que respiramos y dejamos de respirar.

I say good-bye to a girl
whose face I usually see in dreams
lit up by the sad flash
of train lights departing in the rain.

I say good-bye to memory
and I say good-bye to nostalgia—
salt and water
of my aimless days—

and I say good-bye to these poems:
words, words—a little bit of air
stirred by my lips—words
to hide, perhaps, the only truth:
we breathe and we stop breathing.

Wesleyan Poetry in Translation

from Arabic

    Desert Tracings: Six Classic Arabian Odes by ʿAlqama, Shánfara, Labid, ʿAntara, Al-Aʿsha, and Dhu al-Rúmma. 1989. Translated and introduced by Michael A. Sells.

from Bulgarian

    Because the Sea Is Black: Poems of Blaga Dimitrova. 1989. Translated and with introductions by Niko Boris and Heather McHugh.

from Chinese

    Bright Moon, Perching Bird: Poems by Li Po and Tu Fu. 1987. Translated and with an introduction by J. P. Seaton and James Cryer.

from Czechoslovakian

    Mirroring: Selected Poems of Vladimír Holan. 1985. Translated by C. G. Hanzlicek and Dana Hábová.

from French

    Fables from Old French: Aesop's Beasts and Bumpkins. 1982. Translated and with a preface by Norman Shapiro; introduction by Howard Needler.

    The Book of Questions (Vols. I–VII in four books). 1976, 1977, 1983, 1984. By Edmond Jabès. Translated by Rosmarie Waldrop.

    The Book of Dialogue. 1987. By Edmond Jabès. Translated by Rosmarie Waldrop.

    The Book of Resemblances. 1990. By Edmond Jabès. Translated by Rosmarie Waldrop.

from German

    Sonnets to Orpheus. 1987. The poems of Rainer Maria Rilke, translated and with an introduction by David Young.

from Italian

    The Coldest Year of Grace: Selected Poems of Giovanni Raboni. 1985. Translated by Stuart Friebert and Vinio Rossi.

from Lithuanian

    Chimeras in the Tower: Selected Poems of Henrikas Radauskas. 1986. Translated by Jonas Zdanys.

from Navajo

Hogans: Navajo Houses and House Songs. 1980. Translated by David and Susan McAllester.

from Portuguese

An Anthology of Twentieth-Century Brazilian Poetry. 1972. Edited and with an introduction by Elizabeth Bishop and Emanuel Brasil.

Brazilian Poetry, 1950–1980. 1983. Edited by Emanuel Brasil and William Jay Smith.

When My Brothers Come Home: Poems from Central and Southern Africa. 1985. Edited by Frank Mkalawile Chipasula.

The Alphabet in the Park: Selected Poems of Adélia Prado. 1990. Translated and with an introduction by Ellen Watson.

from Serbian

Roll Call of Mirrors: Selected Poems of Ivan V. Lalić. 1988. Translated by Charles Simic.

from Spanish

Times Alone: Selected Poems of Antonio Machado. 1983. Translated and with an introduction by Robert Bly.

With Walker in Nicaragua and Other Early Poems, 1949–1954. 1984. The poems of Ernesto Cardenal, translated by Jonathan Cohen.

Off the Map: Selected Poems of Gloria Fuertes. 1984. Edited and translated by Philip Levine and Ada Long.

From the Country of Nevermore: Selected Poems of Jorge Teillier. 1990. Translated and with an introduction by Mary Crow.

About the author

Jorge Teillier, who has been called the most important Chilean poet of his generation, was born in Lautaro, in the south of Chile, in 1935. Teillier studied history and geography at the University of Chile, and was later made editor of the University's *Bulletin*. He began writing poems when he was twelve, and his first book of poetry, *Para angeles y gorriones* (*For Angels and Sparrows*), was published when he was twenty-one. The author of twelve collections of poems, Teillier has also written many short stories and essays.

Teillier poems focus on the politics of the psyche and are haunted by ill-fated dreams of happiness. Selections from his work have been translated into French, Italian, Rumanian, Russian, Swedish, Polish, and Czechoslovakian. Teillier lives near Santiago, Chile.

About the translator

Mary Crow's interest in Teillier began with a Fulbright research grant to Chile and Peru in 1982. In 1986 Colorado State University, where she is professor of English and director of the Creative Writing Program, awarded her a travel grant to return to Chile to talk with Teillier. She also received an NEA poetry fellowship in 1984 and a second Fulbright to read her poems in Yugoslavia in 1988. She is a graduate of the College of Wooster (B.A.) and of Indiana University (M.A.) and studied at the Writers Workshop at the University of Iowa. She has published three other books of poetry, *Going Home, The Business of Literature,* and *Borders,* and an anthology of poetry by Latin American women poets, which received awards from the NEA and the Columbia University Translation Center. Her home is in Fort Collins, Colorado.

About the book

From the Country of Nevermore was composed on the Mergenthaler 202 in Baskerville, a contemporary rendering of a fine transitional typeface named for the 18th-century English printer John Baskerville. The book was composed by Brevis Press of Bethany, Connecticut, and designed and produced by Kachergis Book Design of Pittsboro, North Carolina.

WESLEYAN POETRY IN TRANSLATION